The Critics Choice

"This Fledgling Series May Soon Do For Travel Guides What Hitchcock Did For Film." ***/Chicago Tribune***

"Sharp Writing And A Thrilling Layout Make It A Guidebook You Can Read From Cover To Cover Without A Yawn." ***/San Francisco Examiner***

"Dripping With Attitude... Cutting Edge..." ***/Atlanta Journal-Constitution***

"It's Hip To Be There – All The Usual Topics From History To Hotels To Shopping But With A Welcome Cutting-Edge Spin." ***/Chicago Sun-Times***

"No Other Guide Captures So Completely And Viscerally What It Feels Like To Be Inside The City." ***/San Francisco Bay Guardian***

"Razzle-Dazzle Design." ***/USA Today***

"An Insider With Attitude." ***/Newsday***

"For Travelers Who've Outgrown The Shoestring Budget Of Their College Days, There's Avant-Guide, A New Series From Itinerant Genius Dan Levine." ***/Elle Magazine***

"Ultra Hip Travel Tomes." ***/Atlanta Journal-Constitution***

"If It's Cutting Edge You Want In A City That Teeters Between Conservative And Revolutionary, This Is The Book To Buy." ***/Toronto Sun***

PICK OF THE MONTH – "Refreshingly Sharp Entertaining Advice." ***/Consumer Reports***

"Opinionated, Mildly Caustic And Very Stylish." ***/Baltimore Sun***

"A Wealth Of Local History And Color." ***/US News & World Report***

"One Guide That Doesn't Shrink From Expressing Opinions." ***/Boston Globe***

fiercely independent!

Each Avant*Guide is created by independent experts who never accept discounts or payments in exchange for positive coverage.

Our visits to restaurants, clubs and other establishments are anonymous, and expenses are paid by Avant*Guide.

FEW OThER GUiDEßOOkS CAN MAkE ThiS CLAIM.

AVANT GUIDE

PRAGUE

Empire ~ New York

Empire Press Media, Inc.
Empire State Building

Web: www.avantguide.com
Email: editor@avantguide.com

Editor-in-Chief: Dan Levine
Photo Editor: Julie Denesha

Design: »0« Mowshe
Gregorini (mig) | Kleček (li6®) | Matyáš (on)

Cover: M. Vlček
Cover Imaging: mi | li | on |
Back Cover: Liz Steger

Web Design: Ivan Gosić

Digital Cartography: Copyright © Empire Press Media, Inc.
Films: Generace – 2h

Photography: Julie Denesha, Pavel Šuba,
Kryštof Blažek, Dimír Šťastný, NYCVB

Very Special Thanks:
Fran & Alan Levine, Petra Lustigová, Jan Kurdík, Chronic,
Jonathan Pontell, Marilyn Wood, Babe LN,
David Černý, Jan Svěrák, Jiří X. Doležal,
Tono Stano, Kamilala Mráčková.

Copy Editor: Peter Metzenbaum

ISBN: 1-891603-13-2
Second Edition

Printed in the Czech Republic
Distributed in North America by Publishers Group West

Also From Avant*Guide
Avant*Guide New York City
Avant*Guide London
Avant*Guide San Francisco
Avant*Guide Paris
Avant*Guide New Orleans
Avant*Guide Amsterdam
Avant*Guide Las Vegas
Coming Soon...
Avant*Guide Toronto
Avant*Guide Boston
Avant*Guide Washington, DC
Avant*Guide Barcelona
Avant*Guide Italy
Avant*Guide Cuba

CONTENTS » CONTEN

CONTENTS » CONTENTS » CONT

×01× PRAGUE EXPOSEd
ENGAGiNG

× 01 ×
ENGAGiNG

BOhEMiAN RhAPSODiZING

It's just become so "klee-shay" how absolutely everybody rhapsodizes about the Bohemian capital's beauty; nonetheless, we can't help but nod our proverbial heads in agreement. The very heart of Prague is what enraptures the aesthetes; one historical square-mile that is the most beautiful little city on Earth. Really. Prague is storybook beautiful; made of cobblestone streets, frilly Baroque buildings, a castle on a hill and a river that runs through it. Strolling along the center's narrow lanes, past magically sculpted buildings garnished with golden spires, is like wandering through a giant jewel box. With surprising harmony, gothic churches rub shoulders with renaissance mansions, baroque gardens, cubist office buildings and art nouveau houses. Prague's smorgasbord of evolutionary architecture is a miracle of contrasts and colors that exists nowhere else. Often, just as the sun is setting behind Prague Castle, the heavenly buildings of Old Town shimmer with such brilliant oranges and yellows it almost feels as though the entire city is levitating just a few feet off the ground.

It's a good bet that Prague probably looks better today than at any time in its thousand-year history. Too perfect, some say: The capital of Bohemia has lost its bohemian veneer. On a crumbling yellow wall in Prague's Old Town, alongside posters promoting heavy metal bands and techno parties, there's some graffiti which reads: CAPITALISM = VELVET OCCUPATION! While warning against the seductive onslaught of consumerism, this ironic wall-scrawl also calls attention to a somber truth: From the Germans and the Austro-Hungarians to the Nazis and the Soviets, the Czech people have been under the thumb of one foreign regime or another for more than a thousand years. Now that the Habsburgs are buried, the Nazi Scum are crushed and the Commie Pinkos have been sent packing, have Ronald McDonald and Mickey Mouse stepped-in to fill the void?

01 ENGAGING

ThE CZECh MINd

Nobody returns from a trip to Prague cooing that the locals "are the nicest people in the world." Fact is, Praguers can be downright surly. Some blame it on communism, which rewarded rancor as equally as kindness. In other words, unlike the West, there was no economic benefit to being nice. Others say that Czechs are mean because they've had rotten lives: Things were tough under the Communists, Nazis and Habsburgs. As far back as the turn of the last century, the writer (and friend of Kafka) Max Brod observed that "the inhabitants of Prague have long ago perfected the art of embittering each other's lives."

One thing's for sure: centuries of domination have made Czechs somewhat xenophobic and suspicious of outsiders. A lot of locals, it seems, are uninterested in opening any windows to the world. After all, they reason, they might catch a chill from the draft. And, because they have rarely had much influence over the course of international events, Praguers observe the world around them as if from afar. They glow with cynicism as they gesture towards the castle on the hill and comment with a sneer about what is going on "up there."

Generations of foreign control have also shaped a people inclined towards pragmatism and passivity: When Warsaw Pact troupes rolled through in 1968, Czechs accepted their fate out of both fear and a sense of powerlessness, and not because the masses embraced the Russian Politburo's principles. And perhaps it's the solace which lurks within every liter of beer that explains why Czechs are the greatest pub-going nationals in the world.

bEER: ThE NATiONAL RELIGION?

District	Catholic Churches	Protestant Churches	Synagogues	Pubs
Prague 1	30	6	7	942
Prague 2	10	6	0	702
Prague 3	5	6	0	664
Prague 4	13	10	0	1725
Prague 5	13	7	0	933
Prague 6	4	4	0	764
Prague 7	2	1	0	402
Prague 8	6	7	1	759
Prague 9	13	5	0	763
Prague 10	11	8	0	1069
Total:	**107**	**60**	**8**	**8723**

Sources: Archbishopric of Prague & Galeleo Praha, sro

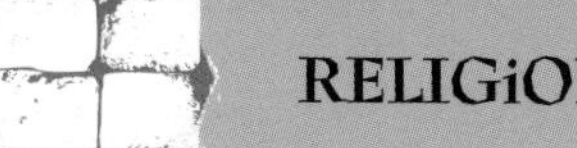

RELIGiON

According to polls, only 33% of Czechs consider themselves "religious" while 40% describe themselves as "atheist." And only a tiny minority say they are "real believers." In Prague, especially, it's hard to find a devout resident who prays to God or goes to church on a regular basis.

But secularism wasn't always in vogue, in fact, as the thousand-year history of Bohemia is closely related to Christianity. For centuries, Prague's archbishops crowned Czech kings, acted as the monarchs' primary advisers, and served as chancellors of the university.

The rift between the church and state began as early as the 14th Century, when the masses protested against the excesses of Roman Catholicism. Religious leaders were further weakened during the 19th Century due to their association to the increasingly unpopular Austrian Empire. And a century later, religion was hammered and sickled under the Communists. The greatest blow was struck on April 14, 1950, when the government launched "Operation K" and, in the course of a single night, closed every convent and monastery in the country. During the next decade, "Scientific Atheism" was installed as the new opiate of the masses and became an integral part of the political curriculum. Lately, in these post-Revolution years, alternative religions, obscure sects and foreign cults have increased in popularity. Bald-headed Krishnas parade across Charles Bridge with regularity, competing for local hearts and minds with L. Ron Hubbard's Scientology and the cults of Sri Chinmoy and Herbalife.

ThE JEWISH CITY

Prague was once considered to be one of Europe's great Jewish cities. Jews have been here since the end of the 10th Century and, by 1708, Jews accounted for about a quarter of Prague's population. In the early 18th Century, there were more Jews here than anywhere else in Europe. And before World War II, about one-fifth of Prague's citizens were Jewish. Most Jews fled just before, or were killed during, the Nazi occupation. Today, Prague's Jewish community numbers about 1500.

COMMUNIST dAZE

A dozen years is apparently not enough time for Czechs to come to grips with their Communist past. The problem is that, to varying degrees, almost everyone in the nation was an accomplice to the criminal Communist Party: When confronted by one-party rule, the overwhelming majority of Czechs rolled onto their backs, then rolled back onto their feet and started trotting along with their oppressors. The Czech people have not put former Communist Party leaders on trial because the masses are not willing to face cross-examination on the witness stand.

When Czechoslovakia fell into the Soviet abyss, it was part of a much larger political game between Russia and the West. Towards the end of World War II, the United States, France and England secretly agreed to let the so-called East-European nations, which included Czechoslovakia, to fall under Russia's sphere of influence. In return, the western Allies got the western European countries. And Germany, as we know, was cut in two. At the time, this arrangement wasn't at all distasteful to most Czechs as the Russians were brothers in arms—it was they, in May, 1945, who liberated Prague from seven years of Nazi terror. Furthermore, liberalism is deep-routed in Bohemia and socialism had wide popular support even before the war. In 1946—in the first elections after the Germans were routed from Czechoslovakia—left-leaning parties filled the entire slate and the Communist Party edged-out its socialist competitors with 38% of the vote. According to European parliamentary custom, Communist Klement Gottwald, the leader of the most-vote-getting party, was crowned Prime Minister and bestowed with the power to form a coalition government. But in 1948, two years after Czechs chose socialism, something went terribly, terribly wrong....

Jiří X. Doležal

Writer, editor and political agitator Jiří X. Doležal is one of the Czech Republic's most outspoken drug advocates and social commentators. Well-known for his work in the enormously popular *Reflex* magazine, Doležal is as extraordinarily candid as he is controversial.

A-G: Did you plant drugs in a police chief's office?
JXD: Well, this is how it happened: There was a Police Director from Liberec (a town in northern Bohemia) who had a political platform that could be summarized as "shoot the drug users." He was a textbook example of drug repression. I won't say he's a pedophile, but when I see him I call my children to come with me. Anyway, I went to his office to interview him about his views on drugs. Then I went home, took a statue of a Buddha, drilled a hole in the bottom and put a little grass in it. Then I filled the hole, glued it over with cardboard and sent [the statue] to him. A week later, we went back to the Police Director's office with a TV camera and asked him "do you still believe the possession of drugs should be illegal?" and he said "yes." "Could [that law] be abused?" we asked, and he said "No." And there was that Buddha on his shelf. So I took the Buddha and broke it, and we filmed the marijuana being found in the office of the Police Director! Soon after, he was kicked out!

A-G: Who is Czech?
JXD: That question doesn't have any meaning anymore. With the Internet, there are no more borders.

A-G: Are you optimistic about the future?
JXD: I am! I am! I believe in the hot ending of the Universe. I don't believe in the cold one!

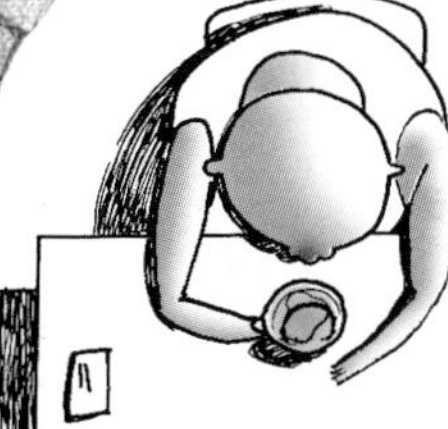

dATELiNE

500BC	Celts settle central Europe.
AD450	Slavs arrive.
870	Bohemia becomes part of Holy Roman Empire; Castle constructed in Hradčany.
973	Bishopric founded in Prague.
1170	First stone bridge (Judith's Bridge) spans the Vltava.
1234	Old Town founded, in what will be Prague's historic center.
1257	Malá Strana established by German colonists.
1306	Přemyslid dynasty ends following the death of heirless King Václav III.
1344	Prague bishopric raised to an archbishopric.
1346	Charles IV crowned King and Holy Roman Emperor; Prague's first Golden Age.
1348	Charles University founded.
1357	Charles Bridge begun.
1403	Jan Hus launches crusade for religious reform.
1415	Hus burned at the stake sparking decades of religious warfare.
1419	First Defenestration—Catholic councilors thrown from windows of New Town Hall.
1434	Radical Hussites defeated in the Battle of Lipany, ending religious warfare.
1526	Roman Catholic Habsburgs gain control of Bohemia.
1541	Huge fire ravages Malá Strana and the Castle District.
1584	Rudolf II makes Prague seat of imperial court; Prague's second Golden Age.
1618	Second Defenestration helps ignite Thirty Years' War.
1620	Czechs defeated at Battle of White Mountain; Czech language & culture declines.
1621	27 leading Czech noblemen beheaded on Old Town Square.
1648	End of Thirty Years' War; Praguers defend city against invading Swedish army.
1784	Prague's four towns united; Czech National Revival begins.
1818	National Museum founded.
1848	Industrial Revolution begins in Prague, drawing people from countryside.
1875	Horse-drawn trams on Prague's streets.

ENGAGING *01*

1881	National Theater completed.
1883	Franz Kafka born in Staré Město; National Theater is opened.
1918	Czechoslovak Republic founded.
1921	Prague's boundaries expanded, encompassing neighboring villages and settlements.
1938	Leaders of Germany, Great Britain, Italy and France give Czech border territories to Hitler's Third Reich.
1939	Hitler occupies Czech lands; puppet Slovak Republic established.
1940s	World War II; 130,000 Czechs are murdered, including over 80,000 Jews.
1944	Prague Uprising fails to liberate capital from Nazi rule.
1945-6	Soviet army liberates Prague; 2.5 million Germans expelled; Communist leader Klement Gottwald appointed prime minister after his party wins 38% of vote.
1948	Communists seize power amid cabinet crisis.
1950s	Top Jewish Communists executed in purge as Stalinism reaches its peak; Giant statue of Stalin unveiled on Letná plain overlooking Prague.
1968	"Prague Spring" reforms; Warsaw Pact troops invade Czechoslovakia.
1977	Czech dissidents form Charter 77 to protest suppression of human rights.
1989	Anti-government protests erupt into revolution; Communist government resigns; Parliament nominates playwright Václav Havel as president.
1990	Free elections held; Havel's Civic Forum Party captures 170 of 300 parliamentary seats.
1993	Czechoslovakia divides in two: Czech Republic is born.
1997	Czech crown floats freely on world markets; "Kolya" wins Oscar for best foreign film; Prime Minister Klaus resigns amid financial scandal.
1998	President Václav Havel re-elected; National hockey team wins Olympic gold.
1999	Czech Republic admitted to NATO.
2000	Widespread riots as IMF/World Bank meets in Prague.
2002	Prague hosts NATO summit.

CZECh-UP

Country:	Česká Republika
Population: Men: Women:	10,278,098 48.66% 51.34%
Capital & Largest City:	Prague (1,186,855)
Other Major Cities:	Brno (383,569) Ostrava (321,264) Plzeň (167,534) Olomouc (103,015) Liberec (99,588) Ústí nad Labem (96,070) Hradec Králové (98,700) České Budějovice (98,926)
Area:	30,450 sq. miles (78,864 sq. km)
Average Elevation:	1,476 ft. (450 m)
Neighboring Countries:	Germany, Austria, Poland, Slovakia
Currency:	Koruna (Crown)
Political System:	Parliament
Nationalities:	Czech (95%),Slovak (3%), Polish (0.6%), German (0.5%), Gypsy/Romany (0.3%), Hungarian (0.2%), Other (0.4%)
Religions:	None (40%), Roman Catholic (39%), Protestant (5%), Orthodox (3%), Other (13%)
Life Expectancy:	Male 69 years Female 76 years
Industry:	Fuels, Power Supply, Ferrous Metallurgy, Machinery & Equipment, Motor Vehicles, Glass, Textile, Chemicals, Armaments.

Ancient History

The word "Bohemia" probably derives from the Latin "Boiohaemum," the name of the area settled by the Celtic "Boii" tribe in the Fourth Century BC.

The First Roman Empire, which existed around the time of Christ, never actually conquered Czech territory—it only got as far north as the Danube River. But, Rome's influence was clearly felt here: Romanesque structures can still be seen in the basements of Old Town and below several churches around Prague.

From the third to the seventh centuries Bohemia was overrun by Slavic people from the steppes of the East; ancestors of today's locals. Slavs founded the Greater Moravian Empire in what is today the Czech Republic (and bits of Poland and Hungary). In AD 863, Cyril and Methodius—two sainted heroes whose arrival is still celebrated with a public holiday—brought Christianity here, along with the written word (Cyrillic). Slavic rulers embraced the new religion and were pleased to discover that their own power increased when they aligned with the Church. The Slavic Přemyslid dynasty took the throne of Bohemia in the 10th Century, founded Prague Castle and held the reigns of power for the next 300 years.

The Luxembourgs & the First Golden Age

The French Luxembourgs began their rule over the Czech lands when John of Luxembourg (1310-1437) married Eliška Přemyslovna, the daughter and lawful heiress of Slavic Přemyslid King Wenceslas III. John is remembered as a good king who loved a good fight. When he died at the battle of Crecy in 1346, John was succeeded by his young son, Charles IV. Charles was not really named Charles; he was named Wenceslas. But he was raised in France, and everyone there called him Charles—after Charamagne—so the name stuck.

Charles was a particularly bright king. Under his enlightened leadership, the city blossomed into what came to be known as the "First Golden Age of Prague." A native Francophone, Charles learned Czech and three other languages, at a time when most people in Europe couldn't even read or write. He had a passion for art and was an avid collector of antiques, especially holy

relics. The king founded Charles University, the first school of higher learning in Central Europe, and funded Charles Bridge. He successfully lobbied to have the Prague bishopric made an archbishopric, then commissioned the building of St. Vitus' Cathedral, which rises up from the center of Prague Castle. Charles proposed the construction of Prague's New Town *(Nové Město)*, and is even said to have had a hand in its layout. Most importantly, the King made Prague the capital of the Holy Roman Empire, all the while working his way through four different wives.

Upon Charles' death, religious strife and political ineptitude devastated the Czech lands. Charles's son, Wenceslas IV (1378-1419), was extremely erratic, perhaps even psychotic. He was also wildly unpopular, imprisoned twice, then stripped of his imperial title.

Meanwhile, a holy feud erupted when Bohemia's pious peasants railed against the Roman Catholic Church for growing excessively wealthy and straying from God. Grassroots passions were fueled by the charismatic Jan Hus, a religious reformer known for fiery sermons inspired by the English agitator John Wycliffe. Needless to say, Hus was particularly unpopular with the Pope, who ordered the "heretic" burned at the stake on July 6, 1415. Hus' brutal murder only served to make him a martyr and swell the ranks of his followers, who came to be known as "Hussites." Their new leaders petitioned the Pope with the Four Articles of Prague, a list of demands designed to promote equality within the faith: All believers should be permitted to receive communion in both kinds (the wine and the wafer); mortal sinners should be punished equally, regardless of their social status; the Word of God should be freely preached; and, most troublesome for Rome, the clergy should give up their worldly wealth.

The Hussite Wars

The relationship between run-of-the-mill Czechs and the foreign-oriented aristocrats who ruled them went from bad to worse. In 1419, Hussite priests took matters into their own hands and began to offer their congregations communion in both kinds. Revolution was in the air, the people were feeling empowered and the movement turned hostile. Whipped into religious fury, a mob of Hussites burst into Town Hall and threw several town councilmen to their deaths from upper story windows, an event written into history as Prague's "First Defenestration." In response, Bohemia's next king, Sigismund of Luxembourg, dispatched five successive waves of warriors to the Czech lands to put down the rebellion. Each time, the king's Roman Catholic crusaders were roundly defeated by the rag-tag Hussite armies, led by the celebrated one-eyed military genius Jan Žižka. Ultimately, the Hussites destroyed *themselves*, when their two main factions started fighting each other. The moderate Utraquists pummeled the radical Taborites at the Battle of Lipany, on May 30, 1434, and then struck a deal with the Roman Catholic Church that imposed an uneasy religious dualism, and a division between the sovereign and the masses that would never be closed.

The Habsburgs

A power vacuum in the 16th Century opened the royal doors to the Austrian Habsburgs who added the Czech throne to their empire. One of the most colorful Habsburgs, Rudolf II (1576-1611), was enamored with Prague and, when he ascended the throne, decided to move the seat of Empire here from Vienna. A huge patron of science and the arts, Rudolf opened his court to many of the world's best and brightest creators and thinkers. He supported eminent astronomers like Tycho de Brahe and Johannes Kepler and collected great art, including works by Michelangelo, Da Vinci and Rafael. The city blossomed intellectually, spiritually and artistically—a time that has come to be known as the "Second Golden Age of Prague." Rudolf was also more than a bit eccentric. He kept a menagerie of exotic pets and had a passion for expensive trinkets that he believed had magical powers. He financed the work of dozens of alchemists and opened his castle to the likes of John Dee and Edward Kelley, English hoaxers who enjoyed the royal treatment while attempting to turn lead into gold. Rudolf crossed that thin line from genius to insanity by 1611, when he was forced to abdicate the throne in favor of his power-hungry brother.

In the 17th Century the monarchy was unstable and Bohemia's aristocratic land-owners began to jostle for power. It all came to a head in 1618, when an angry mob marched up to Prague Castle and threw two Austrian vice-regents and several governors out a window, an event known as Prague's "Second Defenestration." No one was killed—their falls were padded by piles of garbage—but the event marked the beginning of the Rebellion of the Czech Estates (aristocratic land-owners) and was a prelude to the long European tragedy of the Thirty Years' War.

The Bohemian aristocrats were soundly trounced in 1620 at the Battle of the White Mountain, a contest which has come to symbolize the end of autonomy for the Czech people. The Habsburgs tightened their grip on the region, which they held securely for the next three hundred years. Twenty-seven Czech noblemen—leaders of the Estates who fought on the losing side against the Habsburgs—were publicly executed on Old Town Square in May, 1621 (cobblestone crosses mark the spot adjacent to Old Town Hall). Ten of their heads were then skewered on spikes and affixed to the Old Town tower of Charles Bridge where they remained for almost a dozen years as a warning to anyone who might again challenge the authority of Vienna. The Habsburgs then instituted draconian policies which included the confiscation of land owned by Protestants and the establishment of German as the official language of the Czech lands.

The Industrial Revolution & The Czech National Revival

Luckily, it was high time for the Enlightenment to make an entrance. 1781 was a particularly uplifting year. Serfdom was abolished, education was secularized and the Edict of Tolerance called for the free exercise of religion.

The Industrial Revolution, which started at the end of the 18th Century, was in full-swing by the middle of the 19th. The Austrian Empire's first factories were built in the Czech lands' mountainous border regions, where rushing rivers could be harnessed to power the engines of industry.

Industrialization begot prosperity, and prosperity begot new calls for political and social freedom. It was the middle of the 19th Century and rebellion was gripping Europe. It was the French Revolution in 1848 that signaled the beginning of the end for the Austrian Empire. Paris sneezed, the saying goes, and the whole continent caught a cold.

In the second half of the 19th Century, nationalism rose to fever pitch and local leaders petitioned Austria for greater autonomy. Czechs went wild asserting their unique cultural attributes with regards to religion, science and the arts. And they took up nationwide collections for the construction of nationalistic architectural chest-thumpers like the National Theater, the National Museum and the Rudolfinum. This Czech National Revival *(Národní obrozeni)*, as it became known, was a proud time in Czech history; Revivalists remain hugely popular cultural heroes. Writer Božena Němcová is depicted on the 500 Kč note, composer Bedřich Smetana has a major concert hall named for him and lexicographer Josef Jungmann (who compiled the first modern Czech dictionary) is honored with a large statue and a square in the center of the Prague.

World War I & Independence

Czechs weren't the only ones pressing for reform. Citizens of other nations within the Austrian Empire were also agitating for independence. On June 28, 1914, a radical Serbian nationalist assassinated the heir to the Austrian throne, Archduke Francis Ferdinand, precipitating World War I.

During the course of the war, Austria aligned with Germany which only helped unify the Czech people in their opposition to Austrian rule. The resistance was lead by university professor Tomáš Garrigue Masaryk, lawyer Edvard Beneš and Slovak astronomer Milan Rastislav Štefánik. Their political position was strengthened with the establishment of Czechoslovak military units fighting on the side of the Allies, who then recognized the trio as the leaders of Free Czechoslovakia.

At the war's end, the resistance received permission from the Allies to form a new government, provided they also form the new country of Czechoslovakia. Although Czechs and Slovaks had never before been politically connected to each other, the Allies felt that a united Czechoslovakia would provide the stability that Central Europe needed. And so the Czechoslovak Republic was born on October 28, 1918, and Tomáš Garrigue Masaryk was named the country's first President.

The First Republic

If Prague were to have a third Golden Age, it would be the years between the World Wars; a time of economic and political prosperity that locals often look back upon with nostalgia. During those 20 years Czechoslovakia evolved into one of the most advanced countries in Europe. Having inherited virtually all of Austria's industrial base, the Czechoslovak Republic was among the world's ten richest countries and one of the few states in Europe

with a constitutionally-mandated parliamentary democracy. Even the Communist Party, which was an increasingly vocal opponent of democracy, was legally allowed to exist, and won several seats in Parliament.

The young country had its problems too. For starters, ethnic Czechs and Slovaks accounted for only 65 percent of the total population. A full quarter of the population—more than three million—were ethnic Germans (the recent enemy), most of whom lived in the eastern border regions that were to become known as the "Sudetenland." The economic depression that hit world markets at the end of the 1920s politicized the ethnic Germans of the Sudetenland, who called for secession from the Czechoslovak state in favor of an attachment to increasingly-jingoistic Germany.

In 1938, Hitler demanded control over the Sudetenland and Czechoslovakia turned to the outside world for protection. But France and Britain believed appeasement was the best response and, at an notorious meeting that included Germany, Great Britain, France and Italy—but not Czechoslovakia—it was agreed that extensive Czech border regions would be ceded to Germany. Britain's Neville Chamberlain returned to London and told a cheering crowd in an infamous speech that his sly deal meant "peace in our time."

World War II

Within a year all of the Czech lands were overrun by the German army and Slovakia became an "independent" puppet Nazi state.

Reinhard Heydrich, a German Nazi and one of the architects of the "Final Solution," was appointed *Reichsprotektor* of Bohemia and Moravia. A close associate of Hitler's, Heydrich was a dreaded figure who ruled by fear with indiscriminate killing and maiming. In May, 1942, British-trained Czech resistance fighters parachuted into Prague and assassinated Heydrich. The *Reichsprotektor's* death touched off a furious reign of terror: More than 1600 people were executed and thousands more were immediately shipped to concentration camps. The Czech town of Lidice, from where some of the commandos were thought to have come, was then taken off the map; the Germans executed all 339 men of the village, sent the women and children to concentration camps, and plowed the houses into a potato field. A few weeks later, the same thing happened to the village of Ležáky—54 men, women and children were killed, and their village was razed to the ground.

Once it became clear that the Allies would win World War II, Roosevelt, Stalin and Churchill met at Yalta to divide the booty. There it was agreed that the Russian army would liberate Prague, and Czechoslovakia would fall under the Soviet sphere of influence.

After the war, in a spectacular act of retribution, up to three million ethnic Germans were stripped of their Czech citizenship and expelled from Czechoslovakia. Their property and belongings, according to presidential decrees, were put under "national supervision" and redistributed to ethnic Czechs. By 1950, ethnic Germans were reduced to 1.8 percent of the population in the Czech lands.

Politically, the post-war backlash was also intense. In the 1946 parliamentary elections, the Communist Party won 38% of the vote, followed by the National Socialists with 23%, and the People's Party with 20%.

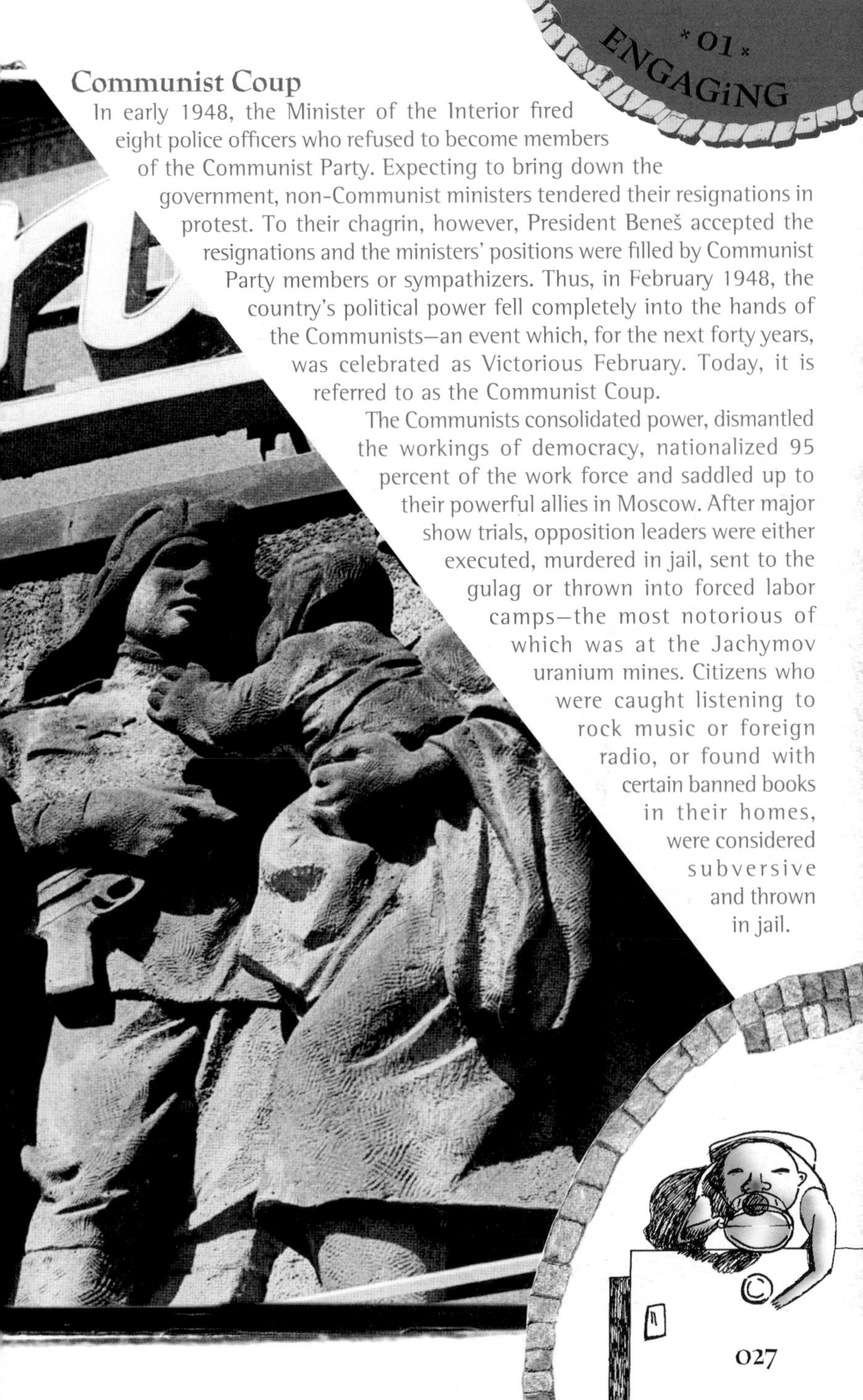

Communist Coup

In early 1948, the Minister of the Interior fired eight police officers who refused to become members of the Communist Party. Expecting to bring down the government, non-Communist ministers tendered their resignations in protest. To their chagrin, however, President Beneš accepted the resignations and the ministers' positions were filled by Communist Party members or sympathizers. Thus, in February 1948, the country's political power fell completely into the hands of the Communists—an event which, for the next forty years, was celebrated as Victorious February. Today, it is referred to as the Communist Coup.

The Communists consolidated power, dismantled the workings of democracy, nationalized 95 percent of the work force and saddled up to their powerful allies in Moscow. After major show trials, opposition leaders were either executed, murdered in jail, sent to the gulag or thrown into forced labor camps—the most notorious of which was at the Jachymov uranium mines. Citizens who were caught listening to rock music or foreign radio, or found with certain banned books in their homes, were considered subversive and thrown in jail.

The Prague Spring & "Normalization"

In the spring of 1968, the government responded to a broadening grassroots movement that was pushing for more economic, political and cultural freedom. The Communist Party's Central Committee publicly criticized its past policies, proclaimed the legitimacy of basic human rights and objected to the persecution of political opponents. Soon, jazz music, rock clubs, pop culture and miniskirts were spotted all over the Czech capital. Alexandr Dubček, the First Secretary of the Communist Party, referred to these reforms as "socialism with a human face." The people called it the "Prague Spring."

Threatened by this compromise in the uniformity of the Communist bloc, Moscow amassed a pan-Soviet invasion force. On the night of August 20, 1968,

Warsaw Pact tanks (with the exception of Romania, which refused to participate) stormed Czechoslovakia. The compassionate Prague government was replaced with hard-liners and the country began a 20-year period of occupation that was referred to by Party members as "normalization." Political purges removed thousands from their jobs and about 150,000 Czechs and Slovaks fled to the West.

In 1976, the members of an apolitical rock band called The Plastic People of the Universe were arrested and charged with crimes against the State. Their imprisonment was the catalyst for a group of dissident writers and artists to create "Charter 77," a petition demanding that the government abide by the international Helsinki Human Rights Accords, to which Czechoslovakia was a signatory. One of the chief spokespeople of the group was playwright Václav Havel.

The Velvet Revolution

In late 1989, Eastern Europe was in turmoil. The Berlin Wall crumbled and totalitarian regimes were tumbling like dominos. On November 17, 1989, students in Prague held a rally and march to commemorate the death of student Jan Opletal at the hands of the Nazi German invaders fifty years previous. The rally soon turned into a demonstration demanding democratic reforms. Riot police swooped down and blocked the marchers on Národni třida, near Wenceslas Square. After a long stand-off, the police moved-in, battering the unarmed crowd and injuring at least 167 people. During the melee, it was reported that one of the students was beaten to death. Although later proven false, the report helped galvanize popular support for the students.

During the next six weeks, mass demonstrations took place throughout Czechoslovakia. The country's theaters canceled performances and instead held public discussions about the country's future. During one of these, at the Činoherní Klub in Prague, *Občanské Fórum* (the Civic Forum) was established with Václav Havel as its leader. The Forum demanded the resignation of the Communist government and the release of prisoners of conscience.

Massive demonstrations and crippling general strikes forced the Communists to hold talks with the Civic Forum on November 28th. That same day, the government agreed to form a new coalition, to delete articles from the Constitution that guaranteed a leading role for the Communist Party, and to rescind a mandate requiring Marxist-Leninist education in schools.

Given an inch, the Civic Forum then went the mile, demanding the resignation President Gustav Husák. He capitulated on December 10th and was replaced by former dissident Václav Havel.

The first free elections in forty years were held in July, 1990. More than 96 percent of the population went to the polls and Václav Havel was elected President.

The new Czechoslovak government set about the huge task of dismantling the old political and economic framework. The pace of change was hotly disputed and split along geographical lines: Czechs wanted to move toward capitalism as quickly as possible while Slovaks weren't willing to make the social sacrifices necessary for fast change. The issue was basically decided at the polls, with the national elections of 1992. Czechs voted overwhelmingly for Václav Klaus, a strict Monetarist of the Milton Friedman school and a fan of Margaret Thatcher. Slovaks voted for staunch nationalist Vladimír Mečiar, whose platform basically consisted of two planks: autonomy for the eastern half of the former Czechoslovakia, and the slowing-down of privatization and painful economic reforms. Czechs and Slovaks wanted such different things from one another that their politicians decided that a shared future for the two nations was essentially impossible.

The next six months were spent dividing the common property that the two partners in the Czechoslovak Federation shared. Like all breakups, this one was somewhat painful and a little bit messy. But, when Czechoslovakia peacefully ceased to exist on January 1, 1993, many observers marveled at the smoothness of the "Velvet Divorce."

The Czech Republic Today

The years just after the Revolution opened a special window in time in which something truly magical happened. In order to begin with a clean slate, one of the first things the new government did was discard most of the laws that were enacted by the Communists. Reasoning that nobody had gotten a fair trial during the previous regime, President Havel signed an executive order releasing most prisoners from jail. The result was a short lived period of benevolent anarchy in which the happiness of being opened to the world was so pervasive it felt like you could cut it with a knife. People smiled at each other on the street, as everything from books and music to religion and ideology was new again. Possibilities seemed endless, travel and work restrictions were lifted, and people from around the world came to visit. By 1996, however, debates began to arise as to whether the post-revolutionary glow was over. Reality set in slowly. Sure capitalism offered boundless opportunity. But it also vanquished the economic safety net that Czechs—especially older Czechs—had become accustomed to. McDonalds colonized the city, along with fashion magazines, pornography and all the trappings of consumer culture. Today, more than ever, the Czech Republic feels like it's well on its way to becoming another successful part of the European Community, a political goal that has its share of dissenters. Anti-globalization activists came out in force during the IMF/World Bank meeting held in Prague in 2000, during which violent protests were answered with police brutality.

* 01 *
ENGAGiNG

President Václav Havel's First New Years' Address to the Nation (Excerpt)

Prague, January 1, 1990

My Dear Fellow Citizens!

Three days ago I became the president of the Republic as a consequence of your will, expressed through the deputies of the Federal Assembly. You have a right to expect me to mention the tasks I see before me as President.

The first of these is to use all my power and influence to ensure that we soon step up to the ballot boxes in a free election and that our path toward this historic milestone will be dignified and peaceful.

As Supreme Commander of the armed forces I want to guarantee that the defensive capability of our country will no longer be used as a pretext for anyone to stand in the way of courageous peace initiatives, the reduction of military service, the establishment of alternative military service and the overall humanization of military life.

In our country there are many prisoners who, though they may have committed serious crimes and have been punished for them, have had to submit despite the goodwill of some investigators, judges and above all defense lawyersto a debased judiciary process that curtailed their rights. They now have to live in prisons that do not strive to awaken the better qualities contained in every person, but rather humiliate them and destroy them physically and mentally. In a view of this fact, I have decided to declare a relatively extensive amnesty. At the same time I call on the prisoners to understand that forty years of unjust investigations, trials and imprisonments cannot be put right overnight, and to understand that the changes that are being speedily prepared still require time to implement. By rebelling, the prisoners would help neither society nor themselves. I also call on the public not to fear the prisoners once they are released, not to make their lives difficult, but to help them in the Christian spirit after their return among us, to find within themselves that which jails could not find in them: the capacity to repent and the desire to live a respectable life.

My honorable task is to strengthen the authority of our country in the world. I would be glad if other states respected us for showing understanding, tolerance and love for peace. I would be happy if Pope John Paul II and the Dalai Lama of Tibet could visit our country before the elections, if only for a day. I would be happy if we succeeded before the elections in establishing diplomatic relations with the Vatican and Israel.

In conclusion, I would like to say that I want to be a president who will speak less and work more. To be a president who will not only look out of the windows of his airplane but who, first and foremost, will always be present among his fellow citizens and listen to them well.

People, your government has returned to you!

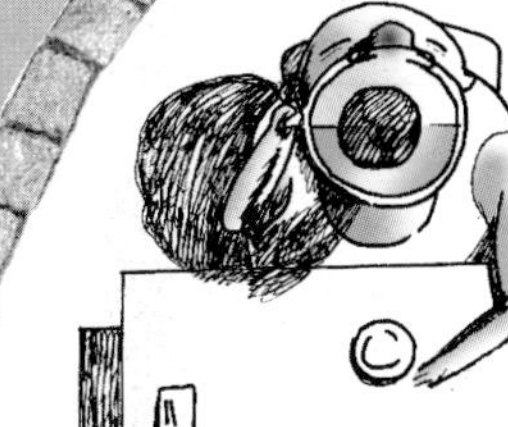

× 02 × ThE LAY Of THE LAND
NAVIGATiNG

KNOW YOUR NEIGHBORHOODS

Bisected by the curvaceous Vltava river, Prague's incredibly sexy historical center is one of the most beautifully built places on earth. But it's surrounded by suburban neighborhoods that grow newer and uglier the farther you move from the city's core. If Prague were a dart board then Old Town, New Town, Malá Strana and the Castle District—the city's first developments—would be the bulls-eye. Vinohrady, Žižkov, Dejvice, Smíchov and Vyšehrad—the oldest suburban neighborhoods—would be the treble ring, and everything else, including the new socialist-era housing estates, would be plain out of bounds. Our advice: Go for the money shot. After you've racked up enough points in the center, fine-tune your knowledge of the city by exploring the outskirts.

ThE CITY CENTER

The city center is comprised of five adjacent neighborhoods, all of which are within the desirable "Praha 1" post code.

Old Town

This is the storybook-beautiful place visitors coo about, and home to restaurants, clubs and pubs that you will get to know well.

Officially founded in the early-13th Century, but settled hundreds of years earlier, Old Town *(Staré Město)* is, well, old. Security-obsessed natives nestled the nascent town inside a right-angle bend in the river, so that it's protected by water like a infant in its mother's arms. On the town's backside, fortifications were built and a moat was dug. A ring of water and walls were the prerequisites for Prague to develop into a cultural, economic and religious island in the middle of the hostile, poor and pagan Mittle-Europa sea. Today, Old Town continues to be the humming city's hub and is still very much an international meeting- and market-place.

* 02 *
NAVIGAtiNG

Josefov

For more than six hundred years, until it was demolished in the late-19th Century, Prague's Jewish ghetto was Old Town's closest neighbor, nuzzling up against the north side of Old Town Square. At the turn of the 20th Century, the streets of the former ghetto were completely restructured, then studded with fantastically-sculpted apartment buildings. The area is now known as Josefov, named after Joseph II, a late-18th century king who passed laws that were relatively tolerant of the city's Jewish population. Pařížská, the quarter's main thoroughfare, is now lined with swanky Madison Avenue shops, and contemporary Josefov is only the faintest shadow of its former self. Only five ancient synagogues and an intensely overcrowded cemetery recall the quarter's roots.

New Town

Because it's wrapped around Old Town, the creation of New Town *(Nové Město)* effectively expanded Prague's borders and made the walls that surrounded Old Town superfluous. Founded by Charles IV in 1348, New Town was created around the same time that Charles Bridge and Charles University were built. There's not much in New Town that remains from the 14th Century and most of the area's office buildings and apartment houses were erected during the last two hundred years. Most of New Town is a work-a-day place that lacks the cobblestone charm of older parts of the city. But some of the city's best shops and restaurants are here, especially on Na Příkopě and Wenceslas Square *(Václavské náměstí)*.

Malá Strana

Across the famous Charles Bridge from Old Town is Malá Strana, an ancient fantasyland with one foot along the river and the other firmly planted on the castle hill. The neighborhood's name translates awkwardly into English as the "Lesser Side," but there is nothing ungraceful about the district's exquisite baroque architecture and perfect antique cobblestone streets. Virtually unchanged for centuries, Malá Strana's narrow lanes are coveted backdrops for dozens of European costume dramas including *Amadeus* and *Les Miserables.* Home to the Czech Parliament, government ministries and lots of foreign embassies, this quarter has the fewest residents and the best restaurants per square foot of any section of town. Dotted with grand aristocratic palaces and riddled with secret gardens, we can think of no better urban activity than to get lost in these dreamlike back streets.

Hradčany

Hradčany, "the Castle District," is perched above Malá Strana and Old Town. This quarter is relatively small and is home to the Castle *(hrad)*, the adjacent Bishop's Palace and other government and religious buildings. Despite its small size, Hradčany is big on visitor entertainment. Other important sights here include the Loreto and Strahov Monastery.

NEARBY SUBURBS

Žižkov

Prague's quintessential working-class neighborhood is famous locally for its plethora of pubs (more per capita than any other section of the city) and fiercely proud residents. Situated adjacent to Vinohrady, the two neighborhoods were united until 1868, when the citizens of Žižkov abruptly proclaimed their autonomy. Žižkov's independent spirit can be traced to the area's namesake, Jan Žižka (c.1360-1424), a one-eyed Hussite general who developed an almost invincible army that successfully repulsed a string of Catholic crusades. (His statue, said to be the world's largest equestrian sculpture, roosts upon a neighboring hill.)

Vinohrady

Vinohrady, once a royal vineyard, was turned into a grape paradise in 1358 on the order of King Charles IV. Respectable vintages were produced here for nearly 300 years. In the 17th century, following the Thirty Years War, developers moved in and transformed the fields into one of the nicest residential neighborhoods in the city. Situated just minutes east of the city center by tram or metro, Vinohrady is known for leafy, tree-shaded streets and unusually spacious apartments with high ceilings. The neighborhood is home to Pavilon, the city's first upscale shopping mall, Ambiente, one of Prague's best wholly-Czech-owned restaurants and Radost, the city's longest-running dance club.

Dejvice

When you want to see how the richest Praguers live, head to this Praha 6 neighborhood, located north of Hradčany hill. Some of the huge mansions here are as fine as you have seen anywhere in the world. Many of these former aristocratic villas have been taken over by international embassies, while others are home to wealthy locals. Particularly noteworthy buildings include the American ambassador's residence (Zikmunda Wintera 3), the Russian Embassy (pod Kaštany 1) and the home of President Václav Havel (Dělostřelecká 1).

Vyšehrad

Perched on a rock above the Vltava river, Vyšehrad ("high castle") was once the seat of Bohemia's Přemyslid princes. Located about two miles upriver from Charles Bridge, Vyšehrad is now home to a beautiful park with sweeping views. The National Cemetery, where some of the Czech nation's most outstanding personalities are buried, is here too.

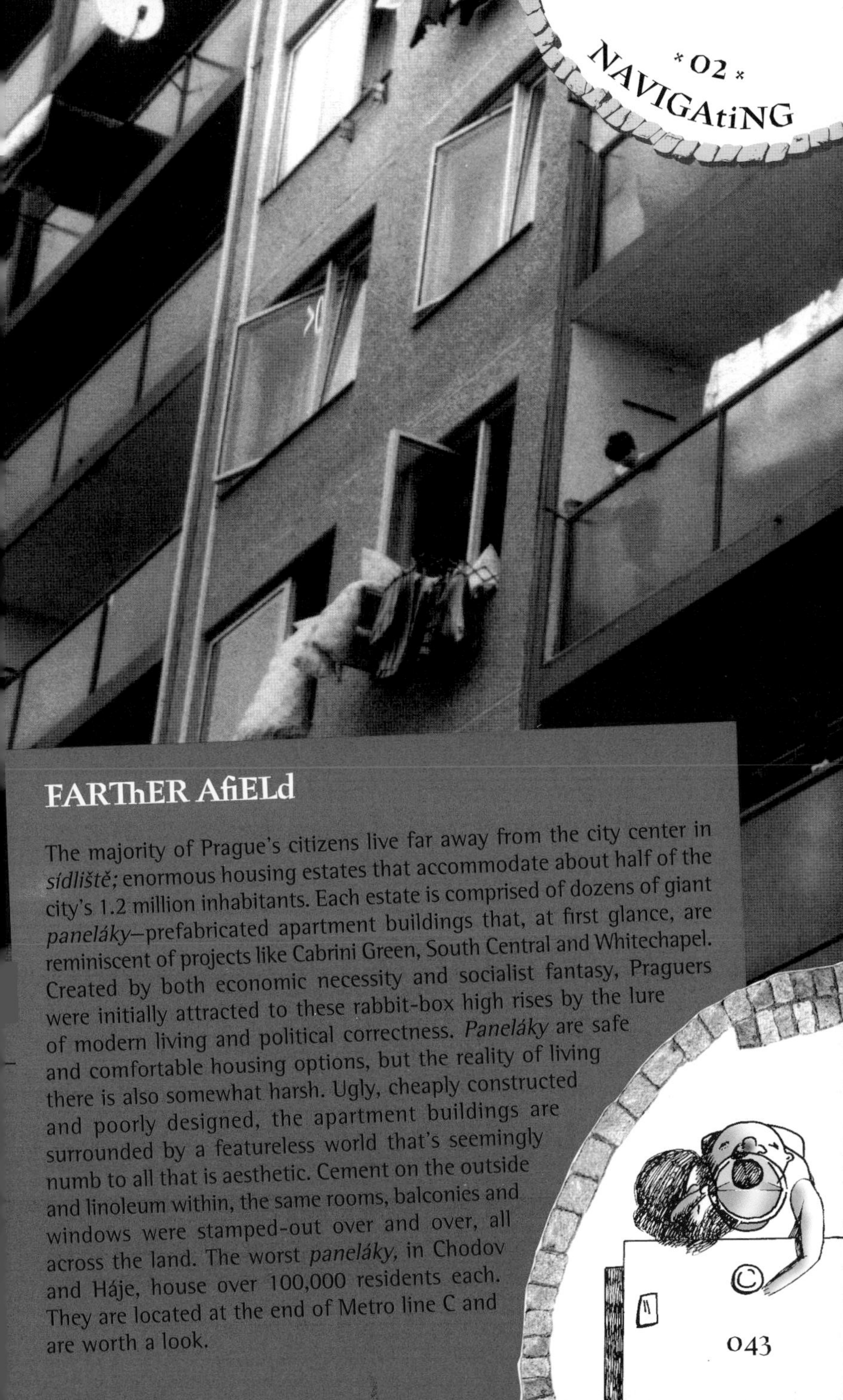

FARThER AfiELd

The majority of Prague's citizens live far away from the city center in *sídliště;* enormous housing estates that accommodate about half of the city's 1.2 million inhabitants. Each estate is comprised of dozens of giant *paneláky*—prefabricated apartment buildings that, at first glance, are reminiscent of projects like Cabrini Green, South Central and Whitechapel. Created by both economic necessity and socialist fantasy, Praguers were initially attracted to these rabbit-box high rises by the lure of modern living and political correctness. *Paneláky* are safe and comfortable housing options, but the reality of living there is also somewhat harsh. Ugly, cheaply constructed and poorly designed, the apartment buildings are surrounded by a featureless world that's seemingly numb to all that is aesthetic. Cement on the outside and linoleum within, the same rooms, balconies and windows were stamped-out over and over, all across the land. The worst *paneláky,* in Chodov and Háje, house over 100,000 residents each. They are located at the end of Metro line C and are worth a look.

ARRIVING

The Airport

Just a few years ago, landing in Prague's tiny airport felt comparable to touching down in some small place like Athens (Georgia, not Greece). It wasn't until late 1997 that a snazzy new terminal opened; one that looks and feels like a real big-city airport. Designed to accommodate an anticipated surge in foreign visitors much later in this century, the airport now seems awfully big and empty.

There are plenty of places to **exchange money** in the airport, but their rates are inferior to those offered by downtown banks. If you need crowns immediately, change a minimum amount and wait until you get into town to trade the big bucks. ATMs are located in the arrivals hall too.

Getting to Town

Mafia Taxi	600–700 Kč
City Taxi	300–350 Kč
Airline Shuttle	100 Kč
City Bus	12 Kč

By Taxi "Official" taxis line up just outside the arrivals terminal. These late-model Volkswagens are part of a taxicab mafia that "somehow" won the exclusive right to overcharge incoming travelers. You'll pay them 600-700 Kč to the city center.

For those who like their funky foreign experiences to begin immediately upon landing, exit the airport and turn right, along the sidewalk. When you are out of view of Mafia cabs, step out into the street and flag-down an empty normal city cab that has just dropped-off its passengers. There are plenty of them and they'll know exactly what you're up to. Negotiate a fare of 300 to 350 Kč. The driver may not know much English, but he will be a whiz at numbers.

By Airline Shuttle Buses operated by the national airline ČSA dash between the airport and the airline's city center office near náměstí Republiky every 30 minutes from 730am to 730pm. It costs about 100 Kč per person and is convenient if you are traveling light.

By City Bus Local bus 119 travels between the airport and Dejvicka, which is the last stop on the Metro's "A" line. Buses operate daily between 427am and 1140pm and take 21 minutes. When returning to the airport from the center, make sure you leave the bus at the very last stop as the first buildings you'll see with airport signs are almost two miles from the passenger terminal. A single trip is 12 Kč.

network is condensed into eight lines with different routes and numbers than their daytime counterparts. Like bees returning to their hive, all night trams converge on Lazarská, located in New Town near the Tesco department store.

Tickets can not be purchased on trams. If you remembered to buy one at either a Metro station or a newsstand beforehand, validate it in the machine immediately upon boarding.

Metro

Prague's chrome-plated, Soviet-built Metro was completed in 1974. The forty-six underground stations are strung along three color-coded lines that intersect beneath the city's center. The system is so simple that even the most street-unwise people can negotiate it with ease. Trains run daily, every two to seven minutes, from about 5am to midnight. Validate your ticket by inserting it, in the direction of the arrows, into the yellow date-stamping machine before descending to the train platform.

Buses

Unless you're visiting an unlucky friend who lives in the outer reaches of suburbia, it's unlikely you'll ever get on a bus in Prague. Regular bus service stops at midnight, after which selected routes run reduced schedules (usually only once per hour).

Taxis

Monkeys go to the zoo and gorillas become taxi drivers. At least, that's the way it is in Prague, where finding an honest ride is as difficult as encountering someone who admits to having once been a Nazi sympathizer or a member of the Communist Party. When it comes to performing meter tricks, almost every driver is a Houdini. Passengers who can't speak Czech are particularly susceptible to their mischievous slights-of-hand. Fares are supposed to be no more than 30 Kč upon entrance and 20 Kč per kilometer. The only way to protect yourself from meter-tampering, however, is to watch the *odometer*. Even better, negotiate a flat fee before you go anywhere (remembering that the long ride to the airport should only cost about 350 Kč).

You'll never get a reasonably-priced ride from the taxis lounging at the curbs by Old Town Square, Charles Bridge or Wenceslas Square. These are mafia cabs, manned by Neanderthals who are happy to beat to a pulp any non-dues-paying cabby who tries to pick-up a fare on "their" turf. Find a moving cab with an illuminated "TAXI" sign on its roof. Negotiate hard and don't overpay or you'll make it even worse for the rest of us.

For an almost guaranteed honest ride at no additional charge, phone for a taxi *yourself*. If you let the person at the front desk of your hotel phone for you, you'll pay a higher fare, as surely *someone* at the hotel will be getting a kick-back (In Prague it sometimes feels like everyone is on the take!). Reputable companies with English-speaking dispatchers include **AAA Taxi** (tel. 3311-3311) and the unfortunately-named **ProfiTaxi** (tel. 6131-4151).

Cashing In

The koruna (crown) is the coin of the realm, fractionated into relatively worthless *halíře* (hellers).

In the city center exchange places are almost as common as cobblestones, but exchange rates and commissions can be as shocking as the contents of a street-stand sausage. Don't be fooled by an attractive exchange rate, always ask what the *commission* is first and refuse to pay more than two percent. Banks generally offer the best rates, but American Express and some private exchange offices are not far behind.

If you do allow yourself to be suckered into changing money at an all-nite change shop, ask how much everything costs before handing over your crowns. And don't take the map or you'll pay for it.

The Biggest Bank for Your Buck

On a recent afternoon we ran around the city and asked the following currency exchange places how many crowns they'd give us for $100 bill:

Rate	Name	Address (Praha 1)	Open
3810 Kč	Živnostenská Banka	Na příkopě 20	Daily 830am-5pm
3737 Kč	Komerční Banka	Na příkopě 33	Mon-Fri 8am-5pm
3650 Kč	InterChange	Rytířská 26	Daily 835am-1140pm
3575 Kč	American Express	Václavské nám. 56	Daily 9am-7pm
3369 Kč	Chequepoint	Staroměstské nám. 21	Nonstop

Credit Cards and ATMs

There is absolutely no need to carry a bundle of cash when traveling to Prague, or any other major European city for that matter. In fact, you can travel to Prague without a penny in your pocket and obtain all the dough you need from hundreds of ATMs that work seamlessly with banks around the globe. Connected to the Cirrus and Plus networks, Prague's 900-plus cash machines communicate in English, allow 24-hour access to your accounts, and offer excellent

midpoint exchange rates. Your bank will charge between $1 and $3 for each withdrawal. Almost half of the city's ATMs also accept Visa or MasterCard (make sure you have a PIN).

Credit cards are widely accepted in Prague's restaurants, hotels and shops, and their use will usually result in an exchange rate that's superior to the one you'll get from the banks when trading cash. **Cash advances** on your Visa and MasterCard can be obtained from Komerční Banka, Na příkopě 33 (open Mon-Fri 8am-5pm).

Traveler's Checks

Travelers Checks are obsolete. You don't use them at home, why embarrass yourself with these clumsy dinosaurs when you're away? Any company that claims their travelers checks are as good as cash is lying. Even the tellers at American Express may refuse to exchange *their own* checks without your passport in tow. Stick to ATMs and credit cards. If you still insist on giving interest-free loans to major multinational corporations in exchange for their private-issue money, you'll find the best exchange rates at **American Express**, Václavské nám. 56, Praha 1 (tel. 2421-9992), where checks from all issuers are exchanged commission-free. Some restaurants and many hotels will exchange traveler's checks, but their rates are always much worse than banks'.

Black Market Money

Foolishness and adventure are the only two reasons we can think of to change money on the so-called "black market." Because the crown floats freely against world currencies, street trading has become the exclusive province of an unscrupulous band of money-launderers. If you're tempted to exchange money on the street in order to save a small commission, be very sure you know what Czech money looks like or you may get ripped-off with counterfeit, invalid or foreign banknotes. Want to give it a whirl? Head to Můstek (at the foot of Wenceslas Square), look pitifully lost, and you'll almost certainly be approached by the money men.

When All Else Fails

Western Union, Václavské náměstí 15, 2nd floor, Praha 1 (tel. 2422 2954) is the address to which daddy should wire money. It's open Mon-Fri 8am-10pm, Sat 9am-5pm, Sun 10am-4pm. M Můstek/Muzeum.

What's a crown worth? For today's exchange rates, check out the Avant-Guide CyberSupplement at www.avantguide.com

INFORMATION

Before heading out on your trip, check-out our online CyberSupplement™ at www.avantguide.com. Continuous updates include up-to-the-moment links to music, theater, film and other cultural events. Once in Prague, you can obtain English-language information from several sources:

The most comprehensive listings are contained in the monthly **Culture in Prague**, available from most bookshops and at many newsstands in the center. The ***Prague Post***, the city's weekly English-language newspaper, contains the most obvious cultural listings but is wanting when it comes to the late night dance scene. It's available from newsstands throughout the city center. For a look at the current club scene, find a copy of **Think**, a free, American-made monthly 'zine that's distributed at popular expat pubs (*see* Chapter 9 for complete information).

Prague Information Service, Old Town Square, inside Old Town Hall, Staroměstské nám. 6, Praha 1 (tel. 2448-2202); and Na příkopě 20, Praha 1 (tel. 544-444), offers several free government-published brochures focusing on upcoming cultural events.

Dozens of tour and ticket sellers are located throughout Prague's tourist center. Though they're often disguised as information agencies, these outlets are primarily interested in sales. The largest of these is **Čedok,** Na příkopě 18 and Václavské náměstí 53, Praha 1 (tel. 2419-7111), the holder of the tour operator monopoly under communism, and now the country's biggest private travel agency.

For straightforward answers to typical touristic questions, approach a concierge at one of the city's major hotels. You don't have to mention it if you are not sleeping upstairs.

ESSENTIAL SERVICES

Credit Cards American Express (tel. 2421-9992); MasterCard/EuroCard (tel. 2424-8110); Visa (tel. 2412-5353).

Emergencies Police (tel. 150); Fire (tel. 158); Ambulance (tel. 155). **Canadian Medical Center**, Veleslavínská 1, Praha 6 (tel. 0602/335670, or 3536-5297). **American Medical Center**, Janovského 48 , Praha 7 (tel. 807-7569).

Embassies US Embassy, Tržiště 15, Praha 1 (tel. 5753-0663), open Mon-Fri 8am-4pm. **Canadian High Commission**, Mickiewiczova 6, Prague 6 (tel. 7210-1800), open Mon-Fri 830am-1230pm. **British Embassy**, Thunovská 14, Praha 1 (tel. 5753-0278), open Mon-Fri 9am-noon. **Australian Honorary Consulate**, Klimentská 20, Praha 2 (tel. 2431-0743), open Mon-Thurs 830am-5pm, Fri 830am-2pm.

Eyewear/Contact Lenses **Fokus Optik**, Mostecká 3, Praha 1 (tel. 2421-0818). In addition to fitting Czech sports stars and actors with the latest models by Armani and Ralph Lauren, the shop offers a full range of clear and tinted contact lenses from Johnson & Johnson and Bausch & Lomb. Doctors are on site Mon, Thurs and Fri (appointments required). Open Mon-Fri 9am-6pm, Sat 10am-1pm.

Branches: Štěpánská 19, Praha 1; Vodičkova 36 (pasáž Lucerna), Praha 1; Hybernská 8, Praha 1; Na poříčí 33, Praha 1; Revoluční 5, Praha 1.

Film Processing/Photography
AZ Foto, Celetná 8, Praha 1 (tel. 2423-9170) is the flagship of Prague's largest comprehensive photo chain, selling state-of-the-art equipment and offering one-hour developing. Other Praha 1 branches are located at Vodičkova 39 (in Světozor passage), and Senovážná 8.

Internet Internet Cafe Prague, Národní 25, Praha 1 (tel. 2108-5286), is a webspace with 21 computers where you can download your email to disk. They're open Mon-Fri 9am-11pm, Sat-Sun 10am-11pm. **Café Electra**, Rašínovo nábřeží 62, Praha 2 (tel. 229-7038), has 18 computers and is AOL friendly. They're open daily 8am-midnight and charge 40-80 Kč/hour.

The local access number for **CompuServe** is tel. 2210-1010.

Laundry/Dry Cleaning Several shops offer American-style self- and service-washes. **Laundry Kings**, Dejvická 16, Praha 6 (tel. 312-3743) is open Mon-Fri 6am-10pm, Sat-Sun 8am-10pm. From Hradčanská Metro station, take the "Prague Dejvice" exit and turn left. **Prague Laundromat**, Korunni 14, Praha 2 (tel. 2251-0180) is open daily 8am-8pm. Walk two blocks east from Náměstí Míru Metro station. **Laundryland**, a self-service place in pasáž Černá růže, Na Příkopě 12, Praha 1 (tel. 2101-4632) offers a convenient delivery service. They're open Mon-Fri 9am-8pm, Sat 9am-7pm, Sun 11am-7pm. M Můstek.

Lost Property It's probably gone for good, but you might as well try visiting the city's **Lost Property Office**, Karolíny Světlé 5, Praha 1 (tel. 2423-5085).

Luggage Storage The **Ruzyně Airport Luggage Storage Office** (tel. 2011-1111) is open nonstop and charges 80 Kč per item, per day. You can also leave luggage at almost any downtown hotel. At an average cost of 50 Kč per item, your bags can stay at the Savoy, even if you can't.

Pharmacies The most centrally-located pharmacy *(lékárna)* is at Václavské nám. 8 (tel. 2422-7532). For essentials like pantyhose, toothpaste, tampons and Donald Duck bubble bath, try **Rossmann**, Pařížská 16, Praha 1 (tel. 2482-6344), open Mon-Fri 8am-8pm, Sat 9am-8pm, Sun 1-8pm.

Photocopying **Copy General**, Národní 11, Praha 1 (tel. 2207-5650) is the Kinko's of Prague, offering a full range of copy services. They're open daily 7am-10pm. M Národní třída. A smaller branch at Senovážné nám. 26, Praha 1 (tel. 2423-0020) is open nonstop.

Postal Services/Express Mail

The Main Post Office *(Hlavní pošta)*, Jindřišská 14, Praha 1, 110 00 (tel. 2113-1111), just a few steps from Václavské náměstí, is open nonstop. Other Praha 1 post offices are located in **Old Town** at Kaprova 12 (near Staroměstská Metro station); in **Malá Strana** at Josefská 4 near Charles Bridge; and opposite St. Vitus' Cathedral in the Third Courtyard of **Prague Castle**. You can buy stamps at Tabák shops all over town.

DHL, Běžecká 1, Praha 6 (tel. 2030-0111); **Federal Express**, Klimentská 46, Praha 1 (tel. 4400-2200); **UPS**, Výtvarná 4, Praha 6 (tel. 3300-3111).

Telecommunications

Local telephone numbers contain anywhere from four to eight digits. Most public phones operate exclusively with a **Phonecard**, available from post offices and newsstands in denominations ranging from 175 Kč to 320 Kč for 50 to 100 impulses. You can use cardphones to dial direct to almost anywhere in the world (for international calls dial 00 first).

To call the US via AT&Ts USA Direct, dial (tel. 0042/000-101). The same service is also offered by MCI (tel. 0042/000-112) and **Sprint** (tel. 0042/087-187).

There are three **cellular phone** networks in the Czech Republic: **Eurotel** (tel. 6701-6701; www.eurotel.cz), **Paegas** (tel. 2162-0128; www.paegas.cz); and **Oskar** (0800/177177; www.oskar.cz). All three work on the European-standard GSM. To **rent a cellphone** in Prague, visit the EuroTel Shop, Jindřišská 24, Praha 1 (tel. 2422 7283). It's open Mon-Fri 8am-7pm, Sat 9am-1pm.

Video

PAL is the video standard. English-language tapes and multi-format machines can be rented from **Video To Go**, Vítězné nám. 10, Praha 6 (tel. 312-4096). They're open daily 10am-10pm.

× 03 ×

WhERE TO STAY
SLEEPiNG

Although a recent hotel-construction boom has significantly eased Prague's housing crunch, scoring the perfect room at a price you can afford is still a bit of a challenge. While most everything else in the city is far cheaper than Western Europe, accommodations remain uncharacteristically pricey. The best of the city's new hotels are locally-owned charmers in Old Town and Malá Strana, carved from beautifully-reconstructed old buildings. The best places tend to be relatively small, so getting a reservation can be tough–especially in late Spring and early Fall. Quality ranges from Spartan to spectacular and is usually–but not always–reflected by price.

All the hotels listed below share one thing in common: they have enviable locations and are within walking distance to most everything. Hotels that are far from the center, or difficult to reach by public transportation, are not listed–we wouldn't want to stay in them.

The hotels in this book represent the very best in each price category that Prague has to offer. All present something special in the way of local color and character. And we have gone to great lengths to flush out the very best of the city's budget hotels. Every establishment listed here meets our strict criteria for service, facilities and value. Hotels get extra points for shower power, room service reaction time, a sound system when you want it, and silence when you don't. Then, of course, there's the cool factor....

Got Reservations?

In Prague there is really no such thing as a "rack" rate. Sure, some hotels publish their highest tariffs but, in reality, the price is determined by availability (read: supply and demand). If there are a lot of people in town the price goes up; if there aren't, the price goes down. Simple. Because of travel agent commissions and corporate and club discounts, many hotel rooms are sold for substantially less than the rates listed below. A stay of one week or more is also worthy of a reduction.

The best way to reserve a hotel room is to phone, fax or email and ask for their "best corporate rate." To compare prices and save time, contact several hotels concurrently and then immediately cancel the ones that don't work for you. The country code for the Czech Republic is 420. The city code is 02. Drop the second 0 when phoning or faxing from outside the Czech Republic (from the US dial 011-420-2 plus the local number; from Great Britain dial 00-420-2 plus the local number).

If you're willing to take the chance of not getting a room in your first choice of hotel, then arriving in the city without reservations puts you in a great position to negotiate a lower rate. Hotel rooms are perishable commodities and become worthless if they go unsold. It is not unreasonable for a walk-in customer to expect a 40% to 60% reduction in the hotel's standard rates, especially during the off-season. And if you ask to see the room before committing, chances are you'll be shown to a better room than if you don't.

Apartment Rentals

Because hotels in Prague are so expensive, many visitors prefer to hole-up in a centrally-located apartment; an excellent option that will give you more room at exceptionally lower rates. Apartments are comfortable, but basic, usually with a separate living room and full kitchen. Plumbing can be dodgy and there's often no telephone or maid service, but you'll get a good feel for how some typical Praguers live.

Accommodations Service (tel. 02/231-0202; fax 02/231-6640; www.telecom.cz/accommodation) is the best rental agency in the city, with good prices and a long list of places on offer. Expect to pay about 2000 Kč/night for their best places in the center (for two people). Cheaper apartments are located outside the historical center.

hOTELS bY AREA

The cost (*) reflects the average price of a double room

*	= Under 5000 Kč	***	= 7000–9000 Kč
**	= 5000–7000 Kč	****	= Over 9000 Kč

OLD TOWN		page
Betlem Club	*	078
Casa Marcello	***	066
Dům U Staré Paní	*	078
Four Seasons Hotel Prague	****	063
Inter-Continental Praha	****	061
Klášterní Dvůr	*	079
Maximilian	**	072
Hotel Paříž	****	064
Hotel Ungelt	**	076
Hotel U Zlatého Stromu	*	082
MALÁ STRANA		
Dům U Červeného Lva	**	071
Hotel Čertovka	**	070
Hotel U Krále Karla	**	072
Hotel U Modrého Klíče	**	071
Hotel U Páva	**	075
Pension Dientzenhofer	*	081
Hotel Pod Věží	**	075
Residence Nosticova	**	076
Sidi Hotel	*	082
Hotel U Tří Pštrosů	***	068
Hotel U Zlaté Studně	***	067
NEW TOWN		
Hotel Axa	*	078
Bílá Labut' Best Western	**	070
Evropa Hotel	*	081
Hotel Harmony	*	079
Prague Marriott Hotel	**	066
The Palace	****	064
Renaissance Hotel Prague	***	074

Inter-Continental Praha

nám. Curieových 1, Praha 1. Tel. 02/2488-1111. Fax 02/2481-1216. www.interconti.com Rates: 11,600-12,600 Kč single/double; suites from 16,000 Kč. Parking 850 Kč. AE, MC, V. M Staroměstská

Served by a doting staff with an eager-to-please philosophy, this member of the internationally respected chain is easily the best-managed property in the neighborhood. Uniformly well-decorated rooms and a fine location—one long, wonderful block from Old Town Square—makes the Inter-Conti attractive to individuals, groups and business travelers. There are lots of older tourists here, mixed in with airline personnel, diplomats and the occasional touring rock band. Hillary Clinton has stayed here, as have Michael Jackson, R.E.M., U2 and Luciano Pavarotti. From the outside, the hotel is something of a concrete horror. But the interior is far more appealing. Neutral colors and dark vertical stripes give average-size guestrooms a sleek, club-like appearance. Each is styled with medium-quality wood-and-cloth furniture, marble baths and interesting original art. Book a room facing Old Town, as these have better views than those overlooking the river. Junior Suites are just larger rooms, while Business Suites are actually split with a wall, like they're supposed to be. The Inter-Conti also has one of the best fitness clubs in town (*see* Chapter 6/Recreation & Exercise), which includes an indoor swimming pool, workout room and saunas.

364 Rooms: Air-conditioning, cable TV, telephone, modular jacks, hairdryer, minibar, radio, room service (24 hours), concierge, 2 restaurants, bar, business center, fitness center, swimming pool, wheelchair access.

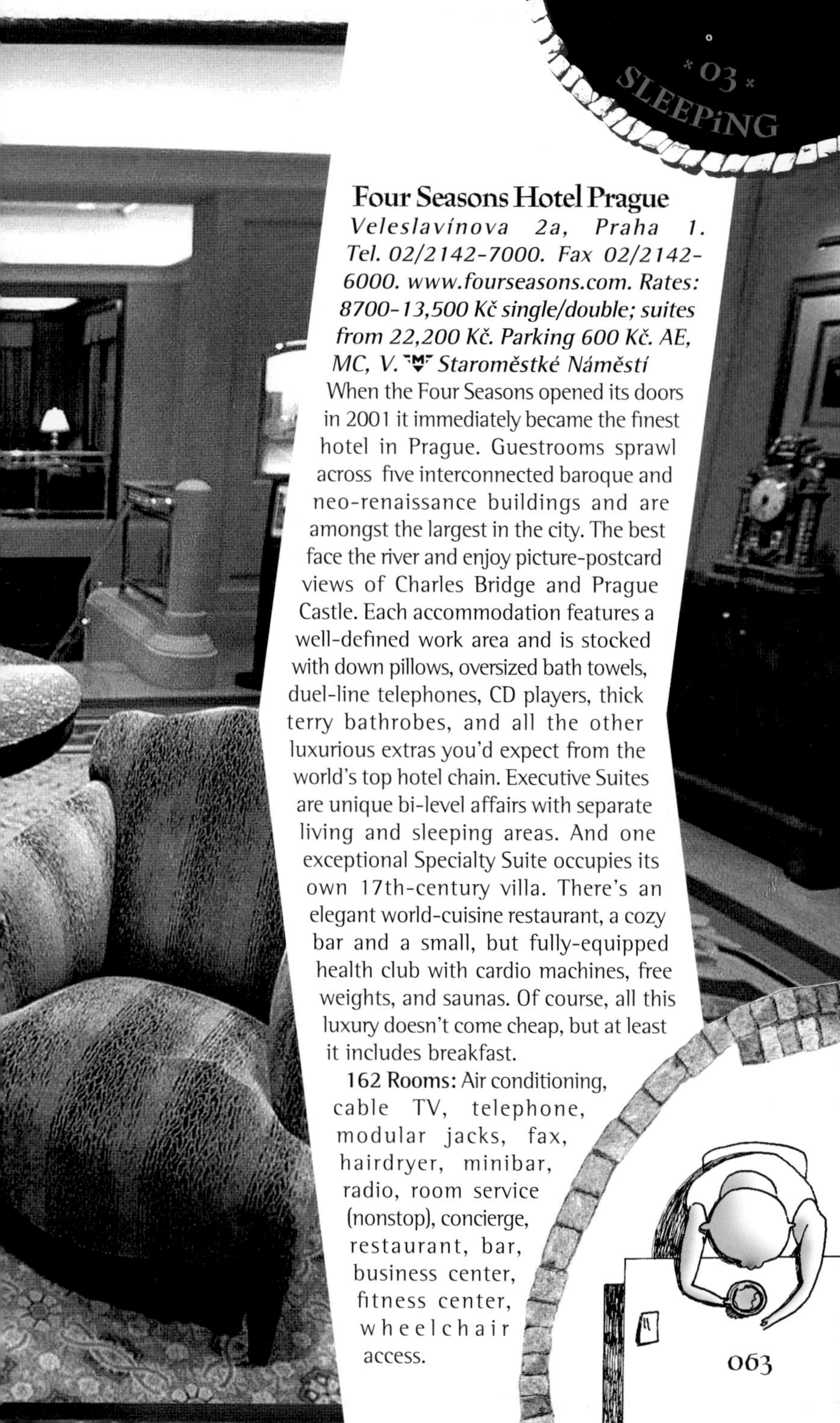

Four Seasons Hotel Prague

Veleslavínova 2a, Praha 1. Tel. 02/2142-7000. Fax 02/2142-6000. www.fourseasons.com. Rates: 8700-13,500 Kč single/double; suites from 22,200 Kč. Parking 600 Kč. AE, MC, V. M Staroměstké Náměstí

When the Four Seasons opened its doors in 2001 it immediately became the finest hotel in Prague. Guestrooms sprawl across five interconnected baroque and neo-renaissance buildings and are amongst the largest in the city. The best face the river and enjoy picture-postcard views of Charles Bridge and Prague Castle. Each accommodation features a well-defined work area and is stocked with down pillows, oversized bath towels, duel-line telephones, CD players, thick terry bathrobes, and all the other luxurious extras you'd expect from the world's top hotel chain. Executive Suites are unique bi-level affairs with separate living and sleeping areas. And one exceptional Specialty Suite occupies its own 17th-century villa. There's an elegant world-cuisine restaurant, a cozy bar and a small, but fully-equipped health club with cardio machines, free weights, and saunas. Of course, all this luxury doesn't come cheap, but at least it includes breakfast.

162 Rooms: Air conditioning, cable TV, telephone, modular jacks, fax, hairdryer, minibar, radio, room service (nonstop), concierge, restaurant, bar, business center, fitness center, wheelchair access.

The Palace

Panská 12, Praha 1. Tel. 02/2409-3111. Fax 02/2422-1240. palhoprg@mbox.vol.cz Rates: 9000-10,000 Kč single/double; suites from 11,500 Kč. Parking 650 Kč. AE, MC, V. M Můstek

The ultraconservative Palace can always be counted on for impeccable service and the highest standards. On the plus side, this means intense attention to detail, top-quality furnishings and a concierge that's famously well-connected for reservations and tickets. Both George Bush (The Elder) and the Rolling Stones have enjoyed the Palace's airy rooms, European art and handy toilet-side telephones. Guestrooms are opulent. But their dull designs and muted colors will win no fast-forward style awards. The white-marble bathrooms are large, but contain only one sink, and bedrooms are devoid of stereos or VCRs—accouterments that are increasingly common in less orthodox hotels. Lady Queen Rooms, which are priced the same as doubles, are slightly larger than others. The Palace is centrally located, within walking distance of all the major sights, but its immediate neighborhood is neither quaint nor quiet.

124 Rooms: Air-conditioning, cable TV, telephone, modular jacks, fax, hairdryer, minibar, radio, room service (24 hours), concierge, 2 restaurants, bar, business center, sauna, wheelchair access.

Hotel Pařiž

(Hotel Paris) U Obecního domu 1, Praha 1. Tel. 02/2422-2151. Fax 02/2422-5475. www.vol.cz/hotels/pariz/ Rates: 10,800 Kč single/double; suites from 15,600 Kč. Parking 700 Kč. AE, MC, V. M Náměstí Republiky

Harking back to the golden time between the world wars, the Hotel Pařiž is built with regal architecture, set with stiff linen and fronted by tailcoated doormen. Opened in 1923, the hotel is an historical landmark trimmed with elaborate cast iron railings and gilded accessories, and packed with eye-catching elements of art nouveau. Until the communists began their 40 years of mismanagement, the hotel functioned as the city's superintendent of traditionalist wealth. Today, the etched-glass doors are once again opening to the world's old- and new-rich, which basically boils down to German industrialists and American holiday-makers. Although it lacks the services and facilities to qualify for "world-class" ranking, the Pařiž remains an exceedingly pleasant place to stay. Guestrooms are uniquely styled and amply sized, which is a welcome departure from typical cookie-cutter hotel rooms. Each is handsomely decorated with fabulous First Republic furnishings and seriously comfortable beds and is exceedingly private, shielded with double sets of wooden doors. The largest rooms are on the top floor. Depending on your mood, you can drop down to the lobby cafe for a pricey cocktail, or head to the Sarah Bernhardt restaurant for an elegant meal.

93 Rooms: Air-conditioning, cable TV, telephone, modular jacks, hairdryer, minibar, radio, room service (630am-midnight), concierge, restaurant, fitness room and sauna.

HOTEL PARIZ

EXPENSIVE

Casa Marcello

Řásnovka 738 (Haštalské nám.), Praha 1. Tel. 02/231-1230 or 02/231-0260. Fax 02/231-3323. www.casa.marcello.cz. Rates: 9500 Kč single/double; suites from 10,500 Kč. Parking 600 Kč. AE, MC, V. M Staroměstská

When Hotel Paříž owner Antonin Brandejs decided he needed more guestrooms, he chose privacy over pretension and renovated Casa Marcello. A small, high-quality hotel on one of Old Town's most secluded squares, this sprawling, whitewashed three-story complex makes for both a great base and a silent night's sleep. Built around a central courtyard over 500 years ago, the hotel rambles across two adjacent buildings, united with arched ceilings, well-chosen furnishings and an unmistakable sense of being someplace special. Services and facilities are few, but guestrooms—each of which are unique in character, color and shape—are larger than most in the city. Suites, which are significantly larger than standard rooms, are well worth the additional crowns.

31 Rooms: Air conditioning (some), cable TV, telephone, modular jacks, hairdryer, minibar, radio, room service, restaurant, sauna.

Prague Marriott Hotel

V Celnici 8, Praha 1. Tel. 02/2288-8888. Fax 02/2182-2333. www.marriotthotels.com. Rates: 8800 Kč single/double; suites from 14,500 Kč. Parking 600 Kč. AE, MC, V. M Náměstí Republiky

Purposely built for the Marriott chain, this marble monolith is strictly business; meaning well-planned boxy rooms and a good location, walkable to most everywhere. As you step inside this hotel on the outskirts of Old Town you could convince yourself you're in almost any city in the world. That's both the greatest benefit and the top drawback of this thoroughly serviceable chain hotel in which all the rooms are all rectangle and CNN is on TV at all times. You can often find excellent corporate rates here, and weekend specials too. There's a decent restaurant, a comfortable lounge, and even a casino in the cellar.

297 Rooms: Air-conditioning, cable TV, telephone, modular jacks, hairdryer, minibar, radio, room service (nonstop), concierge, restaurant, bar, business center, fitness center, wheelchair access.

Renaissance Hotel Prague

V Celnici 7, Praha 1. Tel. 02/2182-2100 or 02/2481-0396. Fax 02/2182-2333. www.renaissancehotels.com Rates: 7800 Kč single/double; suites from 12,000 Kč. AE, MC, V.
M Náměstí Republiky

A quintessential top business hotel, this suit-oriented chain hotel is a somewhat sterile but functional place that's both well-conceived and inoffensive. The hotel's most outstanding features are good closets and bright lighting, neither of which make for great letters home. Most rooms are identically well-dressed with light Scandinavian furnishings and original contemporary art. Although they cost the same, king-bedded rooms offer a bit more space than doubles. Corner rooms are larger still. Suites, all of which are on the top floor, are exceptionally spacious and have sizable bathrooms. Excellent prices and lots of uniformity make this hotel popular with tour groups and touring comeback bands like Kiss.

309 Rooms: Air-conditioning, cable TV, telephone, modular jacks, hairdryer, minibar, radio, room service (nonstop), concierge, 3 restaurants, bar, business center, fitness center, small swimming pool, wheelchair access.

Hotel U Zlaté Studně

(At the Golden Well) U Zlaté Studně 4, Praha 1. Tel. 02/5701-1213. Fax 02/5753-3220. hotel@zlatastudna.cz. Rates: 6800-9500 Kč single/double; suites from 9500 Kč. Limited free parking. AE, MC, V.
M Malostranská

You'd never find this place if we didn't tell you about it because the Hotel at the Golden Well is hidden at the end of the smallest street in Malá Strana. Set in the foothills just below Prague Castle, the hotel wows with wonderful views of Prague and top-quality rooms designed for privacy and comfort. Every room in this excellent hotel is different, and each has it's own recommendable charm. Many have ancient beamed ceilings and all are furnished with top-quality faux-antiques. Bathrooms are particularly special, built with heated floor tiles and Jacuzzi tubs, some of which are large enough for three. Breakfast, included, is served in one of the most enchanting rooms in Prague.

20 Rooms: Air-conditioning, cable TV, telephone, modular jacks, hairdryer, minibar, radio, room service (nonstop), restaurant, bar.

Hotel U Tří Pštrosů

(At the Three Ostriches) Dražického nám. 12, Praha 1. Tel. 02/5753-2410. Fax 02/5753-3217. www.utripstrosu.cz. Rates: 5500 Kč single, 7000 Kč double; suites from 9000 Kč. Limited free parking. AE, MC, V. M Malostranská

A great choice for travelers who are late to bed and early to rise, this five-story gem at the foot of Charles Bridge is so close to the street musicians and trinket peddlers you can almost reach out and clobber them on their heads without even getting out of bed. Once owned by a feather dealer who decorated the house with depictions of ostriches, the hotel has preserved its renaissance-era painted wooden ceilings and gaggle of interior frescos. The light and airy guestrooms are a perfect fusion of contemporary and antique, designed with beautiful wooden furnishings, large windows and plenty of ancient architectural elements peeking from most every corner. The best rooms, on the top floor, offer views of both Charles Bridge and Prague Castle, and the ample-sized suites are particularly recommendable. Film directors David Lynch and Miloš Forman are among the many Hollywood types who have stayed here.

18 Rooms: Cable TV, telephone, modular jacks, hairdryer, minibar, radio, room service (7am-11pm), restaurant, bar.

MOdERATE

Bílá Labuť Best Western

(The White Swan) Biskupská 9, Praha 1. Tel. 02/2481-1382 or 02/232-8692. Fax 02/232-2905. cchotels@login.cz. Rates: 5000 Kč single, 5600 Kč double; suites from 6000 Kč. Parking 400 Kč. AE, MC, V. *Náměstí Republiky/Florenc*

A miraculous transformation from dilapidated apartment house to modern hotel has made this contemporary charmer into a respectable, value-priced member of the Best Western chain. A clean, plush little lobby gives way to immaculately tidy guestrooms fitted with new plumbing and smart decorations. Smallish rooms and positively tiny closets are drawbacks, but they are fully functional and well-maintained. Suites include a small living room and tiled bathrooms with double sinks. There is a modest fitness center and sauna on the roof.

54 Rooms: Air-conditioning, cable TV, telephone, hairdryer, minibar, radio, room service (7am-2am), restaurant, bar, fitness center, sauna, wheelchair access.

Hotel Čertovka

(Devil's Stream) U Lužického Semináře 2, Praha 1. Tel. 02/5753-2235 or 02/5753-0265. Fax 02/5753-4392. www.certovka.cz. Rates: 4500 Kč single, 6000 Kč double. AE, MC, V. *Malostranská*

Named for the romantic stream it overlooks, the Čertovka is one of the newest hotels in Malá Strana. This charming place, just a cobblestone's throw from Charles Bridge, offers wonderfully contemporary rooms with superior furnishings and dense soundproofing. Wood floors, quality carpeting and a bright, cheery atmosphere make this one of our top recommendations. And it ranks very high on our value-meter. Every accommodation is different, but most are ample sized and have enjoyable views. The best and biggest are top floor corners.

21 Rooms: Cable TV, telephone, hairdryer, minibar, safe, wheelchair access.

Dům U Červeného Lva

(House at the Red Lion) Nerudova 41, Praha 1. Tel. 02/5753-3833. Fax 02/5753-2746. www.starshotelsprague.com. Rates: 6000-7000 Kč single/double; suites from 8500 Kč. AE, MC, V. M Staroměstská

The "House at the Red Lion" was built as a single-family home for a local tradesman. Apparently a well-connected tradesman, considering the house's fabulous location on the Royal Way, close to Prague Castle. A wine bar in the well-preserved basement dates from the gothic period. And guestrooms upstairs, with their painted wood-beam ceilings and carved reproduction furnishings, appear to be straight out of the Renaissance. Historical elements are perfectly restored throughout the house and enhanced with wooden floors and well-chosen spreads and upholstery. Standard rooms are not particularly large, but each feels uniquely special. Suites are liberally sized and contain a separate sitting area. The best room is the top floor double, which is capped by a cathedral ceiling.

8 Rooms: Cable TV, telephone, hairdryer, minibar, room service, restaurant, bar.

Hotel U Modrého Klíče

(At the Blue Key) Letenská 14, Praha 1. Tel. 02/5753-4361. Fax 02/5753-4372. www.bluekey.cz. Rates: 4800 Kč single, 6000 Kč double, 10,00 kč suite. AE, MC, V. M Malostranská

Situated in the center of Malá Strana, the Blue Key offers contemporary rooms at decent prices and scores high in the value-for-money category. There's not much creativity to the IKEA decor and there are no views to speak of. But rooms are clean and comfortably furnished, and the prices are low for the neighborhood. Because they're almost directly on top of the tram racks, rooms in front are a light-sleeper's nightmare. Check-in here only if you can secure accommodations in the back.

28 Rooms: Air-conditioning, cable TV, telephone, modular jacks, hairdryer, minibar, whirlpool, sauna.

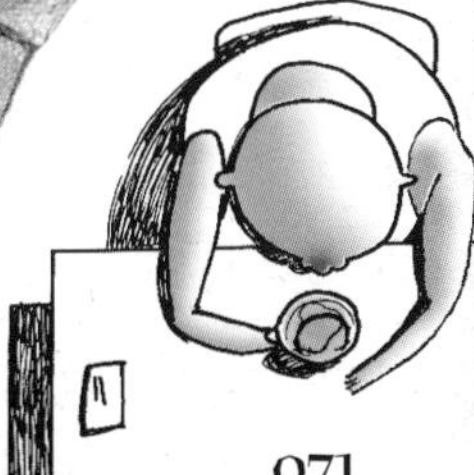

Hotel U Krále Karla

(At the King Charles) Úvoz 4, Praha 1. Tel. 02/5753-2869 or 02/5753-0484. Fax 02/5753-3591. www.romantichotels.cz. Rates: 6000-6500 Kč single/double; suites from 7000 Kč. Limited free parking. AE, MC, V. Ⓜ Malostranská

Among the prettiest little hotels anywhere, the King Charles feels romantic and regal, offering well-sized rooms fitted with beamed ceilings, stained-glass windows, antique furnishings and massive wood beds with intricately-carved headboards and satin coverings. U Krále Karla was originally a gothic building owned by Benedictine monks. It still has the feeling of a sanctuary, decorated with plush furnishings, plenty of wood and lots of art from centuries past. The hotel is located close to the main entrance of Prague Castle, which puts it at the top of the beautiful, but steep, Nerudova Street. Guests of the American Embassy check-in here with regularity, and rocker Annie Lennox and other vacationing celebrities have been spotted in the breakfast room. The hotel is not a good place for babies, dogs and other ankle-biters.

19 Rooms: Cable TV, telephone, modular jacks, hairdryer, minibar, radio, room service (8am-9pm), restaurant, bar.

Maximilian

Haštalská 14, Praha 1. Tel. 02/2180-6111. Fax 02/2180-6110. maximilianhotel@hotmail.com. Rates: 6500-7500 Kč single/double; suites from 7500 Kč. Parking 500 Kč. AE, MC, V. Ⓜ Staroměstská

Situated on a small and handsome square in the hidden depths of Old Town, the Maximilian is a thoroughly recommendable gem packed with comfort and charm. The hotel's warm, art nouveau public areas lead to top-quality, contemporary-styled guestrooms. Strict attention to detail translates into acoustically-padded bedrooms fitted with polished cherry wood furniture, king-size beds, and classical Italian drapes and coverings. Stereos are connected to loudspeakers in the bathrooms and non-smoking rooms are available. The best accommodations are on the top floor and have slanted ceilings with skylights. Suites are simply large rooms with additional seating. Although it's popular with businesspeople, this hotel would certainly be filled with more leisure travelers, if they only knew about it. For location, price and style, the Maximilian can't be beat.

72 Rooms: Air-conditioning, cable TV, VCR (on request), telephone, fax, hairdryer, minibar, radio, bar, room service (drinks only), safe, wheelchair access.

* 03 *
SLEEPiNG

Hotel U Páva

(At the Peacock) U Lužického Semináře 32, Praha 1. Tel. 02/5732-0743 or 02/5731-5867. Fax 02/5753-4187. www.romantichotels.cz. Rates: 5400-6400 Kč single, 5900-6900 Kč double. Limited free parking. AE, MC, V. M Malostranská

We love U Páva, a friendly, intimate hotel with a family-run atmosphere on a beautiful Malá Strana backstreet. The hotel's refined historical ambiance is augmented by dark nutwood furnishings, crystal chandeliers, beamed ceilings and carved pillars. And original old works of art and Oriental carpets make the hotel feel like a mini-museum. Top floor rooms peer over the walls of a secret garden, and up to Prague Castle rising over the quarter's red rooftops.

27 Rooms: Cable TV, telephone, modular jacks, hairdryer, minibar, radio, room service (8am-10pm), fitness center, restaurant.

Hotel Pod Věží

(Hotel Under the Tower) Mostecká 2, Praha 1. Tel. 02/5753-2060. Fax 02/5753-2069. Rates: 5500-7000 Kč single/double; suites from 9500 Kč. Parking 400 Kč. AE, MC, V. M Malostranská

A fine boutique hotel with a great location, Pod Věží luxuriates in the shade of the gothic tower on the Malá Strana side of Charles Bridge. Particularly nice bedrooms are designed with Renaissance-era molded plaster ceilings, placid pinstripe wallpaper and excellent beds that are as firm as they are large. The property itself is a beautifully restored baroque house that feels tailor-made for artists and writers (including Milan Kundera who was once a guest here). Most of the time, the hotel is filled with well-healed visitors from nearby Germany and Austria. Front rooms have bridge views while the quietest accommodations are in back.

12 Rooms: Cable TV, telephone, hairdryer, radio, room service (7am-10pm), minibar, safe (most), restaurant.

Residence Nosticova

Nosticova 1, Praha 1. Tel. 02/5731-2513 or 02/5731-2516. Fax 02/5731-2517. www.nosticova.com. Rates: 6500 Kč single/double; Suites from 9500 Kč. Free parking. AE, MC, V. Malostranská

Precisely because it is one, Residence Nosticova feels just like a high-quality home. All ten individually-owned condominium-style apartments are rented to the public when their masters are away. On-site management services the residences, each of which is equipped with a living room and full kitchen, and fitted with antique furnishings and well-chosen works of art. All the apartments are terrific, and the roof-top Imperial Suite, with a balcony and terrific views of Malá Strana, is one of the premiere places to stay in the entire city. An Italian bar on the ground floor serves jumper-cable espressos to get you started in the mornings. We love this place.

10 Rooms: Cable TV, telephone, modular jacks, minibar, room service (8am-11pm), restaurant, bar.

Hotel Ungelt

Malá Štupartská 1, Praha 1. Tel. 02/2482-8686. Fax 02/2482-8181. www.ungelt.cz. Rates: 5500 Kč single suite, 6500 Kč double suite. Parking 300 Kč. AE, MC, V. Náměstí Republiky

First the good news: Ungelt is one of the city's best-located hotels, on an exciting little backstreet, a single block from Old Town Square. It's a large building with only a few spacious rooms, each of which feels like part of a baroque palace, which, in fact, they are. Unfortunately, the hotel needs an extensive renovation to bring it into the twenty-first century. Each one- and two-bedroom suite includes a living room, a full kitchen, and an antiquated bathroom. Like the rest of the house, bedrooms are scantily clad with communist-era furnishings, augmented by a few antique odds and ends.

9 Rooms: Air conditioning, Cable TV, telephone, hairdryer, minibar, room service (7am-7pm) radio, snack bar.

Hotel Axa

Na poříčí 40, Praha 1. Tel. 02/2481-2580. Fax 02/2421-4489. www.vol.cz/IDC/AXA Rates: 2600 Kč single, 3800 Kč double; suites from 4500 Kč. AE, MC, V. M Náměstí Republiky/Florenc

A well-kept and tightly managed eight-story Functionalist lowrise, Axa offers 11-dozen pristine rooms in the middle of a busy central business district. Guestrooms are not large, frills are few and so are towels. But they're extremely practical, set with good beds and soundproofed windows. And no place in town has better health club facilities. There's a large weight room and a 75-foot indoor heated swimming pool.

135 Rooms: Air conditioning, Cable TV, VCR, telephone, 2 restaurants, bar, fitness center, swimming pool, wheelchair access.

Betlem Club

Betlémské nám. 9, Praha 1. Tel. 02/2222-1575. Fax 02/2222-0580. betlemclub@login.cz. Rates: 2800 Kč single, 3800 Kč double; suites from 4000 Kč. MC, V. M Národní Třída

One of the least-expensive hotels in Old Town, Betlem Club enjoys a premiere location on a quiet cobblestone square, surrounded by plenty of bars, restaurants, cafes and clubs. Like the church across the street, parts of the hotel date from the 13th Century, as evidenced by the gothic cellar breakfast room. The bedrooms upstairs are functional and clean, though far from special. Each contains simple, firm beds and other conspicuously inexpensive furnishings.

22 Rooms: Cable TV, telephone, hairdryer, minibar, radio.

Dům U Staré Paní

(House at the Old Maid) Michalská 9, Praha 1. Tel. 02/2422-3301 or 02/2422-8090. Fax 02/2422-6659. www.ustarepani.cz. Rates: 3500 Kč single, 4000 Kč double; Suites from 5000 Kč. AE, MC, V. M Staroměstská

Most locals know the House at the Old Maid only for its excellent jazz cellar, which is one of the best-loved jive rooms in the city. What few realize, however, is that the majority of this four-story Functionalist building is a hotel, catering to knowledgeable visitors with more sense than dollars. The rectangular rooms are sparse, designed with white walls and light furnishings, but they are also clean and pleasant and fantastically located, on an extremely central Old Town backstreet. Each of the four suites is approximately the size of two standard guestrooms, which makes them particularly good buys. And don't fret about noise—the basement festivities end around midnight.

18 Rooms: Cable TV, VCR, telephone, modular jacks, minibar, restaurant.

Hotel Harmony

Na poříčí 31, Praha 1. Tel. 02/232-0016. Fax 02/231-0009. Rates: 2700 Kč single, 3700 Kč double; suites from 3900 Kč. AE, MC, V. M Náměstí Republiky/Florenc

This eight-story hotel's simple, clean lobby and equally modest rooms are conscientiously cared for by particularly hospitable management. Guestrooms, which contain little more than a bed, desk and chair, are reasonably sized. Corner rooms on higher floors are both larger and brighter. Hotel Harmony is not for everybody; it's decidedly unfancy, and most of the motel-quality rooms face a busy urban street. But if you're happy with basic accommodations and relish being right in the heart of the hustle, this hotel is thoroughly recommendable.

60 Rooms: Cable TV, telephone, hairdryer, minibar, radio, room service (7am-10pm), restaurant, bar, wheelchair access.

Klášterní Dvůr

(Cloister Court) Bartolomějská 9, Praha 1. Tel. 02/2421-1020. Fax 02/2421-0800. www.cloister-inn.cz Rates: 3000 Kč single, 4000 Kč double, 1100 Kč per person in dorm; suites from 4500 Kč. Parking 250 Kč. AE, MC, V. M Staroměstská

Once a medieval Jesuit convent, this ancient cloister was bequeathed to the Sisters of Mercy (the nuns, not the rock band) in 1856. During the communist regime the grounds were taken over by the dreaded Secret Police, and political prisoners were routinely incarcerated here: Václav Havel was jailed in concrete cell P6. Returned to the nuns after the Revolution, the building was spruced up, window bars were removed and the cloisters were transformed into a hotel. The former basement brigs are now 6-bed hostel-like dorm rooms. And upstairs offices have been converted into cheery doubles that are bright but basic, designed with simple wooden beds and bargain furnishings. The location—on a relatively quiet street at the edge of Old Town—is great. And prices can't be beat.

73 Rooms: Cable TV, telephone, hairdryer.

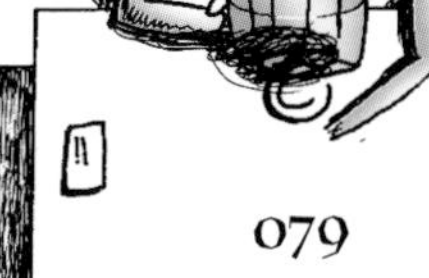

Evropa Hotel

Václavské nám. 25, Praha 1. Tel. 02/2422-8117. Fax 02/2422-4544. Rates: 3000 Kč single, 4000 Kč double; suites from 5000 Kč. Parking 350 Kč. AE, MC, V. M Můstek/Muzeum

Rebuilt in the art nouveau style in 1905, and little changed since, the historical Evropa is the grand dame of modern Prague hotels. It's a pleasure to explore the heavily-decorated public rooms and enjoy tea in the famous bar. But up in the guestrooms, age and neglect have taken an obvious tolls. In keeping with its old-world ambiance, there are no televisions, direct-dial telephones or radios. And the antiquated plumbing and cracks in the ceiling require more than a cosmetic nip-and-tuck. Still, most guestrooms are dressed with Louis XVI-style furnishings, and the Evropa remains one of the most magnificent turn-of-the-century structures in Prague. Be forewarned that not all rooms are created equal. The biggest and loudest are doubles facing the front of the hotel, a half-dozen of which have balconies overlooking Václavské náměstí. The smallest and quietest rooms, in back, are narrow as a hallway and not much larger than a closet. And some singles don't even have windows. Unfortunately, the only way to ensure acceptable accommodations here is to show up in person and ask to see a room before committing.

75 Rooms: Restaurant, cafe, room service (10am-10pm).

Pension Dientzenhofer

Nosticova 2, Praha 1. Tel. 02/531-672 or 02/538-896. Fax 02/5732-0888. dientzenhofer@volny.cz. Rates: 2800 Kč single, 3700 Kč double; suites from 4000 Kč. Parking 180 Kč. AE, MC, V. M Staroměstská

This 16th-century house was the birthplace Kilian Ignaz Dientzenhofer (1689-1751), one of Bohemia's greatest baroque architects. Today, it's a family-run bed-and-breakfast, offering a handful of homey rooms. All are relatively simple, fitted with heavy wooden furnishings, firm beds and precious little decoration on the white walls. The location is great, on a quiet Malá Strana street, but this is not the kind of place where you'll want to lounge around all day.

8 rooms: Cable TV, telephone, bar, wheelchair access.

Sidi Hotel

Na Kampě 10, Praha 1. Tel. 02/5753-1332. Fax 02/5753-1332. www.hotel-kampa.cz. Rates: 5000 Kč single/double; Suites from 6000 Kč. No cards. M Staroměstská

O.K., so the name is unfortunate. But this tiny three-story house—fronting a quaint Malá Strana square and backing onto the Vltava River—is far from shabby. There are only two standard rooms and two suites, each of which are relatively spare, but well proportioned. It's very private, too. Almost no services are offered, but there is a restaurant and bar on the ground floor and all of Prague is at your feet.

4 Rooms: Cable TV, telephone, hair dryer, modular jacks, room service (11am-11pm) minibar, restaurant, bar.

Hotel U Zlatého Stromu

(At the Golden Tree) Karlova 6, Praha 1. Tel. 02/2222-0441. Fax 02/2222-0441. www.zlatystrom.cz. Rates: 4000 Kč single, 4500 Kč double; Suites from 6000 Kč. AE, MC, V. M Staroměstská

The place to stay for late-night veterans and those who like to party, this fine hotel rocks around the clock with a 24-hour restaurant and a cellar club that spins until 6am. Winning high marks for both comfort and style, the hotel flaunts every crown's worth of its multi-million-dollar renovation. Each of the well-sized rooms is different, but all are unusually large, beautifully designed and well-equipped with sparkling tiled bathrooms and plenty of creature comforts. Because they're biggest and brightest, our favorites are on the top floors, and the duplex suites represent some of the best values in the city. The Golden Tree has an amazing location on the street that crosses Charles Bridge. The only problem here is the incessant muffled pulsating of the music below: This place is definitely not for light sleepers.

23 Rooms: Cable TV, telephone, minibar, safe, room service (24 hours), restaurant, bar.

hOSTELS

Travellers Hostels (www.travellers.cz), a growing local chain of cheap sleeps, has some of the least-expensive and best located beds in town. All of their hostels offer basic accommodations at unbeatable prices, and each has its own unique character. Breakfast, linens, lockers and showers are always included.

Roxy

Dlouhá 33, Praha 1. Tel. 02/2482-6662 or 02/2482-6663. Fax 02/2482-6665. Open year-round. Per Person Rates: 480 Kč double, 350 Kč triple, 320 Kč quad, 270 Kč dorm. 120 beds.

Situated on a great street, just above the Roxy nightclub, this is one of the coolest places to stay in the city. It's a terrific place to meet people and, because they have so many different types of rooms, during the off season you're likely to snag one all to yourself.

Újezd

U Lanové dráhy 3, Praha 1. Tel. 02/533-160. Fax 02/2482-6665. Open Jun 20-Sept 25 only. Per Person Rate: 220 Kč. 77 beds.

This cheapest of sleeps is an easy, friendly place, situated in a park at the bottom of Petřín Hill. The dorm accommodations are simple, but the location is great and Bohemia Bagel and a good Internet cafe are located just across the street.

Růžová 5

Růžová 5, Praha 2. Tel. 02/2421-6771. Fax 02/2482-6665. Open May 15-Sept 10 only. Per Person Rate: 260 Kč. 65 beds.

This vast dorm room situated close to the main train station has an on-site bar where lunches and dinners are served.

Husova Pension

Husova 3, Praha 1. Tel. 02/2222-0078. Fax 02/2482-6665. Open July 2-Aug 25 only. Per Person Rates: 550 Kč double, 400 Kč quad. 40 beds.

The Pension is the smallest, quietest and most "respectable" of the Travellers Hostels.

Island Hostel

Střelecký ostrov. Tel. 02/2491-0188 or 02/2491-4849. Fax 02/2482-6665. Open Jun 20-Sept 10 only. Rates Per Person: 320 Kč. 75 beds.

This hostel has an amazing location, on a private, wooded island in the Vltava, right in the heart of the city. The accommodations—large dorm rooms—are kind of skanky, but that's the price you pay for location. There's a terrific garden pub, an occasional open-air cinema, and even a tennis court. This place is truly unique.

× 04 × THE TOP SIGHTS

SIGHTSEEING

CRUCIAL PRAGUE

PRAGUE CASTLE

(Pražský hrad) Hradčany, Praha 1. Tel. 2437-3368. Open (except where noted) Apr-Oct, daily 9am-5pm; Nov-Mar, daily 9am-4pm. The Castle grounds are open Apr-Oct, daily 5am-midnight; Nov-Mar, daily 6am-11pm. Royal Gardens are open April-Oct, daily 10am-6pm. Southern Gardens are open Apr-Oct daily 10am-6pm. Admission: Grounds & Gardens free; Interiors 120 Kč. Additional admission fees where noted. The ticket office is located inside the Castle's Second Courtyard. From Malostranské náměstí walk up steep Nerudova Street to the castle's front entrance. Alternatively, from Malostranská Metro station, walk up the Old Castle Steps, or take Tram 22 to Pražský hrad and enter the Castle's North Gate.

Visitors to Prague often look up at the little city of buildings that crown Hradčany hill and ask "which one is Prague Castle?" The answer is that it's the whole enchilada; the entire, elongated conglomeration of houses, towers, churches, courtyards and monuments; including the huge cathedral that sticks up out of the center. To Kafka, the enormity and mystery of the Castle was the frightening epitome of an unknowable faceless bureaucracy. The Communists further sullied the Castle's reputation by turning it into their party's headquarters (though the Parliament was relegated to an electronic-bug-riddled building in New Town) and ensuring that vast portions of the complex remained off-limits to the general public. By the time the Velvet Revolution rolled around, the Castle had such a bad reputation that the democratically-elected Parliament decided to move their offices closer to the people, down in Malá Strana. When Václav Havel became President, he pledged to make the Castle as accessible to the public as possible; a promise that's kept with generous opening hours and token admission fees.

Prague Castle was founded by Přemyslid Prince Bořivoj in A.D. 875. Making wise use of the protective natural

• 04 •
SiGhTSEEiNG

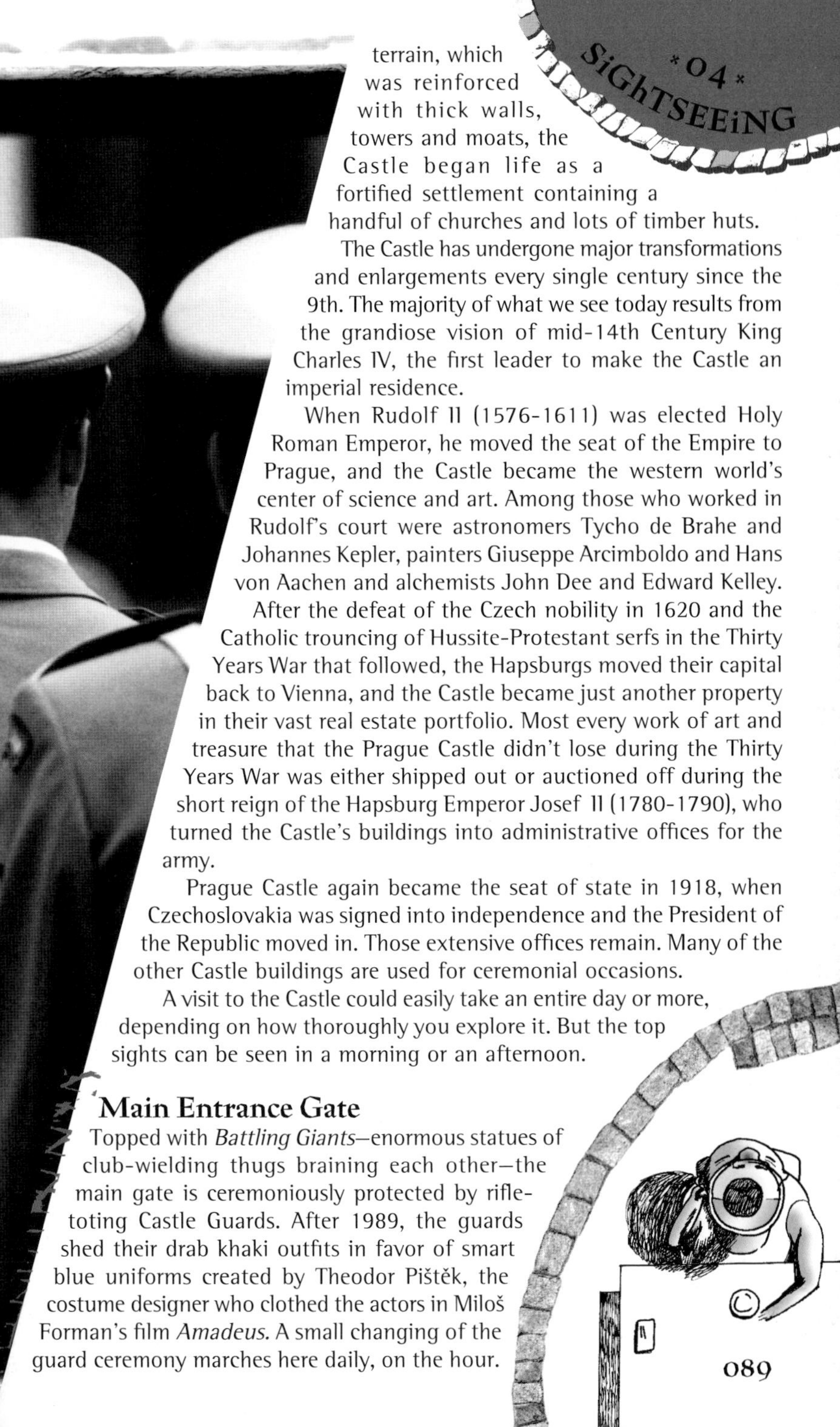

terrain, which was reinforced with thick walls, towers and moats, the Castle began life as a fortified settlement containing a handful of churches and lots of timber huts.

The Castle has undergone major transformations and enlargements every single century since the 9th. The majority of what we see today results from the grandiose vision of mid-14th Century King Charles IV, the first leader to make the Castle an imperial residence.

When Rudolf II (1576-1611) was elected Holy Roman Emperor, he moved the seat of the Empire to Prague, and the Castle became the western world's center of science and art. Among those who worked in Rudolf's court were astronomers Tycho de Brahe and Johannes Kepler, painters Giuseppe Arcimboldo and Hans von Aachen and alchemists John Dee and Edward Kelley.

After the defeat of the Czech nobility in 1620 and the Catholic trouncing of Hussite-Protestant serfs in the Thirty Years War that followed, the Hapsburgs moved their capital back to Vienna, and the Castle became just another property in their vast real estate portfolio. Most every work of art and treasure that the Prague Castle didn't lose during the Thirty Years War was either shipped out or auctioned off during the short reign of the Hapsburg Emperor Josef II (1780-1790), who turned the Castle's buildings into administrative offices for the army.

Prague Castle again became the seat of state in 1918, when Czechoslovakia was signed into independence and the President of the Republic moved in. Those extensive offices remain. Many of the other Castle buildings are used for ceremonial occasions.

A visit to the Castle could easily take an entire day or more, depending on how thoroughly you explore it. But the top sights can be seen in a morning or an afternoon.

Main Entrance Gate

Topped with *Battling Giants*—enormous statues of club-wielding thugs braining each other—the main gate is ceremoniously protected by rifle-toting Castle Guards. After 1989, the guards shed their drab khaki outfits in favor of smart blue uniforms created by Theodor Pištěk, the costume designer who clothed the actors in Miloš Forman's film *Amadeus*. A small changing of the guard ceremony marches here daily, on the hour.

Kohl's Fountain and Well

The Early Baroque fountain in the middle of the Second Courtyard dates from 1686. The adjacent well used to be the only source of drinking water for the Castle.

Prague Castle Picture Gallery

The Emperor Rudolf II amassed one of the best art collections in Europe and displayed his masterpieces at Prague Castle. During the Thirty Years War, most of the works were hidden or stolen, effectively dividing the collection amongst the royal courts of Austria, Sweden and other countries. What's left are several paintings by Tintoretto, Rubens and Veronese, as well as the celebrated *Portrait of a Girl* (1605-10) by Hans von Aachen, depicting the artist's daughter.

Most of the paintings at the Prague Castle Picture Gallery are from European and Czech artists from the 16th and 18th centuries. The museum is great for art history majors looking to fill in some blanks. But, in general, the Czech art that hangs here feels derivative of finer French and Italian works.

The Gallery is located in the former Imperial Stables, which were once home to Rudolf IIs favorite Spanish horses.

St. Vitus Cathedral

Forget the separation of Church and State. In London, Paris and Rome the Church's headquarters are within close proximity to the seat of government. In the Czech lands, the country's main church is smack-dab in the heart of the corridors of power.

St. Vitus Cathedral, which rises up from the very center of the Prague Castle, is named for the Patron Saint of Bohemia, a deep-pocketed Sicilian who was thrown to the lions in the Fourth Century.

The Cathedral is considered to be a pioneering gothic masterpiece. Its foundation stone was ceremoniously laid by soon-to-be King Charles IV in 1344. For design work, Charles called on the services of French architect Matthew of Arras, who was succeeded after his death by 23-year-old Petr Parléř, one of the leading builders of the Gothic era. St. Vitus was not completed and

04
SiGhTSEEiNG

consecrated until 1929, almost 600 years after it was begun. After a 40-year hiatus during socialism, the Prague Archbishop once again conducts regular services here.

Before entering, notice the front doors which feature ornamental sculptural reliefs depicting scenes from the lives of St. Wenceslas and Vojtěch and the construction of St. Vitus's Cathedral.

Once inside, turn left and look up at the second stained-glass window on your left. Called *Allegory of the Slavs,* this colorful work was created in 1931 by art deco legend Alfons Mucha. Of the twenty-one chapels contained within this massive gothic cathedral, the highlight is the Chapel of St. Wenceslas (1362-67), which was built directly above the tomb of the saint. It's an outrageously decadent room, encrusted with more than 1300 stones of jasper and amethyst set into the walls. In a corner of the chapel a door leads to the Crown Chamber, where the Czech Crown Jewels are stored. There are seven locks on the door; the keys to each are held by seven different governmental institutions.

The fate of the Bohemian monarch's 14th-century crown, sword and assorted other sundries has been dramatic. From 1420 to 1434 they were kept in Hungary by the Emperor Sigismund. In the 15th and 16th centuries they were housed in Karlštejn castle, 20 miles southwest of Prague (see Chapter 10/The Best Day Trips). From the first half of the 17th Century the Crown Jewels were in Vienna, and at the end of the 18th Century they were moved back to Prague again. Copies of the jewels are displayed in the Castle's Lobkovic Palace (see below).

There are several notable items surrounding the high altar. The ancient candlesticks originated in Jerusalem and were brought to Prague in the middle of the 12th Century. To the left of the altar is a fantastic 17th-century wood carving depicting the *Flight of Frederick of Palatine from Prague after the Battle of White Mountain.* To the right of the altar is an excessively ornate two-ton silver tomb that tops the remains of St. John of Nepomuk, who was thrown into the Vltava in 1393 and sainted in 1729. Nepomuk's canonization was aggressively sought by Hapsburg rulers, who bet that a local martyr would raise the stock of Roman-Catholicism in the region.

A stairway leads down to the Royal Crypt, which contains tombs of some of the most famous Czech Kings.

You can climb to the top of the Cathedral via a claustrophobic staircase that leads to the Renaissance Gallery, an ambulatory under the copper dome. From here you can step outside for a fantastic view of the Castle and Prague below.

The Monolith & Statue of St. George

The giant granite phallus in the Third Courtyard is a monument dedicated to victims of World War I. Nearby is another freestanding sculpture: a diminutive depiction of St. George on a horse, slaying a dragon. It is a copy of a sculpture from 1373 that has the distinction of being the first official monument ever commissioned by the City of Prague. It's famous in the art world for being one of the precious few gothic statues that's not attached to a wall.

Powder Tower

The Castle's largest and most powerful gun tower was erected in the 15th century. Cannon loopholes face three ways and are protected from enemy shots by slanting shields.

The ground floor was designed to accommodate a small carriage and several horses, employed to manipulate the artillery.

During the 16th Century, Tycho de Brahe, Johannes Kepler and other scientists and alchemists worked here. Today there's a decent permanent exhibit on the evolution of science and art during the reign of Rudolf II, including some equipment and tools of alchemy. Other noteworthy items from the exhibition are objects from Rudolf's coffin, including dishes for his heart and brain.

Old Royal Palace

The Old Royal Palace is a compact collection of buildings that was home to Bohemian kings and princes for over 700 years. It was the most significant part of the entire castle until the 16th Century, when newer kings' quarters were built in the western part of the castle.

The largest room in the Royal Palace is **Vladislav Hall**, a large late gothic banquet room completed in 1502. It's a huge place with large windows that are over 500 years old. The decorative rib-vaulted ceiling is considered to be a masterpiece of the early Renaissance.

Coronation balls took place here, often accompanied by jousting tournaments. And Emperor Rudolf II held art exhibitions and sales here. The hall was also where commoners had audiences with the King and, not incidentally, where Václav Havel was elected as Czechoslovakia's first post-communist President.

From Vladislav Hall we can step out onto the observation terrace adjoining the chapel, which

offers a great view of the Castle Gardens, below, framed by all of Prague.

At the east end of Vladislav Hall is the **All Saints Chapel**, designed in the 14th Century by Petr Parléř after the Sainte Chapelle in Paris. It was enlarged and rebuilt in the Renaissance style after a fire in the 16th Century. The tomb by the entrance houses the remains of St. Procopius, the first Abbot of the Sázava monastery.

Vladislav Hall is connected by a (sometimes closed) staircase to the **Old Legislative Hall**, which housed the Imperial Court, the highest organ of medieval Czech jurisprudence. The affairs of the whole Holy Roman Empire were ruled from here at the time of Rudolf II. His portrait, along with those of other leading Hapsburgs, hang on the walls. It was in this hall that the final verdict was pronounced upon the twenty-seven Czech noblemen who were executed in Old Town Square after losing the Battle of White Mountain (*see* Chapter 1/The Habsburgs).

Back on the ground floor is the **Old Diet Hall**, which dates from the 16th century. The arrangement of the 19th-century furniture is meant to mimic a legislature in session. You can see the royal throne, the chair of the archbishop, and benches for clergy on the right, and seats for the supreme clerks along the walls. Benches for the nobility are opposite the throne.

In the Old Diet Hall is a staircase leading down below Vladislav Hall. The descent is a grand tour of architectural history that goes backward in time from the 20th Century to Renaissance to Gothic to Romanesque. You encounter the beautiful vaulted chambers of Charles' Palace, before descending further to the Princes' Palace of Soběslav and Vladislav.

St. George's Basilica

Founded in 920 and rebuilt in 1142, this ancient building includes a three-story, three-nave basilica that is the oldest and best-preserved Romanesque structure in Bohemia. The Baroque facade was glued on in the 17th Century.

The oldest part of the building is the **Chapel of St. Ann**, which contains tombs of the abbesses from the convent next door. The adjacent **Chapel of St. Ludmila** is dedicated to St. Wenceslas' grandmother, the first Bohemian Christian martyr. Above the double staircase lies tombstones of the Přemyslid Kings, including Vratislav I and Boleslav II.

St. George's Convent

(Klášter sv. Jiřího), Open Tues-Sun 10am-6pm. Admission 50 Kč.

Built in 973, St. George's was the first convent in Bohemia. Part of the building has been adopted by the National Gallery to house a permanent exposition of Baroque painting and sculpture, represented by such local luminaries as Hans von Aachen and Josef Heinz. This is not the most exciting museum in Prague, but a good place to get a handle on Central European art in the 17th and 18th centuries.

Lobkovic Palace

Open Tues-Sun 9am-5pm. Admission 40 Kč.

An aristocratic palace from the second half of the 16th century, this huge home is named for its most important occupant, Wenceslas of Lobkovice, who was Secretary to the Emperor Leopold I. The building is now the largest Czech historical museum, exhibiting over 2000 pictures, artifacts and documents from antiquity to 1848. Look for everything from Hussite weapons and copies of the coronation jewels to old musical instruments, astronomical devices and historical prints. But unless you have a particularly strong interest in Bohemian history, the palace is only worth a quick walk-through.

Golden Lane

This cute and colorful 16th-century lane is full of tourist shops and great photo ops. The enchanting magic of the street comes from its movie-set appearance and toy like dimensions, which are a surprising counterpoint to the massive proportions of the castle complex within which it's located. Here you can practically touch the rooftops. Originally, there were cottages on both sides and the narrow lane was only about half as wide. But those were demolished at the request of the nuns of adjacent St. George's Convent, who complained about all the mess, noise and smoke that was being generated.

Popular legend holds that Golden Lane *(Zlatá ulička)* takes its name from Rudolf IIs alchemists, who worked in a building nearby. In truth, this tiny street was named for castle sharpshooters, who lived here while moonlighting as goldsmiths. Later, tailors and restaurateurs moved in, transforming Golden Lane into a busy shopping street.

Franz Kafka lived in the tiny house at number 22 during the winter of 1916–17. He didn't know Golden Lane to be such a colorful place, however, as the cottages were only painted in their current vibrant scheme during a major renovation in the 1950s.

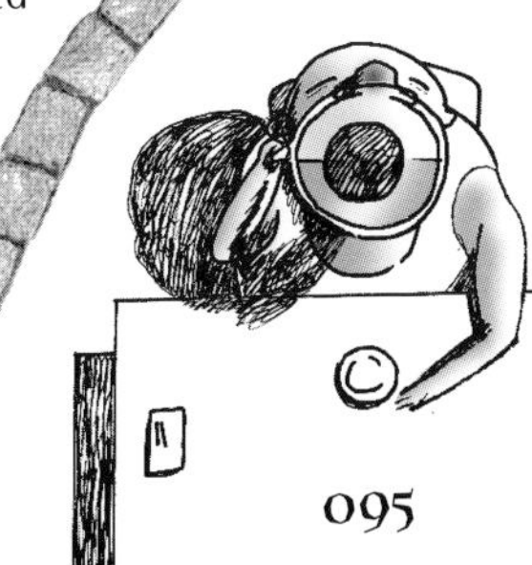

Royal Gardens

(Královská zahrada), Open April-Oct only, daily 10am-6pm.

This large, formal green rectangle on the Castle's east side was created in 1534 on a site that was once the sovereign's vineyards. During Rudolf IIs day, such "exotic" plants as tulips were grown here, which later found their way to Holland. Later, greenhouses were built for lemon, orange, fig and other non-native trees.

Near the Gardens' main entrance is **Lion Court,** built at the end of the 16th century to house Rudolf IIs menagerie, which included twelve camels, two leopards, and several tigers, wolves and bears. The Emperor's favorite lion was kept here as well. Tycho de Brahe, the Emperor's personal astronomer, once prophesied that the lion and Rudolf would share the same fate. The lion died on the 18th of January, 1612, just two days before the Emperor drew his last breath.

If you walk the length of the gardens, you will come to the **Royal Summer Palace** (a.k.a. The Belvedere), a remarkable piece of architecture that's considered to be the most beautiful manifestation of the Italian Renaissance north of the Alps. The roof is designed like an upside-down hull of a ship, covered with copper plates. And the extraordinary vaulted room is as unique for its artistic conception as it is for its excellent condition. During the Hapsburgs' reign, the Summer Palace was used to host seasonal banquets. Rudolf II also enjoyed spending time here, observing the stars in the company of his astronomers. Today the building is an art gallery and temporary exhibition space that has housed shows ranging from Anatolian carpets to photographs by Josef Sudek. Whatever's on, it's usually worth a look. The large fountain in front of the Summer Palace is known as **Singing Fountain.** It's named for the sing-song sound that's made when drops of water fall into the fountain's large bowl. What most people don't know, however, is that you have to actually crawl *under* the fountain to get the intended effect. Don't be shy.

Southern Castle Gardens

Open Apr-Oct only, daily 10am-6pm.

The Southern Gardens open up over all of Prague and are one of our most favorite strolling places in the city. In the lowest part of the gardens stands a table that was regularly used by Czechoslovakia's first President, T.G. Masaryk, who liked to work here. The view is unparalleled.

The gardens were created gradually, as the old fortifications were dismantled.

Daliborka Tower

Situated at the far end of Golden Lane, Dalibor's Tower is another relic from the Castle's ancient fortifications. Built as a cylindrical turret, the tower has served many functions but is best remembered as a prison for the nobility. It's named for its first inmate, the knight Dalibor of Kozojedy, who was locked-up here in 1498. Popularized as a kind of Czech Robin Hood who incited a rebellion by Bohemian serfs, the knight is immortalized by Bedřich Smetana's 1868 opera *Dalibor.*

Prague Castle Riding Hall

Usually open Tues-Sun 10am-6pm.

Situated just across the moat from the Castle, This early-Baroque horse-riding hall has been transformed into one of the National Gallery's principal venues for major exhibitions by Czech artists. Temporary shows run the gamut from individual retrospectives to ensemble projects like Ten Centuries of Architecture. Stop by, or check the *Prague Post,* to find out what's being mounted while you're in town.

ChARLES BRIdGE

According to contemporary legend, when the Dalai Lama walked across Charles Bridge (Karlův most) soon after the Revolution, he said something about standing in the very center of the universe. OK, we wouldn't be surprised if he says that everywhere, but there is no denying that Charles Bridge is an incredibly powerful stone magnet which seems to attract almost everyone in the world.

Throughout summer, the ancient crossing can get so choked with pedestrians that many locals prefer to take alternative routes across the river. But not us. Despite plenty of griping, we're in love with Charles Bridge. The journey across is a swoony stroll through a four-dimensional picture postcard; the fourth dimension being time.

A wooden bridge was laid across the River Vltava near this spot as early as AD 932, then replaced by a spindly stone span several years later. After that bridge was destroyed by flood, King Charles IV ordered a big sturdy one built. Heeding court astrologers' recommendations, the foundation stone was laid at 5:31 on the morning of July 9, 1357, a time that was c…sidered auspicious because it corresponds to …merical palindrome 1357 9.7 5:3.1. In the …iddle Ages, people believed that truth and …nity could be deciphered from the

to Malá Strana

St. Wenceslas, Patron Saint of Bohemia

Sts. Ivan, John of Matha and Felix of Valois

St. Adalbert, first Bishop of Bohemia

St. Lutigarde

St. Nicholas of Tolentino

Sts. Vincent Farrer and Procopius

St. Francis of Assisi

St. Ludmila

St. Francis Borgia

St. Christopher and baby Jesus

St. Xavier and four pagan princes

St. Joseph and Jesus

Jesus, The Madonna, St. John and Mary Magdalene

Sts. Barbara, Margaret, and Elizabeth

St. Ives, Patron Saint of lawyers

orderliness of the heavens, which, according to the old Pythagorean system, could be expressed in numbers.

For the next five centuries, until 1941, Charles Bridge was the only Prague bridge connecting the two banks of the Vltava.

Mostly between 1683 and 1714, the Jesuits (who understood marketing and promotion better than most) lined the bridge with thirty statues of saints. The entire collection is the work of just eight sculptors, including Ferdinand M. Brokoff and Matyáš B. Braun, two masters who are considered to be among the best carvers of their time. All of the statues are now copies, as the originals were carted off to museums long ago. But it hardly seems to matter. As a collective installation, the long rows of martyred saints make a powerful impression.

The do-gooders represented on Charles Bridge were a particularly unlucky lot: St. Ludmila holds the veil with which she was suffocated; St. Judas Thaddeus is palming the club with which he was fatally beaten; St. Vitus stands beside the lions who ate him; and St. John Nepomuk is positioned near the spot from which he was thrown into the river.

Artistically, not all of the figures are gems, but there are some standouts:

The group of **St. John of Matha, St. Felix of Valois and St. Ivan**, created in 1714 by Ferdinand M. Brokoff, was commissioned by the Trinitarians, a religious order

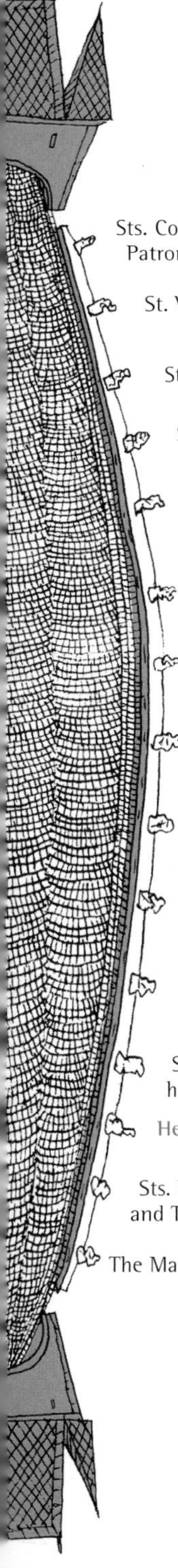

04
SiGhTSEEiNG

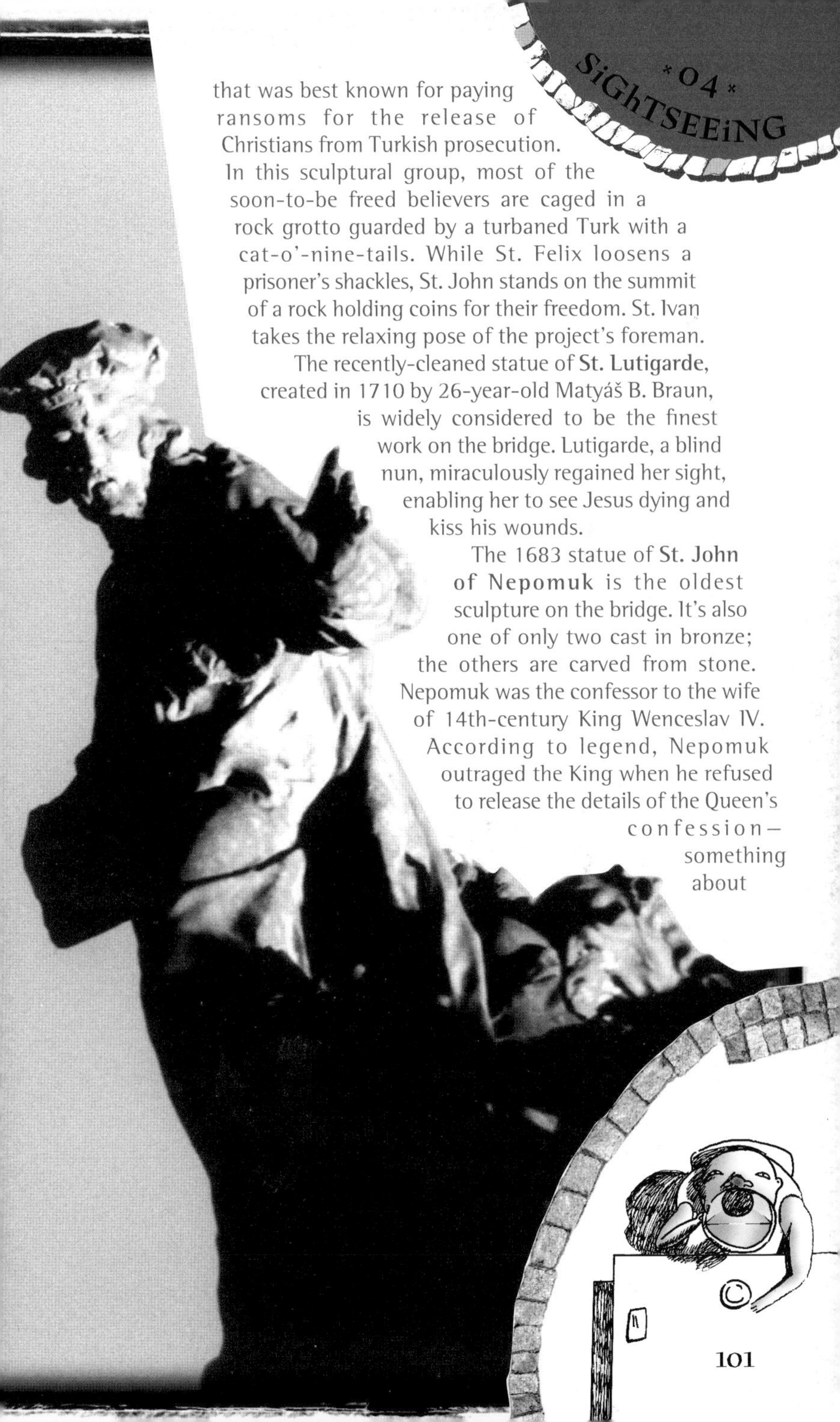

that was best known for paying ransoms for the release of Christians from Turkish prosecution. In this sculptural group, most of the soon-to-be freed believers are caged in a rock grotto guarded by a turbaned Turk with a cat-o'-nine-tails. While St. Felix loosens a prisoner's shackles, St. John stands on the summit of a rock holding coins for their freedom. St. Ivan takes the relaxing pose of the project's foreman.

The recently-cleaned statue of **St. Lutigarde,** created in 1710 by 26-year-old Matyáš B. Braun, is widely considered to be the finest work on the bridge. Lutigarde, a blind nun, miraculously regained her sight, enabling her to see Jesus dying and kiss his wounds.

The 1683 statue of **St. John of Nepomuk** is the oldest sculpture on the bridge. It's also one of only two cast in bronze; the others are carved from stone. Nepomuk was the confessor to the wife of 14th-century King Wenceslav IV. According to legend, Nepomuk outraged the King when he refused to release the details of the Queen's confession—something about having another lover, perhaps? The clergyman's throat was slashed and his body was tossed into the river from the middle of Charles Bridge (the spot is marked by a small bronze cross on the wall about two statues up). Sadly, the truth is far more mundane: Nepomuk, it seems, was on the wrong side of a power struggle with the King concerning the appointment of a new archbishop. But fact shouldn't get in the way of a good story, so it's the myth that endures in this statue's two pedestal reliefs, both of which now shine brightly from the millions of hands that touch it each year for good luck. Ironically, John of Nepomuk is now the Patron Saint of swimmers.

The 1711 statue of **St. Francis Xavier** is another Brokoff creation. The co-founder of the Jesuit order is shown here being carried on the shoulders of an Indian, a Tartar, a Chinese and a Moor—pagan princes of cultures targeted for conversion.

Lots of visitors are bewildered by the **statue with Hebrew letters around a huge bronze crucifix**. The inscription, which translates as "holy, holy, holy God," was paid for under duress by a Jewish man, who is said to have mocked a wooden crucifix that once stood on this site. This anti-semitic story is now commemorated by bronze plaques affixed to the bridge wall just below. When England's Queen Elizabeth saw this statue, she too was dismayed. Not by the alphabet encircling the cross, but by the sexiness of the loin clothed Jesus that dangles from it.

The best times to visit Charles Bridge are between 6pm and 8pm, when tour groups are eating dinner, and after 11pm, when they are snugly tucked into bed. On warm summer nights, after the sun has set, the bridge becomes a bastion of hippydom, flooded with an eclectic mix of bongo-banging dredlocked travelers, pierced-bellied earth muffins and shoeless dancing wood nymphs. Bring a bottle of wine, and a guitar if you have one. Most people depart before midnight when the Metro stops and trams become scarce. Then the bridge blushes with romance, simultaneously uniting more couples than a Moonie marriage ceremony. Stroll on by after 3am, and you might have the span all to yourself.

David Černý

Born in Prague in 1969, David Černý's fame began immediately after the Revolution when he coated a Soviet tank–which, for years, was displayed monument–style in a main square–in pink paint. In 1990, Černý memorialized the flight of East Germans to the West with his sculpture *Quo Vadis*, which put a Trabant car on legs. Later, he spent two years in New York City in the Whitney Museum Independent Study Program. Now one of the best–known sculptors in the Czech Republic, Černy regularly receives international grants and commissions to create large-scale works.

Avant-Guide: Is there a particularly Czech style of contemporary art?

David Černý: No. It's the same the world over. The main difference between Prague and New York art is, if you are in New York City you can say to Barbara Gladstone "come to my studio." If you are in Prague you have to telephone and say "Look at my slides."

AG: Are you saying that the art world is the same in Prague and New York?

DČ: Of course they are different. In Prague, artists think they're supposed to suffer from the Kafka syndrome – sitting and suffering, with piles of papers in a drawer. In New York, everyone is into self-promotion. You meet someone at a party in New York and they say "Hi, I'm an artist. I'm going to have fifteen shows. I'm really good." The artists who were at the Whitney were totally hypocritical, because all anyone cared about was getting into galleries.

04 SiGhTSEEiNG

Old TOWN SQUARE

Basking in both Gothic gloom and Baroque brilliance, Old Town Square *(Staroměstské náměstí)* is both the geographical and emotional heart of Prague. All of Old Town—and by extension, the entire city—was born from this plaza, where Bohemian noblemen were beheaded, Kafka was born, and the Communist Party announced their coup. Every building here secrets a story, and antiquity reeks from every cobblestone.

Astronomical Clock

The Astronomical Clock *(orloj)* that hangs onto the side of Old Town Hall Tower is one of Prague's greatest crowd-pleasers. Tourists pack in front of it at the top of each hour (from 8am to 8pm only) to watch a short parade of statuette Apostles bow to adoring camera-clickers below.

While each of the twelve saints has his turn, eight politically incorrect allegorical figures perform a kind of medieval morality play. The statues on either side of the clock's upper dial represent the four evils according to ancient society: death, vanity, corruption and greed, which are represented by a skeleton, a mirror, a Turk and a Jew. On either side of the lower dial are statues representing the learned city's four messiahs: reading, writing, arithmatic and religion.

The clock's statuette showmen get most of the attention, but it's the quiet timepiece that is the real phenomenon. Designed in the early 15th century by a bevy of court astronomers, the clock is one of the earliest depictions of the heavens in motion, interpreting the movements of the sun, moon and stars in relation to Earth's horizon. In doing so, it also tells time in three different ways:

The top dial, with a painting of Earth in the middle, is the **astronomical dial.** The Sun Hand, which carries a golden orb, revolves around the Earth. A finger at the end of the hand points to the current time.

Old Central European Time, closest to what we use today, is shown with Roman numerals that run twice, from one to 12, in a single ring around the clock's perimeter. In summer, during Daylight Savings Time, it will be off by one hour.

Old-Bohemian or Italian Time is depicted on the outermost dial, a mobile disk which carries the Arabic numbers 1 to 24 written in Gothic script. Old-Bohemian time begins at sunset. At that time, the finger on the Sun Hand will point the number 24, regardless of the actual hour. Of course, the time the sun sets changes with the seasons and so does the rotating outer ring, which moves both clockwise and counterclockwise. You can tell what time the sun will set on any given day by locating the number 24 and seeing which Roman numeral it aligns with.

Babylonian Time is told according to the Arabic numbers that are painted in black just inside the Roman numerals. It's based on the principle that each daylight period is divided into twelve "hours," regardless of how long the sun is up in the sky. Therefore, Babylonian daylight hours are longer in summer than in winter. There are no Arabic numbers in the bottom half of the dial because nights were not measured by Babylonian time.

The ring of the zodiac represents the starry heavens. Its movement corresponds to the then-presumed revolution of the sky around Earth. The golden sun moves away from, and closer to, the Earth during the course of the year. The moon, which is carried by another hand of the clock, rotates on its own axis in order to show its correct phase.

The Astronomical Clock's **calendar dial**, below, was added in the 19th century. It indicates today's day and date and shows the corresponding month and sign of the zodiac. The rotating disk ring is divided in to 365 fields, each of which is marked with the particular saint who is associated with each day of the year. Today's date is indicated by the little golden pointer fixed at the top.

Old Town Hall

(Staroměstská radnice) Staroměstské nám. Tel. 2448-2909. Open Apr-Sept, Mon 11am-530pm, Tues-Sun 9am-530pm; Oct-Mar, Mon 11am-430pm, Tues-Sun 9am-430pm. Admission 30 Kč. M Staroměstská

The big stone clock tower that lords over Old Town Square belongs to Old Town Hall, an ancient government office that has grown over the last few centuries to include six adjacent buildings of various architectural styles. Of all the towers in the city you can climb, this one is best, offering unparalleled views over the red rooftops of Old Town and beyond.

Begun in 1338, Old Town Hall was founded in a corner house on one of the busiest market squares in town. Like any good municipal headquarters, this one was built with a chapel (consecrated 1381) and plenty of architectural frills. Check-out the richly ornamented late-Gothic front door. Then look up and to your left at the ancient emblems of Prague and the Czech Kingdom's coat of arms that decorate the adjoining window.

The complex used to be twice as big as it is now. But in May 1945, the Hall's main building, which fronted the west side of Old Town Square, was blown-up by the German army just days before it rolled out in defeat. Now it's a small park.

Jan Hus Monument

The monumental statue in the center of Old Town Square is a great place to hang out and one of the best outdoor meeting places in the city. On sunny days, the benches surrounding the monument's steps are filled with Italians in expensive sunglasses, American biftads in fraternity shirts, and travelers from all over the globe, eating, drinking, smoking and writing postcards home.

Few realize that the bronze man above them, standing defiantly against hurricane-force winds, was tethered to a stake and roasted alive in 1415—an event that touched off decades of warfare between reform-minded nationalist Hussites and the country's German-oriented Roman Catholic leaders. To Czechs, Hus has come to represent national pride and triumph against foreign aggressors. The statue was unveiled in 1915 at the culmination of the Czech National Revival, an intense nationalist movement that resuscitated the almost-extinct Czech language and reinforced local culture.

In 1968, when Soviet-led Warsaw Pact tanks rolled through this square, someone wrapped a blindfold around the statue's eyes so Hus wouldn't have to witness yet another foreign invasion.

St. Nicholas Church

Open Mon noon-4pm, Tues-Sat 10am-4pm, Sun noon-3pm.

A Soft Serve dollop of highly concentrated baroquetry, this stubby charmer at the northwest corner of Old Town Square was completed in 1735. When it was built, St. Nicholas was dwarfed by several larger buildings, including a massive Old Town Hall, which stood on the site of what is now a bench-dotted little park. The architects, who never imagined the church would be openly visible from the center of Old Town Square, designed St. Nicholas to be viewed from no more than twenty paces away. That's why the statues of saints, high up on the building's facade, are looking down towards the pedestrians and not off into the distance. St. Nicholas has been a Hussite church since 1920, but functions more frequently as a classical music concert hall.

Týn Church

The Church of Our Lady Before Týn (rhymes with *spleen*) is the ultimate gothic ghoul and a total knockout. Towards the end of each day, the gold stars that top each of the church's tall spires blaze brilliantly as they catch the last of the sun's rays. At night, the old yellow stones are white-lighted like a film set, which contributes to the somewhat Disneyesque character of Old Town Square. After midnight, when all the floodlights are extinguished, the massive church becomes the Phantom of the Piazza, a shadow of it's day-lit self.

Founded in 1385, Týn was a hotbed of Hussitism until 1620, when the Hussite "heretics" were slaughtered to near extinction by the ruling Roman Catholics. The following year, twenty-seven of Bohemia's most prominent Protestant noblemen were beheaded just across the square (Xs mark the spot). Catholic Jesuits then made this church their own by recasting the Hussite-named bells that hung in the towers and replacing the sect's symbolic golden chalice with the ten-foot-tall Mary that's nailed-up between the towers today.

While you're looking up, notice that the church is not perfectly symmetrical; the tower on the right is thicker than the one on the left. This is typical of gothic architecture, in which the "masculine" side (on the south) protects the "feminine" side from the strong rays of the midday sun.

Týn's interior (open 30 minutes prior to services, which begin Mon-Fri at 530pm, Sat at 1pm and Sun at 1130am and 9pm) is far less exciting then the awesome facade, but entrance is free and it's worth the price of admission. The majority of what you see is from the Baroque period because the central nave and most of the altars were rebuilt after a disastrous fire in 1679.

As in any good church there are dozens of tombs here, the most famous of which belongs to Danish astronomer/mathematician Tycho de Brahe (1546-1601). Despite his disagreement with Copernicus, who had a sneaking suspicion that the Earth was not the center of the universe, Brahe was one of the leading scientists of his time, creating astronomical tables and formulating laws on the movements of the planets. He was also one of the most flamboyant characters in the court of Emperor Rudolf II. The quirky court scientist walked around with a metal nosepiece after losing the tip of his beak in a duel. Brahe died at the dinner table when his bladder burst during a meal. Court protocol at the time did not allow anybody to leave the banquet room before the Emperor finished his supper. He is buried to the right of the high altar under a salmon-colored marble relief.

The church's other main sites are particularly notable for their great age. The metal tureen in the southern nave is Bohemia's oldest font, dating from 1414. Adjacent is a 15th-century gothic pulpit, which in turn is next to a 16th-century carving of Christ.

04
SiGhTSEEiNG

Old Jewish Cemetery

(Starý židovský hřbitov), U Starého hřbitova. Tel. 231-0302. Open Apr–Oct, Sun–Fri 9am–6pm; Nov–Mar, Sun–Thurs 9am–430pm, Fri and before Jewish hols 9am–410pm. Admission 280 Kč. M Staroměstská

The Old Jewish Cemetery just might be the most photographed site in Prague, which says a lot in a city where a sunny day practically translates into higher stock prices for Fuji and Eastman Kodak.

Jews were obliged to live in Prague's ghetto when they were alive, and forced to be buried there when they died. Opened for business in 1439, this cemetery's first customer was scholar and poet Avigdor Kara. Over the next 400 years, some 20,000 locals were buried in a space barely large enough for a tenth that amount. As a consequence, bodies and tombstones were piled one on top of the other, sometimes as many as twelve deep. The result is dramatic, both emotionally and visually.

The Cemetery's two most famous permanent residents are Kabala master and Golem maker Rabbi Löew (died 1609), and financier Markus Mordechai Maisel (died 1601), banker to Emperor Rudolf II and once one of the richest men in Europe. Both their graves are recognizable by the large quantity of pebbles, and prayers on scraps of paper, that are placed on their tombs to this day.

Since 1990, the Jewish Museum in Prague has been conserving and restoring the Cemetery's 12,000 remaining tombstones, most of which have been seriously damaged by air pollution. The stones are decaying, and their ornamental reliefs and texts are gradually disintegrating. But if you look closely at the headstones you can still see decorative reliefs that symbolize names and occupations of the deceased. Cohens are represented by benedictory hands, while a tailor's grave might be marked with a carving of a pair of scissors.

The admission price for the cemetery includes access to all the sights of the Jewish Museum, including the Maislova, Španělska, Pinkasova, and Klausova synagogues. See Chapter 5/Walking Tours for an in-depth look at the old Jewish quarter.

St. Nicholas Church

(Kostel sv. Mikuláše), Malostranské nám., Praha 1. Open Apr–Oct, daily 9am–430pm; Nov–Mar, daily 9am–4pm. Admission: Church 45 Kč; Belfry 30 Kč. M Malostranská

The greatest Baroque spectacle in a city full of Baroque spectacles, the magnificent Church of St. Nicholas smacks you upside the head with a massiveness and pomposity that is virtually unmatched anywhere in the world.

The flamboyance of St. Nicholas was intended to recapture the hearts and minds of Bohemia's troublesome Catholic flock through an orgiastic display of conspicuous consumption. But the complex required the destruction of two Gothic churches, a school, a number of businesses and several homes—which didn't do much good for Catholicism's already flagging popularity in the neighborhood.

Built in the early 1700s, the vast structure is the work of local architect Kryštof Dientzenhofer. The church is built with titanic statues of assorted saints and holy men, eccentric cornices atop giant piers and one of the largest ceiling frescos in Christendom. The statue above the high altar is of St. Nicholas. At its sides are the altars of St. Ignaz of Loyola and St. Frank of Xaverius. The most celebrated work of art is the painting of St. Cross by Karel Škréta, in the first chapel to the left from the entrance.

For a terrific view over the red roofs of Malá Strana, climb the adjacent belfry. During socialism, this spot was a spy nest from which the secret police monitored the comings and goings at Western embassies.

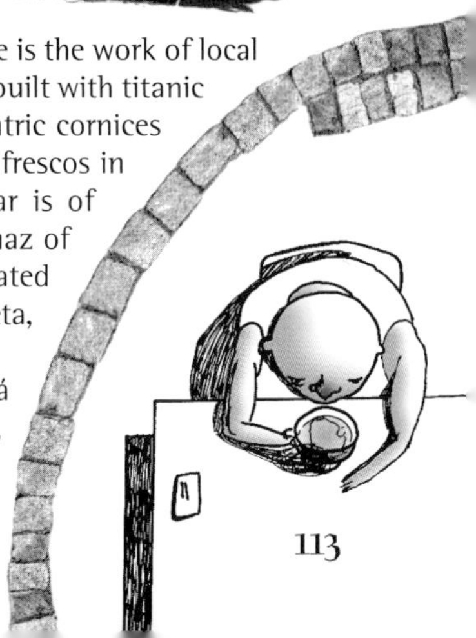

The Municipal House

(Obecní Dům) nám. Republiky 5, Praha 1. Tel. 2200-2100. Open daily 10am-6pm. Admission 150 Kč. M Náměstí Republiky

Completed in 1911, toward the end of the art nouveau fad, the Municipal House is the world's most exuberant celebration of this whimsical and intricate style. A direct result of the Industrial Revolution, art nouveau highlighted innovative new building materials, like iron and curved glass, that unlocked infinite possibilities for flamboyant flourishes and artistic embellishments.

The construction of the Municipal House is also inextricably related to the Czech National Revival, a thirty-year-long nationalistic movement that reclaimed Czech culture from German imperialism. And the importance of the building as a Czech cultural symbol was solidified when the Czechoslovak state was signed into independence here in 1918.

The Municipal House was built as a collaborative project, designed by scores of leading Czech artists, architects and sculptors. Bohumil Kafka made the entrance foyer, Josef V. Myslbek and Jan Preisler created Palacký Hall, Ladislav Šaloun fashioned the 1500-seat Smetana Concert Hall (which is home to the Prague Symphony Orchestra), and Alphonse Mucha's stunning work can be seen in the City Mayor's Hall.

This building is so rich with detail it's too much to grasp in a single look. Catch your first eyeful from across the street. The two lamp holders above the main entrance are particularly spectacular, as is the concave gable mosaic *Allegory of Prague Life.*

Exploring the building's interior is really a treat, as it's an extravaganza of whimsical murals, swirling mosaics, stoic sculptures, kaleidoscopic stained glass and playful iron work. On the ground floor is a dazzling cafe and a great-looking French restaurant (with mediocre food in both). Downstairs is that most rare of things: a sparkling clean Czech pub.

The building fits Prague like a glass slipper and is worth a special visit after sundown, when the spectacular detailing, shiny metalwork, glass screens and sparkling chandeliers shine like a jewel box.

A guided tour is the only way you'll get to see the building's most spectacular rooms and tour times are erratic. Make the effort though. Stop by the information desk, in the rear of the foyer, or telephone for reservations and tickets.

Loreto Palace

(Loreta), Loretánské náměstí 7, Praha 1. Tel. 2051-6740. Open Tues-Sun 9am-noon and 1-430pm. Admission 80 Kč. Tram 22 to Pohořelec

In the 13th century, the Christ family home was lifted from Nazareth by angels and flown to Loreto, Italy to protect it from non-believers who occupied the Holy Land. At least that's the way some religious folks tell it. And Bohemia's 17th-century Catholic leaders liked the story so much, they chose the Loreto cult as a device for the re-Catholicization of the Czech lands. Consequently, Prague's Loreto Palace is supposed to inspired by Mary and Joseph's cottage, and is just one of more than 50 near-replicas that have been constructed in what is now the Czech Republic.

The Loreto's facade is decorated with statues of over a dozen little cherubs, along with history's four best-selling authors: Matthew, Mark, Luke and John. And the carillon in the bell tower belts-out a well-known Marian hymn every hour on the hour (from 9am-5pm).

Inside you'll find the remains of two Spanish saints, St. Felicissimus and St. Marcia, each of whom is wearing a macabre wax mask. And look for the painting of St. Apolena—a.k.a. Appollonia—a 3rd-century deacon who had her teeth knocked out for refusing to renounce Christianity. She is often portrayed with a gold tooth and is the patron saint of dentists. There are lots of treasures here as well, including garnet-encrusted chalices and unique gold-and-diamond monstrances—holders for the consecrated bread of the Eucharist.

Find your way to the Chapel of Our Lady of Sorrows, where you'll discover an 18th-century painting of a bearded woman hanging on a cross. This is St. Starosta—a.k.a. Vilgefortis—a devout young princess whose father betrothed her to the pagan king of Sicily. God took pity on the girl, and, with the seemingly misguided assumption that Italian men don't like a lot of facial hair, caused her to grow a full beard. In any event, the princess's father was so disgraced that he encouraged his daughter to crucify herself. Starosta is now the patron saint of unhappily married women.

Strahov Monastery

(Strahovský klášter), Strahovské nádvoří. Tel. 2051-6671. Open daily 9am-1145am and 1pm-445pm. Admission 50 Kč. Tram 22 to Pohořelec

The Strahov Monastery libraries are some of the world's most beautiful bookrooms. Almost one million volumes are archived in ornate, gilded chambers decorated with carved wood and frescoes. Under the Baroque-era Philosophical Library's 46-foot-high ceilings is one of the world's best collections of theological texts, including many illuminated manuscripts and ancient first editions. The core collections date from the 17th and 18th centuries and are a sight to behold. The adjacent Monastery Picture Gallery contains a valuable collection of liturgical paintings.

Strahov Monastery was founded around 1140 by the relatively progressive Premonstratensians, a scholarly order closely related to the more easily pronounceable Jesuits. They were established by St. Norbert, who settled in the French valley of Pratum monstratum-Premontré in 1120. By 1790 the order was all over Europe and even undertook missions to America and Africa. Wherever they went, their activities emphasized science and education, and the establishment of schools for all grade levels. Through royal patronage this monastery—conveniently located by the Castle—became an important learning center for Prague's future leaders.

The Premonstratensians lost most of their monasteries in the during the 15th-century Hussite Wars. To this day, however, Strahov Monastery is headed by a General Abbot, and you can still see monks running around in white frocks.

Spanish Synagogue

(Španělská Synagoga) Vězeňská, Praha 1. Tel. 02/2481-0099. Open Nov-Mar, Sun-Fri 9am-430pm, Apr-Oct, Sun-Fri 9am-6pm. Admission 280 Kč.
Staroměstská

With its trademark keyhole windows, crennelated roof and faux mineretes, the Moorish-style Spanish Synagogue is the most beautiful and whimsicle house of worship in Prague. Built in 1868, on the site of the city's oldest Jewish prayer hall, the temple served Prague's Sphardic community until the Nazi occupation, after which it served as a storehouse for items confiscated from Czech Jews. The synagogue remained closed, and in terrible disrepair, until 1998, when an enormous reconstruction was completed by the Jewish Museum in Prague. The exhibit inside details the history of Jews in Bohemia and Moravia from the 18th century to the present day.

04
SiGhTSEEiNG

Old-New Synagogue

(Staronová Synagoga), Červená 2. Tel. 231-7191 or 231-0302. Open Apr-Oct, Sun-Thurs 9am-6pm, Fri 9am-5pm; Nov-Mar, Sun-Thurs 9am-5pm, Fri 9am-2pm. Admission 200 Kč M Staroměstská

Built in the 13th century, the Old-New Synagogue was originally just called the "New Synagogue," to distinguish it from even older ones that no longer exist. The *Staronová Synagoga* is now the oldest surviving synagogue in Europe. Orthodox services, which are still conducted here (weekdays at 8am, Fridays at sundown, and Saturdays at 9am), have been held almost continuously for over 700 years, and were interrupted only between 1941 and 1945 during the Nazi occupation.

While the outside of this rectangle gothic God-box is architecturally cold, the interior is positively intimate, warmed by soft lighting and oak seats which line the walls around a central *bema*, a stage that's protected by a medieval grille. Latch onto a tour and you will learn about ancient architecture that's loaded with religious symbolism.

When entering the Old-New Synagogue, notice that you have to walk down a small flight of stairs. That's because most of Josefov and Old Town have been raised about 10 feet over the last few centuries. The Synagogue, however, has preserved its original floor. The high admission fee is more than halved if you claim Czech citizenship. Get a local to purchase tickets for you.

Petřín Hill

(Petřínské sady), Praha 1. Tel. 5732-0112. Tram 12 or 22 to Újezd, then walk or take the funicular to the top.

During hot summer afternoons, locals take to the hills that surround the city center. Filled with fruit trees and wonderful winding pathways, Petřín is one of the most popular. From down below, in Old Town or Malá Strana, you can see the hill's Hunger Wall, a lengthy, decaying 21-foot-high stone wall that sticks out above the trees. It was commissioned in the 14th century by King Charles IV as a kind of medieval WPA project to employ the city's poorest citizens.

The easiest way to reach the top is by funicular, a steep cable car that dashes up and down the hill every 10 minutes or so, daily from 915am to 845pm. The funicular only makes two stops: the first is in the middle of the hill at Nebozízek Restaurant (*see* Chapter 8/Eating). Riders use the same tickets used for the city's trams and busses.

Once on top, you can climb the **Petřín Lookout Tower** (Open Apr-Sept daily 10am-530pm; Oct-March daily 10am-5pm. Admission 30 Kč), a one-fifth scale copy of Paris' Eiffel Tower that was erected for the 1891 Jubilee Exhibition, a chest-thumping nationalist expo meant to highlight the brains and beauty of Bohemia and Moravia. Made of recycled railway track, the free-standing column functioned as the city's main telecommunications tower until 1992, when the bigger and uglier Emir Hoffman tower was built in Žižkov. Most Praguers think the Petřín Lookout Tower is a terrible eyesore, an aesthetic shared by Adolf Hitler, who once commented that the tower spoiled the otherwise perfect view from Prague Castle. Views from the top are particularly awesome around sunset.

The Labyrinth (Open Apr-Aug, daily 10am-530pm; Sept-Oct, daily 10am-5pm; Nov-Mar, Sat-Sun 10am-5pm. Admission 30 Kč), located near the Lookout Tower, was also built for the Jubilee Exhibition. Work your way through a dilapidated funhouse of mirrors, and you'll reach the real booty: a gigantic art installation depicting the last fight of the Thirty Years' War, a battle between Praguers and Swedes that took place on Charles Bridge in 1648.

The nearby **Štefánik Observatory** (tel. 5732-0540) (Open Tues-Fri 2-6pm and 8-10pm; Sat-Sun 10am-noon, 2-6pm, and 8-10pm, closed Mon. Admission 20 Kč), was built in 1930 for the purpose of bringing the stars to the people. Inside is a museum of solar magnifiers. A 90-year-old working telescope views the sun during the day, and stars and planets at night. If you've never been to an observatory before, this is a good one to check out because it's small and crowds are rare. The tour leaders are mainly students, most of whom speak English.

The Olšanské Cemeteries

Two important contemporary cemeteries lie side-by-side, on Jana Želivského, Praha 3, at the M Želivského.

The **New Jewish Cemetery** *(Nový židovský hřbitov)* is where Franz Kafka is buried. His tombstone is one of the world's few Cubist cemetery stones. Its crystal form represents matter overcoming weight, and is meant to be full of energy and mystery. Stop at the main gate and ask the attendant for directions or a map. According to Jewish custom, men are asked to cover their heads. It's open Sun-Fri dawn to dusk.

Directly across the street you'll find the **Olšanské Cemetery** *(Olšanské hřbitovy)*, the final resting place of many of the city's most prominent former residents. Though not as old or overgrown as the Old Jewish Cemetery in Josefov, this tree-filled marbletown is a far cry from the manicured lawns that typify most modern burial grounds. The grave of Czechoslovakia's first Communist President, Klement Gottwald, is here, as is the tomb of Jan Palach, a young anti-Soviet martyr who, in January, 1969, doused himself with gasoline then struck a match. It's open daily dawn-dusk.

Lebodour & Pálffy Gardens

Entrance from Valdštejnské nám. 3, Praha 1. Open Jan-Oct, daily 10am-6pm. Admission: 25 Kč. Malostranská

Few places in Prague are more hidden then the back gardens of Malá Strana's aristocratic palaces. Although most of these gardens belong to embassies and are off-limits to the masses, two of them– Pálffy and Lebodour–were opened to the public in late 1997 after massive reconstruction that was funded, in part, by the Prince of Wales' Prince's Trust. Concealed behind two adjacent 18th-century Baroque palaces, these twin, terraced gardens climb steeply up castle hill to offer truly magnificent views over the rooftops of Malá Strana. In the Pálffy's backyard you'll also find a formal flat garden which, from an architectural point of view, conforms to a very sophisticated Italian design.

Few visitors means lots of solitude: bring a good book or a good friend.

National Memorial & Žižka Monument

(Národní památník) Vítkov Hill, Žižkov

Built as a mausoleum, this grotesquely enormous granite monument once contained the pickled bodies of former Communist leaders including Czechoslovakia's first pinko president, Klement Gottwald, who was entombed here in 1953. Actually, his body was in such poor condition when he died that, after nine years of embalming work, only his hand could be saved. It was displayed here in a jar, beside the urns and ashes of other high-ranking comrades. Check-out the monument's massive doors, decorated with bronze reliefs depicting Czech life during the brutal Nazi regime and the triumphant liberation of Prague by the Soviet Army.

Outside the mausoleum is yet another visual assault: a colossal equestrian statue that is one of the largest bronzes in the world. The mammoth 17-ton sculpture depicts Jan Žižka (c.1360-1424), a Hussite General who led Czech armies in five battles against Roman Catholic crusaders. Because most locals associate this place with former president Gottwald and Communist idolatry, the National Memorial is now largely mocked and was the perfect venue for a post-Revolution techno party that attracted thousands of revelers.

The Müllerova Villa

Nad Hradním Vodojemem 14, Praha 6. Tel. 2431-2012. Open Apr-Oct, Tues, Thurs, Sat-Sun 9am-6pm; Nov-Mar, Tues, Thurs, Sat 9am-5pm. Admission 300 Kč.

Completed in 1930 for Prague businessman Františik Müller, this amazing villa is the work of Adolf Loos, one of the top European architects of the early 20th century. Loos not only designed the house, but created every detail of the interior and supervised the building's construction. The result is a masterpiece that is celebrated for its departure from the traditional vertical arrangement of space into floors, working instead with individual rooms of different heights, all arranged around the house's imaginary axis. The house was recently restored to its original condition and filled with a permanent exhibition of Loos' work. Phone ahead to arrange a guided tour in English (which will cost an additional 100 Kč).

Fred & Ginger

Rašínovo nábřeží 80. Praha 2.

Affectionately called The Dancing Building by its supporters, this quirky construction overlooking the Vltava remains one of Prague's most controversial contemporary structures. It's a striking piece of architecture, built with a curvy corner cylinder of swirling and articulated glass that resembles a flared dancing skirt with a pinched waist. Purists see the design primarily as an advertisement for its creators, Los Angeles-based Frank O. Gehry & Associates, and their Czech partner Vladimír Milunič. The coveted site, at the corner of Jiráskovo náměstí, was cleared at the end of the Second World War by Allied bombing. Locals differ as to whether the dynamic design is appropriate adjacent to the much more staid turn-of-the-century apartment buildings with which it shares the block. Inside are offices, shops, and an overpriced rooftop restaurant.

THE BEST MUSEUMS & EXHIBITION SPACES

Prague's museums and exhibitions run the gamut from terrific to absurd. The National Gallery, which operates a half-dozen spaces in town, is the city's primary player. There are also lots of specialty museums and exhibition spaces managed by public and private agencies.

All the museums listed below either own excellent collections or mount high-quality temporary shows.

To find-out what's on while you're in town, check avantguide.com or pick-up a copy of the *Prague Post*, which has excellent gallery and museum listings.

Most museums are open Tuesday through Sunday from 10am to 5pm and are closed Mondays. Some keep shorter hours in April and September, and many are closed on the day following a national holiday. It can't hurt to telephone before heading out.

Center For Modern And Contemporary Art

Veletržní palác, Dukelských hrdinů 47, Praha 7. Tel. 2430-1111. Open Tues-Wed & Fri-Sun 10am-6pm, Thurs 10am-9pm. Admission 90 Kč; free first Wed of each month. M Vltavská

This terrific National Gallery collection began in the 1920s, when Prague was following Paris in seemingly everything cultural except cuisine. Housed in a Functionalist building, the truly excellent collection of contemporary works is what makes this a particularly exciting museum. Most of the new stuff is of Czech origin and is full of humor, irony and intelligence. The multi-story exhibition space is capable of displaying out-scaled art works the size of billboards, automobiles and more. There's always something new and provocative here, making this one of the very best museums in the city.

The modern art side is particularly long on French painting from the 19th and 20th centuries. The collection was founded with the intention of presenting significant landmarks in the development of French art, including the Romantic paintings of Eugéne Delacroix (1798-1863), and artists of the Barbizon School such as Camille Corot (1796-1875) and Théodor Rousseau (1812-1862). Several early Picasso's are here, along with lesser-known paintings by Cézanne, Gauguin, Chagall, Braque, and Dufy, and a famous self-portrait of Henri Rousseau.

Docent tours are not routinely available, but may be arranged by calling (tel. 2430-1014).

Museum of Cubism

Celetná 34 (at Ovocný trh 19), Praha 1. Tel. 2421-1732. Open Tues-Sun 10am-6pm. Admission 35 Kč.
M Náměstí Republiky

In Paris, where the cubist movement began, practitioners like Pablo Picasso and Georges Braque confined the art form to painting and sculpture. But in Bohemia, cubism extended to architecture and interior design. In and around Prague, dozens of unusual, angular buildings were constructed and fitted with similarly sharp furnishings. This museum, which celebrates that brief artistic period from 1911 to 1919, is located in House at the Black Madonna, Prague's most prominent cubist building. The permanent art collection here features the biggest names of the genre, most notably a fantastically unique series by sculptor Otto Gutfreund (1889-1927). There are lots of works by Czech cubist painters too, but the most brilliant displays are the couches, tables and other furnishings that took cubist decorative art into the third dimension.

Galerie Rudolfinum

Alšovo nábrezí 12, Praha 1. Tel. 2489-3205. Open Tues-Sun 10am-6pm. Admission 80-100 Kč M Staroměstská

Our favorite Prague gallery has no permanent collection, just an excellent exhibition space with a progressive booking policy. The Rudolfinum specializes in 20th-century art, especially in cooperation with foreign galleries. Shows almost always feature contemporary art that is relatively unknown in the West. Recent exhibits included Czech art from Soviet days and paintings from Maoist China. The gallery is located inside the same building as the Rudolfinum concert hall, home to the Czech Philharmonic Orchestra.

Old Town Hall Gallery

Staroměstské nám. Tel. 2448-2159. Open Mon 11-6pm, Tues-Sun 9-6pm. Admission free-100 Kč. M Staroměstská

This terrific gallery space is located right on Old Town Square, a couple of doors down from the Astronomical Clock. Exhibitions change frequently, and are usually regional in theme. No stranger to controversy, this city gallery regularly displays art that would repel most American politicians, including graphic photos of Russian abortion clinics, and Mafia slayings.

Because the gallery has large picture windows facing the square, you can get a good idea of what's on before going inside.

Bertramka Mozart Museum

Mozartova 169, Praha 5. Tel. 5731-8461. Open Apr-Oct, daily 930am-6pm; Nov-Mar, 930am-5pm. Admission 90 Kč Tram: 2, 6, 7, 9, 14 or 16 from M Anděl to Bertramka

Originally built as a vineyard homestead, the Bertramka villa became the property of the singer Josefa Dušek and her pianist/composer husband František Xaver Dušek in 1784. The couple struck-up a friendship with Wolfgang Amadeus Mozart, who visited them on multiple occasions. Mozart completed the score of Don Giovanni here and got help from the Dušeks with the Prague productions of his operas Entführung aus dem Serail and the *Marriage of Figaro.*

Bertramka is now a Mozart museum displaying many of his personal possessions, including arias written in his own hand and a harpsichord on which he composed. There's even a lock of Mozart's hair encased in a glass cube.

The villa's Salla Terrena, which served as a music salon in Mozart's day, continues to be used for chamber music concerts. The program is usually comprised of works by Mozart and Czech composers. Telephone for concert times.

National Museum

(Národní muzeum), Václavské náměstí 68, Praha 1. Tel. 2449-7111. Open May-Sept, daily 10am-6pm; Oct-Apr, daily 9am-5pm. Admission 70 Kč. Ⓜ Muzeum

Prague's museum of natural and national history occupies a grandiose neo-Renaissance building at the top of Wenceslas Square. It's so imposing that Soviet troops fired upon it during their 1968 invasion, thinking it was the government's headquarters. While this museum has nothing on New York's Museum of Natural History, there are a lot of great exhibits here that can't be found anywhere else. An enormous collection of rocks, minerals and meteorites includes several radioactive examples, displayed in open cases. And on the second floor you'll find endless zoological and paleontological displays that include hundreds, if not thousands, of stuffed-and-mounted animals. A huge lifelike model of a woolly mammoth is mounted next to the bones of the real thing. We love the large collection of antique hand puppets and marionettes too. It's worth going in just to see the museum's famous grand staircase, which is often the site of choral concerts and excellent private parties.

St. Agnes's Convent

(Klášter sv. Anežky České), U milosrdných 17, Praha 1. Tel. 2481-0628. Admission 100 Kč; free the first Fri of each month. Ⓜ Staroměstská

Tucked away in a corner of Old Town, this complex of early gothic buildings is home to the National Gallery's collection of gothic art, which includes a unique series of Czech panel paintings. As might be expected, the collection is heavy with paintings on wood portraying saints and sinners. Master Theodoric, one of the most distinguished artistic personalities of the 14th century, is well represented here with dozens of remarkable panel paintings. And we like the museum's display of sandstone gargoyles. The convent also houses 19th-century Czech painting and sculpture, works that that were created during a particularly nationalistic period of Czech history. Canonized in 1989, after a 600 year campaign for her sainthood, St. Agnes was a 13th-century princess who became Abbess of the Clariscan abbey she founded. Until the Church finally waived the requirement, Agnes's canonization was hampered due to the impossibility of locating her remains. The convent is located at the end of Anežska Street, off of Haštalské náměstí.

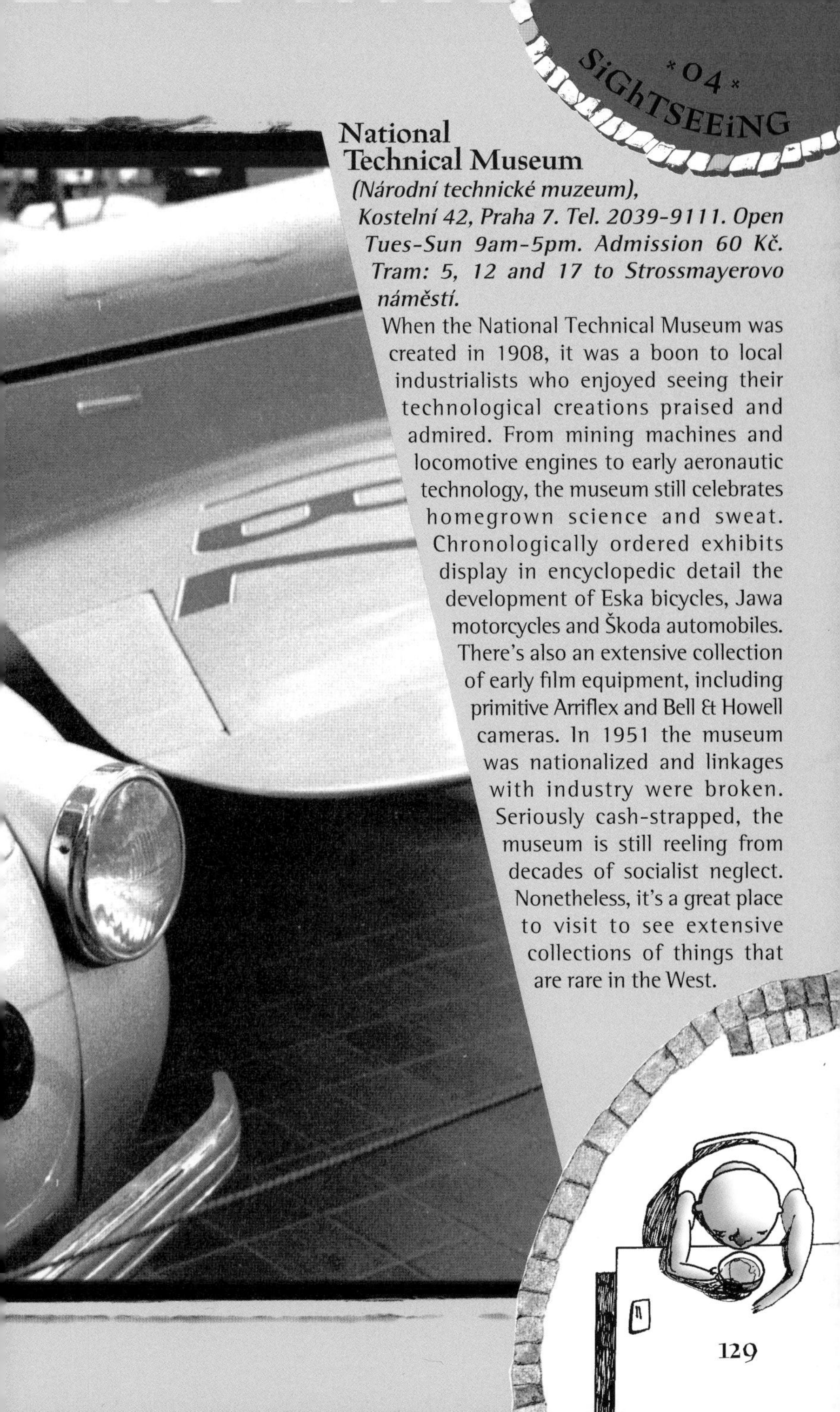

National Technical Museum

(Národní technické muzeum), Kostelní 42, Praha 7. Tel. 2039-9111. Open Tues-Sun 9am-5pm. Admission 60 Kč. Tram: 5, 12 and 17 to Strossmayerovo náměstí.

When the National Technical Museum was created in 1908, it was a boon to local industrialists who enjoyed seeing their technological creations praised and admired. From mining machines and locomotive engines to early aeronautic technology, the museum still celebrates homegrown science and sweat. Chronologically ordered exhibits display in encyclopedic detail the development of Eska bicycles, Jawa motorcycles and Škoda automobiles. There's also an extensive collection of early film equipment, including primitive Arriflex and Bell & Howell cameras. In 1951 the museum was nationalized and linkages with industry were broken. Seriously cash-strapped, the museum is still reeling from decades of socialist neglect. Nonetheless, it's a great place to visit to see extensive collections of things that are rare in the West.

Mucha Museum

Kaunický palác, Panská 7, Praha 1. Tel. 628-4162. Open daily 10am-6pm. Admission 120 Kč. M Můstek/Náměstí Republiky

At no time was Prague and Paris more connected than in the 1920s. And no single artist was associated to both cities as much the world-famous art nouveau painter Alphons Mucha. Even if you've never heard of Mucha, you know his work from the stylish Sandra Bernhardt posters you still see at tourist stalls all over the City of Light. The Mucha Museum celebrates the career of a local boy gone good. Not surprisingly, the best part of this collection are the spectacular Parisian posters that made Mucha famous. There are some great paintings as well, along with a small collection of the artist's personal memorabilia.

Kinský Palace

(Palác Kinských), Staroměstské nám. 12, Praha 1. Tel. 2481-0758. Open Tues-Sun 10am-6pm. Admission 100 Kč Staroměstská

Because of its ultra-accessible location, directly on Old Town Square, this National Gallery exhibition space often hosts popular shows that have included Max Ernst and Rembrandt retrospectives. The National Gallery will sometimes cull some pieces from their own collection of modern masters to mount something special here.

Museum of the City of Prague

Na Poříčí 52, Praha 8. Tel. 2422-3696. Open Tues-Sun 10am-6pm. Admission 50 Kč.

The half-million exhibits in this neo-Renaissance building document life in the city from prehistoric times to the 18th century. The best reason for going is to see the amazing scale model of the city that was made between 1826 and 1837. Taking up an entire room on the second floor, this fantastic creation documents every building in the city and depicts the Jewish ghetto before it was destroyed in the late 19th century.

PRAGUE'S SPECIAL-INTEREST MUSEUMS

Antonín Dvořák Museum
Ke Karlovu 20, Praha 2. Tel. 02/2492-3363. Open Tues-Sun 10am-5pm. M I. P. Pavlova
Portentious ode to Bohemia's most famous composer.

Army Museum
U Památníku 2, Praha 3. Tel. 02/2020-4926. Open May-Oct, Tues-Sun 930am-6pm; Nov-Apr, Mon-Fri 9am-5pm. M Florenc
History of the Czech army from WWs 1 and 2.

Bedřich Smetana Museum
Novotného lávka, Praha 1. Tel. 02/2222-0082. Open Wed-Mon 10am-5pm. M Staroměstská
Original manuscripts, personal possessions, and musical scores activated by laser baton.

Czech Police Museum
Ke Karlovu 1, Praha 2. Tel. 02/298-940. Open Tues-Sun 10am-5pm. M I. P. Pavlova
Celebration of local cops includes lots of temporary exhibitions on the security forces.

Ekotechnické Museum
Papírenská 6, Praha 6. Tel. 02/3332-5500. Open Apr-Oct, Sat-Sun 10am-430pm. M Hradčanská
Voyage back to the steam age in Prague's old sewage treatment plant.

Gasworks Museum
U Plynárny 500, Praha 4. Tel. 02/6717-2482. Open by appointment.
Everything you ever wanted to know about the Czech natural gas industry.

House at The Golden Ring
Týnská 6, Praha 1. Tel. 02/2482-7022. Open Tues-Sun 10am-6pm. M Staroměstská
20th-century Czech art in one of the oldest buildings in Old Town.

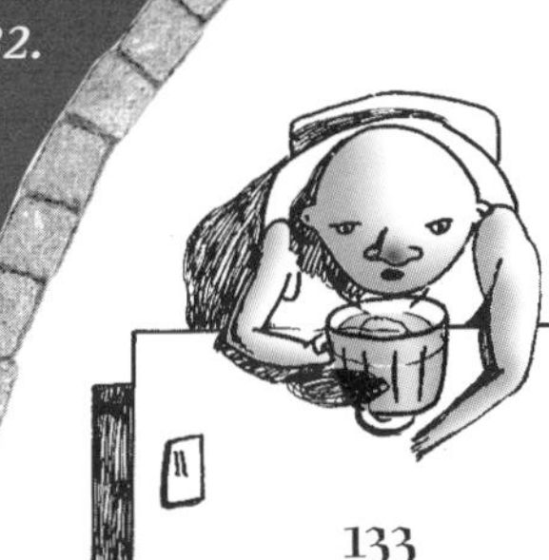

Hrdlička Museum of Man
Viničná 7, Praha 2. Tel. 02/2195-3231. Open Wed 10am-6pm, not public hols.
Ethnographic museum with American Indian masks, Pygmy casts and death masks of prominent Czech scientists.

Jaroslav Ježek Museum
Kaprova 10, Praha 1. Tel. 02/5732-0059. Open Tues 1-6pm. M Staroměstká
Memorial to a major figure of the Czech musical avant-garde in the "blue room" of his former apartment.

Josef Sudek Gallery
Úvoz 24, Praha 1. Tel. 02/5753-1489. Open Wed-Fri 1-6pm, Sat-Sun 10am-noon and 1-6pm. M Malostranská
The work of famed photographer Josef Sudek (1896-1976) in his former home.

Kampa Museum
U Sovových mlýnů, Praha 1. Open Tues-Sun 10am-6pm. M Malostranská
Major collection of Czech modern art in a beautifully-restored, riverfront building in Kampa Park.

Kinský Palace
Staroměstské nám 12, Praha 1. Tel. 02/2481-0758. Open Tues-Sun 10am-6pm. M Staroměstská
The National Gallery's best graphic art and drawings in a late-Baroque Old Town Square palace.

Komenský Pedagogical Museum
Valdštejnská 20, Praha 1. Tel. 02/5753-3455. Open Tues-Sun 10am-1230pm and 1-430pm. M Malostranská
18th-century classroom aids following the development of professional teaching in Bohemia.

Lapidarium of the National Museum
Výstaviště 442, Praha 7. Tel. 02/3337-5636. Open Thurs-Fri noon-6pm, Sat-Sun 10am-6pm. M Nádraží Holešovice
The final resting place of Czech stone sculpture, including originals from Charles Bridge.

Marold's Panorama
Výstaviště Praha, Praha 7. Tel. 02/2010-3204. Open Tues-Fri 2-5pm, Sat-Sun 10am-5pm.
Enormous 19th-century diorama depicting a crusial moment in the 17th-century Hussite Wars.

Museum of Aeronautics
Mladoboleslavská ulice, Praha 9. Tel. 02/2020-4926. Open May-Oct, Tues-Sun 930am-6pm. Českomoravská
Four hangars full of military and commercial aircraft from WW1 to the late 1960s.

Museum of Decorative Arts in Prague
ul. 17. listopadu 2, Praha 1. Tel. 02/5109-3111. Open Tues 10am-8pm, Wed-Sun 10am-6pm. Staroměstská
Glass, porcelain, graphic art, furniture and fashion in a beautiful neo-Renaissance building.

Museum of Historical Pharmacies
Nerudova 32, Praha 1. Tel. 02/5753-1502. Open Apr-Sept, Tues-Fri noon-6pm, Sat-Sun 11am-6pm. Malostranská
Perfectly-restored early 19th century pharmacy with spectacular wooden interior.

Museum of Military History
Hradčanské nám 2, Praha 1. Tel. 02/2020-4926. Open Tues-Sun 10am-6pm. Hradčanská
Bohemian military history from the earliest times to 1918.

Museum of Military Technology
257 42 Lešany, p. Krhanice. Tel. 02/2020-0493. Open Jun-Sept, Sat-Sun 10am-4pm.
Light combat vehicals and other 20th-century equiptment in a former artillery barracks.

Museum of Prague Water Management
Národní 13, Praha 1. Tel. 02/2109-5473. Open by appointment.
800 years of waterworks and Prague's most remarkable example of industrial architecture.

Náprstek Museum
Betlémské nám 1, Praha 1. Tel. 02/2222-1416. Open Tues-Sun 9am-noon and 1245-530pm. Národní Třída
Ecclectic collection of non-European art and artefacts assembled by a 19th-century collector.

National Memorial to Victims of the Heydrich Terror

Resslova 9a, Praha 2. Tel. 02/2492-0686. Open Oct-Apr, Tues-Sun 10am-4pm; May-Sept Tues-Sun 10am-5pm. Karlovo Náměstí

Orthodox Cathedral in which Czech parachutists hid after assassinating the Nazi chief of Bohemia.

National Museum of Agriculture

Kostelní 44, Praha 7. Tel. 02/2030-8200. Open Tues-Sun 9am-1130am and 1230-5pm. Hradčanská

History of food production told with mills, machinery and bakery equipment.

Palacký and Rieger Memoral

Palackého 7, Praha 1. Tel. 02/2449-7376. Open Apr-Oct, Mon 9am-5pm by appointment. Můstek/Národní Třída

Beautiful former apartment of two leading figures of the 19th-century Czech National Revival.

PopMuseum

Besední 3, Praha 1. Tel. 02/5731-4776. Open Fri-Tues 10am-5pm. Malostranská, then tram to Újezd

Czech and Slovak rock, jazz, folk and country hall of fame.

Postal Museum

Nové Mlýny 2, Praha 1. Tel. 02/231-2006. Open Tues-Sun 9am-noon and 1-5pm. Náměstí Republiky

Stamps from the First Republic, Nazi occupation and Russia in a 16th-century building.

Praga Automobile Museum

Pod Kaštany 14, Praha-Zbuzany. Tel. 02/5796-0332. Open Tues, Thurs-Sun 10am-5pm. Luka

70 classic cars, trucks and tractors from Praga, once the largest Czech automobile manufacturer.

Prague Botanical Gardens

Na slupi 16, Praha 1. Tel. 2491-8970. Open daily 10am-3pm. Karlovo Náměstí

Small exhibition of indigenous and exotic flora since 1775.

Public Transport Museum

Patočkova 4, Praha 6. Tel. 02/3332-2432. Open Apr-Oct, Sat-Sun and hols 9am-5pm. Hradčanská

120 years of Prague transit, fron horse-drawn coaches to the Metro.

Šternberg Palace
Hradčanské nám 15, Praha 1. Tel. 02/2051-4634. Open Tues-Sun 10am-6pm. Ⓜ Malostranská
National Gallery collection of old European art from 14th-century Italians to 17th-century Dutch.

Toy Museum
Jiřská 6, Praha 1. Tel. 02/2437-2294. Open daily 930am-530pm. Ⓜ Malostranská
Unique collection of wooden and tin toys, plus dolls and play planes, trains and automobiles.

Tyrš Museum
Újezd 450, Praha 1. Tel. 02/532-193. Open Thurs, Sat-Sun 9am-5pm.
One of the world's first sport museums includes terrific posters, paintings and graphic art.

U Fleků Brewery Museum
Křemencova 11, Praha 1. Tel. 02/2491-5118. Open Mon-Sat 10am-5pm. Ⓜ Karlovo Náměstí
Five-hundred years of beer-making in Prague's most historical brewhouse.

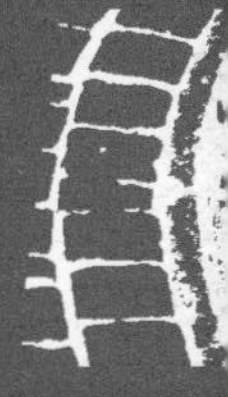

Valdštejnská Jízdárna
Valdštejnská 3, Praha 1. Tel 02/2481-0758. Open Tues-Sun 10am-6pm. Ⓜ Malostranská
National Gallery space for temporary exhibitions about Prague and artistic Praguers.

Villa Bílek
Mickiewiczova 1, Praha 6. Tel. 02/2432-2021. Open May 15-Oct 15, Tues-Sun 10am-6pm; Oct 16-May 14, Sat-Sun 10am-5pm. Ⓜ Hradčanská
Extraordinary early 20th-century home of sculptor and graphic artist František Bílek.

Zbraslav Castle
Zbraslav, Praha 5. Tel. 02/5792-1638. Open Sat-Sun 11am-2pm.
National Gallery's collection of Asian art in a villa on the outskirts of Prague.

IN
GRAFIC
ART

× 05 × WALKiNG TOURS
EXPLORiNG

05 EXPLORING

Walking through Prague is like wandering around inside an enormous jewelry box. Architectural treasures are so intimately knit into the urban fabric that one landmark leads to another as inexorably as arches lead into courtyards, portals to palaces, red-tiled rooftops to the brooding sky. Of Europe's capitals, Prague is probably the least altered by the twentieth century. The city's skyscrapers are still its gothic towers, baroque spires and renaissance domes. And throughout the communist period it remained virtually unchanged, as if frozen in time.

The walks below take you through some of the most magnificent streets in the city. They are designed to point-out the highlights and, at the same time, allow you to make lots of wonderful discoveries on your own.

The best times to see Prague are around sunrise or sunset, when buildings and monuments that are merely stunning at midday appear absolutely otherworldly.

Walk 1

OLD TOWN AND THE FORMER JEWISH QUARTER

from Wenceslas Square to Charles Bridge

When Old Town (Staré Město) was founded in 1234, it was fortified by a thick stone wall and surrounded by a hazardous moat. Today, streets cover the former moat. But if you look at a map, you can see where the channel once lay—under the semi-circle created by the streets Národní, Na Příkopě and Revoluční—connected to the River Vltava at both ends. The creation of New Town (Nové Město) in 1348 made the walls superfluous, and they gradually disappeared over the next century.

Begin your walk at Můstek Metro station, at the foot of

Wenceslas Square *(Václavské náměstí),* which is not a square at all, but a long, sloping boulevard. Topped by the neo-renaissance National Museum (*see* Chapter 4/The Best Museums), the Square has become the crass commercial center of New Town, ringed with shops, restaurants, cinemas and hotels, not to mention a strip club or two. It's an important commercial intersection, and somewhat seedy at night. But it makes an excellent contrast to the bucolic streets of Old Town that you're about to explore.

In the Middle Ages, there were several gates allowing access to Old Town, and one of them was here at Můstek, which in Czech means "little bridge." Drop down into Můstek Metro station (under the glass building with the contemporary clock) where you will see, at the top of the escalators heading down to the platform, the ancient remains of that original stone bridge that spanned the moat. It's a fantastic archeological artifact that was discovered in the 1970s during the building of Prague's Metro.

Return to street level and, with your back to all of Wenceslas Square, walk one block down Na Můstku. Turn right onto Rytířská and walk one block to the green-and-white

* 05 *
EXPLORiNG

Theater of the Estates *(Stavovské divadlo),* one of the most beautiful and historic playhouses in Europe. This Classicist performing arts hall was built at the end of the 18th Century, when national theaters were constructed at all the European courts and in capital cities throughout the Continent. Situated adjacent to the headquarters of Charles University (see below), the Estates Theater is a manifestation of the Enlightenment, when the building of public theaters was perceived to be the moral responsibility of the elite and a demonstration of a nation's cultural importance. The theater was funded by Count Nostic, an aristocratic lover of Italian Opera and German-language drama, both of which were the Estates' primary fare until 1920, when the theater was linked to Prague's National Theater and Czech-language productions became commonplace.

This playhouse will be forever linked with the great composer Wolfgang Amadeus Mozart, who chose this stage to premiere not one, but two of his best-known operas: *La Clemenza di Tito,* in 1791; and a thrilling performance of *Don Giovanni,* on October 29, 1787, which was conducted by Mozart himself.

The interior is usually accessible only to theater-goers but, if the doors are open, try to sneak a peek at the opulent blue-velvet interior, which, incidentally, was featured in the movie Amadeus.

Walk clockwise around the theater into Ovocný trh, or "fruit market" street. The buildings immediately on your left are the

Carolinum, the headquarters of Charles University. When King Charles IV chartered his University in the 14th century, he bestowed the institution with several gothic houses that once stood one this site. The university began with four academic faculties: Philosophy, Medicine, Law and Theology. Their buildings were reconstructed several times; the current look dating from the early 18th century. In the 1950s, the smooth red brick structure with a canopy-like roof was squeezed between the historical houses to accommodate an administrative center and a new office for the chancellor. Today, Charles is considered to be the best university in Central Europe and its campus is spread throughout Prague.

Continue along Ovocný trh, an old market triangle where, on your right, you will see the back entrance of the new Myslbek Shopping Center, and on your left, the back entrances to several Charles University buildings. Ovocný trh curves left, where it meets up with Celetná, one of the oldest streets in Old Town. At the corner of Celetná, on your left, you'll see the

05
EXPLORiNG

House at the Black Madonna, the oldest and most famous cubist building in Prague. In Paris, where Cubism's most famous practitioners were Pablo Picasso and Georges Braque, the artistic movement was confined to painting and sculpture. As an architectural style, Cubism is exclusive to Bohemia, and there are dozens of fine examples throughout Prague. Built in 1911, this house is one of the city's most notable Cubist creations. Shadow play is an important element of Cubist architecture. The recesses, overhangs and carvings that accentuate the building's dimensionality are designed to create interesting angles that seem to change throughout the day. At once bizarre and extraordinary, this house manages to fit well with the older buildings that surround it. Prague is full historical juxtapositions, but the city has always been adept at balancing respect for the past with the shock of the new. The House at the Black Madonna takes its name from the caged statue on the corner of the building that was saved from an earlier structure that stood on this site. Today, the building is home to a worthwhile Cubist Museum (*see* Chapter 4/The Best Museums), and the best gift-book store in the city.

Standing at the corner of Celetná, look to your right where, a one block up you can see the old stone

Powder Tower *(Prašná brána),* once one of the major gateways into walled Old Town. As early as the 11th century, traders from the east would enter Prague through a portal here, on their way to markets in Old Town Square or adjacent Malé náměstí. Because one of the Kings' residences used to be located near here as well, the tower marks the beginning of what was once the Royal Road, a mile-long parade route along which medieval Bohemian monarchs galloped on their way to being crowned in Prague Castle. The Gothic tower you see here was rebuilt in 1475, though much of the decorative exterior was created in the 19th century. You can climb a spiral staircase to the top of the tower, from which there are expansive vistas over both Old Town and New Town. It's only open April to October, from 10am to 6pm. Admission is 30 Kč. Info (tel. 0602/373049).

Rather than walking left, toward Old Town Square, or right, toward náměstí Republiky, cross Celetná, into the vaulted passageway, turn right, and turn left, through the hidden arch that leads into Templová Street (the Radegast Pub will be on your right). Walk to the end of Templová, then turn left, into Jakubská, which is named for the big church on your right. Walk to the end of Jakubská, turn right, and enter

St. James' Church *(Kostel sv. Jakuba),* a massive building containing twenty-one Baroque altars. Just inside the church's front door look up to your right where you'll see a withered human forearm dangling from a chain like a giant stick of jerky. According to legend, the dried appendage belonged to a 16th-century thief who stole into the church one night intent on swiping a pearl necklace from a statue of the Madonna. When the would-be criminal attempted to lift the jewels, however, the statue miraculously ensnared his arm, which could then be extricated only by amputation. So goes divine justice in a place of worship that, ironically, is the church of Prague's butchers' guild. St. James' was founded in 1374, then rebuilt in 1739 after a fire that destroyed much of the surrounding neighborhood. If you happen to be in the area on Sunday morning, you can drop in for a beautiful, and free, 30-minute organ concert, beginning at 1030am.

Exit the church, turn left, and then right, through the archway, into

Týn Court, a beautifully reconstructed courtyard owned by the giant Gothic Týn Church that looms over nearby Old Town Square. From the 11th to the 16th centuries, Týn (which evolved from the same linguistic root as the English word "town") was the site of an inn, a church and several brothels, all of which catered to turbaned traders who came from the East with pelts, spices and slaves. Today, the courtyard still sees far more than its fair share of foreigners. There are four restaurants, a cafe, several upscale shops, and lots of expensive offices upstairs. Architecturally, the courtyard is a blend of Renaissance and Baroque, all of which sit atop Romanesque cellars. It's worth taking a look at one of these deep vaults, which you can see by descending into the basement of the restaurant Metamorphis.

Walk across Týn Court, exit through the arch on the other side, and continue straight, down the narrow passage that opens up into

Old Town Square. If you were to step down into the cellar of any house on the square, you would find yourself in the remains of a dank, stone-pillared Romanesque chamber that was once at ground level. Most of Old Town was purposefully buried during the 13th Century in a radical project meant to ease the periodic flooding of the River Vltava. Today, an entire medieval stone town lies hidden beneath the surface. Most of the cellars of Old Town Square are now closed to the public, but you can still dip into the crypt at Komerční Banka, across from the astronomical clock, or at the White Horse *(Bílý Koníček)* at the corner of Železná Street, which today advertises itself as "the oldest club in Prague."

Walk to the pavement in front of the Old Town Hall clock tower, where you can see twenty-seven white crosses embedded in the cobblestones. These pay homage to noblemen who were beheaded on this spot in 1621, after their failed uprising against the Habsburg monarchy. The names of the nobles are on a large metal plaque that's affixed to the adjacent wall. Another plaque here commemorates the destruction of Old Town Hall, which was blown-up by the Germans in May 1945, just two days before they retreated in defeat. The biggest loss was not the building itself, but its contents, which included centuries of historical records that are now lost forever.

Old Town Square is thoroughly detailed in Chapter 4/The Top Sights.

Our walk now turns down Pařížská Street (which begins at the northwest corner of Old Town Square, just to the right of the Baroque, white church of St. Nicholas). This marks the border of the neighborhood known as Josefov, the former Jewish ghetto which existed for more then six hundred years. It was almost completely demolished in the late 19th century to make room for the fantastically-sculpted apartment buildings that stand today. Pařížská (Paris Street), the quarter's main thoroughfare, is now lined with upscale shops, and contemporary Josefov is only the faintest shadow of its former self.

While strolling down this block, look up at the hill that rises across the river at the end of the street. Called Letná Plain, and now topped by a giant metronome, this hill was once the site of the infamous

Stalin Statue, a frighteningly huge sculpture that briefly dominated the local skyline. The statue was designed by Otakar Švec (1892-1955), a native Praguer who carved out a niche for himself as a designer of monuments and decorator of financial institutions. In a highly prestigious public competition in 1949, Švec won-over the Communist judges with a wedge-shaped monolith in the shape of Czech working people proudly standing behind their Soviet leader. Soon after his designs were chosen, however, the lost creative control to Party partisans who saw the statue as an opportunity to demonstrate their servility to the Stalin cult. The Communists insisted upon grotesque alterations, and Švec fell into the cogs of the Party's political machine. Construction started in February 1953, and though Stalin died in the interim, nothing stopped the enthusiasm of the 600 men and women who worked around the clock for two years completing the marble monument.

* 05 *
EXPLORiNG

Švec, who was under terrific psychological pressure, fell into a deep depression and killed himself shortly before the statue's unveiling in 1955. He bequeathed this entire estate, including his honorarium for the monument, to a hospice for blind children, the only Praguers who would not have to look at the stone monster he had created. The statue loomed over the city for just six years, until 1961, after which Stalin was discredited and the statue was blown-up.

About half-way down Pařížská, on your left, you'll see the Old-New Synagogue, Europe's oldest extant temple, dating from the mid-13th century (described in detail in Chapter 4/Digging Deeper). Turn left, down the stairs that lead past the synagogue's entrance and pause at the corner of Maiselová Street. The Old Jewish Cemetery is straight ahead: You can see some of its tombstones peaking out above the wall on the left. Look up at the clock tower opposite the Old-New Synagogue. This is part of the former

Jewish Town Hall, from which the Jewish quarter was administered. You can see that the clock has Hebrew letters. But what you might not notice is that its hands turn counter-clockwise, because Hebrew is read from right to left. The Jewish Town Hall is the only secular building that remains from the time of the Jewish ghetto. Except for five synagogues, part of the old cemetery and a burial hall, everything else in the neighborhood was demolished at the turn of the last century.

In the 1940s, during the Nazi occupation, the Germans gathered the country's Jewish religious relics and shipped them here to become part of a large Museum of An Extinct Race, a kind of Jewish-theme Disneyland that Hitler envisioned Josefov should become. The Jewish Town Hall, now closed to the public, is the administrative center of the **State Jewish Museum** *(Židovské Muzeum),* which manages the few remaining Jewish synagogues of Josefov. Sometimes, when we see tourists' cameras swing around to shoot Orthodox Jewish visitors here, we can't help but think that Hitler's museum has become a reality.

If you haven't already been to the Old Jewish Cemetery, this is may be a good time to go. The admission price for the cemetery includes access to all the sights of the State Jewish Museum, including the Maislova, Spanělská, Pinkasová, and Klausova synagogues. All are open April-Nov, Sun-Fri 9am-6pm; Nov-Mar Sun-Fri 9am-430pm. Admission is 300 Kč.

With the Old-New Synagogue on your left, walk up Maiselova Street. It's named for the 16th-century Markus Mordechai Maisel, who was Emperor Rudolf IIs banker and once one of the richest men in Europe. One block ahead, on your left, you'll see

Maisel Synagogue, Maiselova 10, which now functions as the State Jewish Museum's primary repository of religious objects such as porcelain goblets, silver torah pointers and rusty circumcision knives. In 1994, these religious objects were assigned to the Federation of Jewish Communities, which recently completed an exhaustive inventory comparing the Nazi's catalogues with the 40,000 items in the current collection. The synagogue dates from the late 16th century.

Turn right, onto Široká Street, where, after a half-block, on your right, you'll come to the entrance of the

Pinkas Synagogue, of which Franz Kafka and his family were once members. Today the *shul* is used for the storage and display of pictures, drawings and graphic works. Built in the Renaissance style in the 16th century, the building was transformed into a Holocaust memorial in 1959, when the names of 77,297 Bohemian and Moravian Jews who were killed by the Nazis were painted on the synagogue's walls. Beneath the synagogue, archeologists have discovered Prague's oldest *mikveh* (a Jewish ritual bath), dating from the 13th century. A second entrance to the Old Jewish Cemetery is located behind the Pinkas Synagogue.

Continue (towards the river) to the end of Široká Street, which opens onto the small, but busy

Jan Palach Square *(náměstí Jana Palacha)*, renamed in 1990 for a 21-year-old philosophy student who burned himself to death in 1969, in protest of the Soviet invasion. An estimated 800,000 Praguers are said to have attended his funeral, and Palach remains a heroic martyr to this day.

Leave the old Jewish quarter by turning left, onto the busy street called 17 listopadu (17th of November), which commemorates both the death of another student, Jan Opletal, at the hands of the Germans in 1939, and the beginning of the Velvet Revolution, on the same day fifty years later. Follow the tram tracks for two blocks, to the foot of Charles Bridge. The two-block-long building on your left is the

Klementinum, a massive former Jesuit college that now houses the Czech Republic's national library. Meant to help re-Catholicize the country's largely Protestant population, the Klementinum's construction necessitated the destruction of dozens of homes, which little to raise the status of the Jesuits' already waning popularity. If the little wooden door at the end of the block (on your left) is open (just opposite Charles Bridge), it's worth strolling into the Klementinum's courtyards. Walk to the second courtyard, where a diminutive door on your left leads into the libraries themselves. Walk assumptively past the security booth and turn right into the grand reading room where students from Charles University study.

Our walk finishes at **Charles Bridge,** which was lined with statues by the same people who brought us the Klementinum. Milan Kundera wrote "The thousands of petrified saints gazing at you from all sides and threatening you, spying on you, hypnotizing you, are the frenzied occupation army that invaded Bohemia three hundred fifty years ago to tear the people's faith and language out of its soul." Today, most people have a hard time seeing that harsh history though the stunningly beautiful views of the Castle and the city beyond.

If you haven't had enough yet, you can cross the bridge guided by the map and description in Chapter 4/The Top Sights. Then pick-up our Malá Strana walk, below, which begins just on the other side of the bridge.

Walk 2

MALÁ STRANA: ThE LITTLE SIdE

from Charles Bridge to the Castle Steps

The destruction of this quarter's romanesque and gothic buildings by fire in 1541 was a blessing in disguise that made room for the baroque showplaces that were built in their place. Today Malá Strana, the "little side" in Czech, is widely regarded as the most purely intact baroque area in the world. The quarter's quiet cobbled lanes are fronted by perfect renaissance and baroque houses, noble palaces and several secret gardens. Director Miloš Forman shot his movie "Amadeus" here because Malá Strana still looks much the way it did over two hundred years ago. But, unlike Venice and Florence, which can feel like mummified villes d'art, this historic center is a vital place that bustles with activity. The Czech Parliament makes its home here, as do dozens of embassies and lots of great restaurants and bars, which are hidden in the dreamlike back streets.

Begin on the Malá Strana side of Charles Bridge under the

Charles Bridge Tower, Malá Strana. In the Middle Ages, a toll was collected for crossing the bridge that, in today's currency, equaled approximately the price of one beer. Collection was enforced by hatchet-carrying guards who stood in this spot. Stand under the tower and look up at the stones. Those deep gashes you see were made from centuries of blade sharpening. On a clear day it's worth paying the small admission fee to climb to the top of this tower, where you can get your bearings and be rewarded with views over the quarter's red rooftops.

Walk onto Charles Bridge, past the fourth statue, to the top of the divided stairway, on your right. Pause for a moment to contemplate the

Balcony at No. 9 Na Kampě, which directly faces the stairs. This strange assemblage is a shrine to the Virgin Mary and includes a painting of the Madonna behind an electric lantern that shines nonstop. The truth about this high altar is shrouded in history, but an interesting legend persists: A washer woman who lived in the house was drying clothes when her fingers got caught in the rollers of the mangle she was using. Her hands went numb and doctors insisted that the condition was permanent. But the washerwoman's faith was strong, and after intense prayers, sensation returned and her hands were healed. So up went the lamp and the picture, along with the rollers from the mangle which now hang on either side of the painting.

Standing on the top of the stairs, look toward the river at the little statue of the knight that stands next to the bridge. This is

Bruncvík, a mythical Crusader about whom multifarious legends abound. According to tradition, the knight wielded an invincible sword, now buried somewhere inside Charles Bridge, that will be miraculously unearthed in Bohemia's moment of greatest need by a stumbling white horse ridden by St. Wenceslas. The crass reality is that Bruncvík was placed here to prop up the shield that is depicted under his left hand. This is the coat-of-arms of Old Town, set on the Malá Strana embankment to demonstrate that Charles Bridge is owned by Old Town which, alone, was empowered by royal decree to control traffic and collect tolls here.

Descend the stairs into the square called

Na Kampě. You are now on Kampa, once known simply as the Island Under the Bridge. It's a narrow islet, washed on one side by the Vltava and on the other by a narrow artificial stream dug-out to power water mills. Filled with acacia trees and newly-minted park benches, the square is lined with sixteenth- and seventeenth-century baroque houses. For centuries, Na Kampě was known for bi-annual ceramics markets, and a pottery shop remains here to remind us of those earlier times.

With the bridge to your back, find the House at the Blue Fox (Na Kampě 1), on your right. The blue fox of the house's namesake is a house sign, located above the front door. House signs depicting animals and objects were used to identify city buildings before the advent of street numbering. This is one of Prague's finest. Stay alert and you'll see reliefs like this one all over town.

Walk the length of the square, where, at the end, on your left, you'll see

Liechtenstein Palace, one of several huge buildings that once belonged to that rich and powerful Liechtenstein family. Their coat of arms is above the front door. Today the building is owned by the federal government and is often used to entertain foreign dignitaries. We've even seen England's Queen Elizabeth II partying here.

* 05 *
EXPLORiNG

Before turning the corner, dip into the adjacent

Kampa Park, the best-loved green in Prague. On warm summer afternoons, this beautiful riverfront park is brimming with young Czippies smoking strong spliffs and chugging cheap wine. There are usually more than a few strolling lovers, and plenty of grandmothers gossiping on benches.

Kampa, from the Latin *campus,* or field, was named in the 17th century by Spanish soldiers who tented here after creaming the locals at the Battle of White Mountain. In the 18th century, the park was made into the private gardens of three noble families who lived around its perimeter. The park was only opened to the public in the 20th century, during the Nazi occupation.

With your back to Liechtenstein Palace's front door, walk straight, turn right onto tiny Hroznová, then left onto the little bridge that crosses

Devil's Stream *(Čertovka),* a narrow waterway that was dug-out to power three water mills that once spun here. The one large wheel you see today was rebuilt a few years ago and turns nothing more than our imaginations. The name Devil's Stream is said to have come from an acerbic-tongued woman who lived in a nearby house called the Seven Devils. Sometimes this area is also called "Prague Venice," and considering how often the river used to flood, there is some truth to that designation. But, unlike the real Venice, which often feels like a dead museum of architecture, Prague's version remains a living, work-a-day kind of place. For proof, look no further than the laundry that's often hung to dry in the wind off the balconies facing the stream. And although several houses have steps down to the water, none has a fancy, private motor launch to scoot them down river.

Before the Vltava was dammed in 1954, floods devastated Malá Strana with alarming regularity. If you look closely throughout the city center, you can see plaques and marks indicating the seriousness of various deluges. Stick your head through the metal bars facing the water wheel and look at the wall on your left. Here you can see two separate reminders of *aqua alta,* from earlier this century. Now turn around and look at the wall where the bridge meets the building. At about head level you can see a small metal plaque marking the water level on September 4, 1891.

Leave Kampa Island and follow the graffiti on your right to

* 05 * EXPLORiNG

Lennon Wall. More than just a great songwriter, cultural icon and a symbol of peace, John Lennon became the Communist world's anti-establishment martyr and saint of disgruntled youth. After his death in 1980, a giant and colorful picture of Lennon's head was painted here, where it became the centerpiece of a unique graffiti-covered wall dedicated to free speech and expression. Needless to say, the Communist authorities were not exactly excited by this unsanctioned Democracy Wall, and the City of Prague regularly dispatched a whitewash crew to cover up the troublesome individualist propaganda. After the Velvet Revolution, the story goes, the French Ambassador (whose embassy is just across the street) asked the Mayor of Prague to call off his rollerboys because he liked to look at the urban scrawl from his office window. In the past few years the wall has been patched-up and re-painted several times. But this little backstreet is not yet ready for the history books. Locals and visitors still add their marks, often affixing poems or posters announcing marches or demonstrations. If you have the talent, you might think about bringing some paint, brushes and a bottle of wine and adding your own wall scrawl. We did.

With Lennon Wall on your right, walk to the end of the square, turn right, and walk a half-block to the

Church of Our Lady Under the Chain *(Kostel Panny Marie pod řetězem),* on your right, facing Maltézské náměstí. Behind a gothic portal and metal gates is the oldest church in the area, built around 1250 by the Knights of Malta, a still-functioning, aristocratic club that can be traced as far back as 1099. It has never been easy to become a member of this exclusive organization, as applicants have to prove they are descended from at least sixteen noble ancestors. In addition to providing care for the sick, the Knights spent their time crusading against heretics and, apparently, acquiring land. A good chunk of Malá Strana (and some important buildings in Old Town) is still owned by the Knights. After the Velvet Revolution, the Knights' substantial real estate holdings were returned to them, and their Grand Prior moved back into their "embassy" next door.

Look at the top of the front gate where you can see an eight-pointed cross, the emblem of the Knights that's emblazoned on facades throughout the neighborhood. The church is usually closed to tourists during the day, but it's open for concerts on most summer nights and for services (in French) on Sundays. If you do get in, notice the church's namesake: chains that were once used to lock the building now hang above the main altar.

With your back to the church, walk straight to the

Statue of St. John Křtitel, a Ferdinand M. Brokoff sculpture depicting the Maltese Knights' patron saint. The Baroque building on the corner, to your right, is the restaurant U Malířů (At the Painter's), which was originally an artist's house and is now the most expensive restaurant in Prague—about $100 a head, without wine. It was one of the first fine-dining restaurants to open after the Revolution. The menu is posted by the door. Make a reservation if you wish, though we honestly think you can get a meal that's twice as good at half the price at several other places in the city.

Leave Maltézské náměstí via Prokopská, the small lane behind the statue, and walk to the corner of Karmelitská, a busy street with tram tracks. Turn left and walk about two blocks to the

Church of Our Lady the Victorious *(Kostel Panny Marie vítězné),* Karmelitská 9. This church is revered in the Italian- and Spanish-speaking world thanks to a peewee-sized Jesus doll known as *Il Bambino di Praga.* The 400 year-old wax baby was gifted to the church by Polyxena of Lobkowicz, a devout Spaniard who married into the local Catholic aristocracy. When the church's nuns were spared of an 18th-century plague that ravaged Prague, they granted the statue "miracle" status. It has answered believers' prayers ever since; over a hundred appreciative plaques attest to the little Jesus' powers. The most bizarre feature of the *Bambino* is its dress collection, which includes dozens of ornate little frocks that have been presented as gifts over the last two centuries. The Order of English Virgins, who take care the statue, have been changing the baby Jesus at sunrise on selected days for the last 200 years.

If you've never heard of the *Bambino,* it may be hard to understand what all the fuss is about. But to Latinos, this church is a miraculous, Lourdes-like shrine. There are so many Spanish tourists here that someone should open a tapas bar across the street. The church is open Apr-Oct, daily 7am-9pm; Nov-Mar, daily 8am-8pm. Admission is free. Info (tel. 5753-3646).

Backtrack along Karmelitská, and just past the expat bar U Malého Glena, turn left onto Tržište. Walk up the hill, past the bored police officers, about two blocks to

Schonborn Palace, home to the American Embassy. It's the huge building on your left. If you can get in the front door, look through the courtyard up at the exquisite gardens behind the palace. At the top of the terraced backyard is a small summer pavilion flying the American flag. Clearly visible from Prague Castle, the stars-and-bars were, for many, an in-your-face symbol of hope and freedom during the communist era. Check out too the embassy's intricately-carved front gates that date from the original construction of the building, in the mid 17th century. In the early 20th century, the building was cut up into an apartment house and Franz Kafka lived in two spacious rooms here for a few months in 1917.

Walk another block up the hill, which becomes Vlašská, to

Lobkovic Palace, one of the city's finest Baroque mansions, and now home to the German Embassy. The palace won headlines in 1989, when thousands of East Germans besieged it, attempting to flee into West Germany via Prague. In their frenzied rush for freedom, many of the would-be refugees

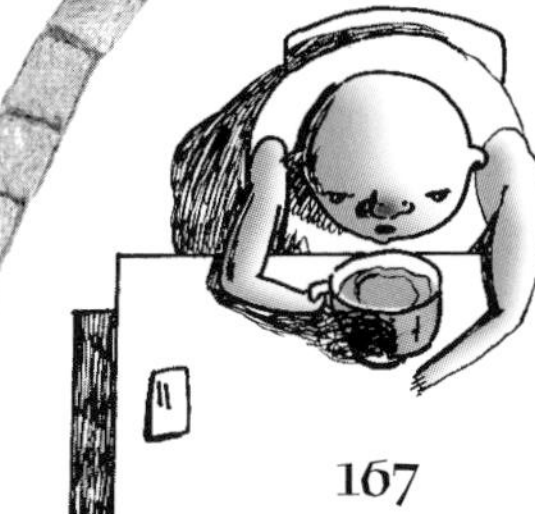

abandoned their flimsy Trabant cars on the surrounding streets, an event commemorated by artist David Černý's clever, footed-Trabant sculpture that now stands in the Embassy's rear garden. To see the sculpture, walk counter-clockwise around the building into the woods, and peer through the iron railing.

Go back down Vlašská Street, and turn left, onto Šporkova. Follow the street down to Jánský Vršek, turn left, and climb the steps to Nerudova street. Turn right, and walk downhill, on what many think is one of the most beautiful streets in Prague. Look closely and you will see some of the finest house signs in Prague—The Moors (#5), The Three Fiddles (#12), The Golden Goblet (#16). At it's end, Nerudova opens up into Malá Strana Square (Malostranské náměstí), broken into upper and lower parts by the Church of St. Nicholas (see Chapter 4/The Top Sights). Continue straight, into the lower part of Malá Strana Square, past the green and white building on your left, which was recently reconstructed as offices for members of Parliament. The faded orange building in front of you is

Malostranská Beseda, or "meeting place," Malá Strana's former town hall. Today it is one of the city's longest-running music clubs. If you walk by at night, you'll likely hear rockabilly or jazz emanating from the upstairs windows.

Walk straight, onto Letenská, then turn immediately left, onto the dead-end street that's home to the

Church of St. Thomas *(Kostel sv. Tomáše),* Josefská 8. This lopsided pink church was built in 1285 for Augustinian monks and became the parish church of *nouveau riche* Malá Strana businessmen. After it was damaged by fire in 1723, no expense was spared in fashioning a new interior, which was shaped by some of the finest artists of the day. Flemish baroque master Peter Paul Rubens created the altar painting *The Martyrdom of St. Thomas*, the original of which is now in the National Gallery. Unfortunately, the interior is only open sporadically, so cross your fingers and try the door.

If it's shut, you can feel heartened that the church was even better known to locals for the excellent and strong beer that its monks brewed in the adjacent monastery. U sv. Tomáše, the alehouse in which it was served, still exists and is located further down the tram tracks.

Continue your walk down Letenská, past the U sv. Tomáše alehouse, and turn left, through the large gates, into

Wallenstein Gardens *(Valdštejnská zahrada)*. This formal green, secreted behind a 30-foot wall, has leafy gravel paths dotted with classical bronze statues and gurgling fountains that fan out in every direction. Laid out in the 17th century, the baroque park was the personal garden of General Albrecht Wallenstein (1581-1634), commander of the Roman Catholic armies during the Thirty Years War. The gardens are part of Wallenstein's Palace—Prague's largest—which replaced 23 houses, three gardens, and the municipal brick kiln. It is now home to the Czech Senate. The gardens are open from March to October from dawn to dusk.

Continue your journey down Letenská and, at the traffic light, turn right, onto U Lužického Semináře. About halfway up the street, turn right, through the gates of

Vojan's Garden *(Vojanovy sady).* When you turn through this discreet, unadorned gateway, you enter Malá Strana's most exquisite secret garden: a lush, shaded fantasyland planted with willows and fruit trees. If you could sneak into the garden at night, it feels like you'd probably see nymphs cavorting with unicorns. It's just a hair less exciting during the day, when the benches are warmed by local grandmothers in house dresses and a few students study on the grass. The garden was laid out in 1248 by Carmelite nuns who used to live next door, on land that is now the backyard of the Ministry of Finance. Just inside, to the left of the entrance, is a grotto-like chapel to the prophet Elijah who, the nuns assert, founded their order in Old Testament days. The garden is open in summer from 8am-7pm, and winter, 8am-5pm.

Back on U Lužického Semináře, you can either turn left and walk past the Malostranská Metro station to the steps of Prague Castle; or turn right, and walk back to Charles Bridge. If you head for the bridge, turn right again, onto Míšeňská, a beautiful curved street that often doubles as a film set. Míšeňská ends at the foot Charles Bridge, the same spot from which this walk started.

* 05 *
EXPLORiNG

×06×

fiTNESS & SPORT

EXERCiSING

Czechs are big fans of biking, hockey, soccer and tennis. But, lets face it, Prague is not an outdoorsy kind of city. The air is awful, and the diet is worse. And because heavy clothes are worn most of the year, there's little incentive to tighten up. It's hard to jog in snow boots, and cobblestones are not exactly conducive to rollerblading.

RECREATION & EXERCISE

Fitness Clubs & Swimming

Nothing in Prague can match the size and scope of the mega-clubs that are all over Los Angeles, but several places have good enough facilities to keep you in tune. Our favorite central-city club is the **Fitness Club at the Inter-Continental Hotel**, nám. Curieových 43, Praha 1 (tel. 2488-9996). Hardware includes Nautilus machines, free-weights, StepMasters and stationary bicycles. It's pleasantly uncrowded and clean, and at 180 Kč per hour the price is right. There's a small sauna and Jacuzzi, and a kidney-shaped swimming pool too. It's open Mon-Fri 6am-11pm, Sat-Sun 9am-10pm. M Staroměstká.

A bit more downscale, and far less elite, is the **Hotel Axa Fitness Center**, Na Poříčí 40, Praha 1 (tel. 232-9359 or 2481-2580), which offers an extensive selection of free-weights and machines in a spacious setting. It costs about 70 Kč per day and is open Mon-Fri 6am-10pm, Sat-Sun 9am-6pm. The adjacent competition-length lap pool is open Mon-Fri 6-9am, noon-1pm, and 5-10pm; Sat-Sun 9am-9pm; cost: 60 Kč per hour. M Náměstí Republiky.

Bowling

Laugh if you must, but **Sportcentrum Duo,** Teplická 17, Praha 1 (tel. 6613-3803) is a great place to take a date. There's a dozen Wisconsin-quality bowling lanes and a few billiards tables. And an adjacent beauty salon/solarium ensures a steady parade of good-looking women traipsing through. They're open Mon 1-11pm, Tues-Fri 11am-11pm, Sat-Sun 10am-11pm. Bowling costs 160-360 Kč per lane, per hour, depending on when you go. Rental shoes are free.

Golf

Golf Club Praha, Plzeňská, Praha 5 (tel. 5721-6584), operates a decent 9-hole course. Constructed in 1926, it was closed in 1950 by communists who resented the bourgeois membership policy. The club reclaimed its grounds after the Velvet Revolution and, although it's a far cry from anything Robert Trent Jones, Jr. ever created, Golf Club Praha's rolling fairways and elevated greens are the most attractive and challenging in the area. Greens fees for members of other golf clubs are under 1000 Kč.

At **Erpet,** Strakonická 510, Praha 5 (tel. 5732-1229), you can make like you're in the South Seas and swing into the palms on a virtual-reality Hawaiian golf course. They're open daily from 9am to 8pm.

The country's best 18-hole courses, in order of difficulty and quality, are: Karlovy Vary (tel. 017/333-1101); Mariánské Lázně (tel. 0165/620251); and Karlštejn (tel. 0311/684716).

Laser Tag

Lazer Game, Národní 25, Praha 1 (tel. 2422-1188) is a fun, multi-level indoor playground in which players don Star Wars-like vests and engage in harmless shoot-'em-ups. Games last about 15 minutes and are scheduled every 20 minutes. It's open Mon-Sat 10am-midnight, Sun 11am-11pm. Admission is 120 Kč per game. M Národní třída

Tennis

Although Czechs are avid tennis players, there are no public courts located in the city center. A ten-minute taxi ride away, **SK Aritma,** Nad lávkou 3, Praha 6 (tel. 2061-2147), offers up nine outdoor clay courts and one hard one indoors. All are lighted for night play. Court fees are about 150 Kč per hour.

Boating

For a romantic, cheap date and a workout too, rent a rowboat or peddleboat from any one of several outlets on Slovanský ostrov, a small island in the Vltava near the National Theater *(Národní divadlo).* The concessions are open only from March through September or October, weather permitting.

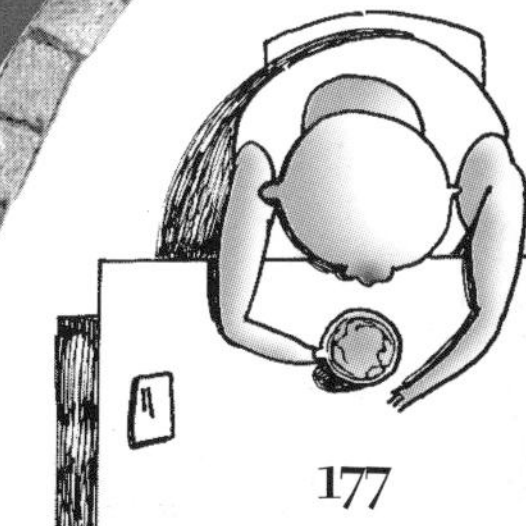

SPECTATOR SPORTS

Tickets for all sporting events are ridiculously cheap and seats for most big games often sell-out long in advance. First try to obtain tickets through normal channels: the event box office or a ticket agency like **Bohemia Ticket International**, Na příkopě 16, Praha 1 (tel. 2421-5031); or **Ticketpro**, Salvátorská, Praha 1 (tel. 2481-8080). If those routes fail, show up to the arena or stadium with a lot of determination and a little extra cash. Scalping is rampant, and even at two or three times the face value of a ticket, you will rarely pay more than 300 to 500 Kč—a steal by Western standards.

Ice Hockey

Sparta and **Slavia** are cross-town rivals in the capital of one of the most hockey-obsessed countries on earth. Sparta, the stronger of the two, lost Jaromír Jágr to a $1.4 million contract as the All-Star forward for America's Pittsburgh Penguins. Plenty of talent remains, and games are regularly SRO. The team skates at Paegas Aréna, at Výstaviště, Praha 7.

Slavia Stadium, Vladivostocká 1460, Praha 10 (tel. 6731-1417), is a relatively intimate ramshackle affair holding just over 6,000 fans.

The hockey season runs from September to April.

Soccer

Football season runs from August to November, and again from February to June.

There are several Prague teams, but **Sparta** is tops, and their games attract the wildest crowds. If their arch-enemy Brno is in town, beg, borrow or steal for a seat. Sparta sports burgundy jerseys and plays at Letná Stadium, Praha 7 (tel. 2057-0323). Tickets costs from 250-600 Kč, and are available at the box office, across the street from the stadium.

With few stars and a crumbling

stadium, **Viktoria Žižkov** is the antithesis of powerful Sparta. Smaller definitely means friendlier, however, and game days are full of community pride. Tickets cost 40-70 Kč, and are available at Stadion Viktoria Žižkov, Seifertova, Praha 3 (tel. 2271-2503).

07 ShOPPiNG IN ThE CiTY
BUYiNG

Prague has come a long way since socialist days, when the only product not in short supply was beer. While this is still not a great shopping city compared to London, New York or Paris, lots of international retailers are beginning to tap into the city's emerging consumer culture. The last few years have seen the opening of company shops like Estée Lauder, Givenchy, Swatch and Benetton. And DKNY and Gianni Versace stores have already come and gone.

In this guide, we focus on locally-owned shops and unusual places, and highlight products that are not readily available everywhere else. Prague's most unique goods are sold at craft and antique shops, as well as at street markets, art studios and galleries. There are over a dozen fine-art galleries in central Prague, and most are within walking distance of Old Town Square. The *Prague Post* lists current shows.

Local Specialties

Garnets, the un-official Czech national gem, are mined near Teplice, about 39 miles northwest of Prague. The deep red stones unearthed here are amongst the finest anywhere. Lots of jewelry shops in Prague create garnet rings and pendants, and offer top quality at reasonable prices (*see* Jewelry/Garnets, below).

Glass, another local specialty, has been produced in the Bohemian countryside since the 14th century. Glass-making was one of the region's most important cottage industries, and many villages are still dotted with tiny glass factories. Quality remains extremely high, and excellent pieces are readily available in Prague for far less than you'd pay back home.

Absinthe, a wormwood distillate that can clocks-in at about 70% alcohol, is one of the city's biggest bar pleasers. Though it's said to be illegal in most other countries of the world, we've never heard of anyone being stopped by customs officers. Dip into most any liquor store or corner food market for a bottle of your own. Or wait until your outbound flight and pick some up duty-free at Prague's Ruzyně Airport.

Marionettes are yet another regional forte. The art of puppetry and marionette-making is a centuries-old Czech tradition. Just after the Revolution, the country's grandmothers cleaned-out their attics and flooded the market with the world's finest antique puppets. Today, you'll find lots of marionette shops around Prague, most of which sell good-quality handmade pieces that make excellent gifts.

Credit cards are widely accepted in Prague and shops are generally open Monday through Saturday from 930am to 7pm. Almost everything is closed on Sundays.

Tax Refunds

Visitors can reclaim up to 17% of the value-added tax (DPH) on most items, provided you spend more than 1000 Kč in a single store and stay in the Czech Republic for less than thirty days. Here's the drill: Pay the tax at the register, ask for a Tax-Free Shopping Cheque, present it to customs officials at the airport before checking-in, then cash it at the airport's Thomas Cook office. There are refund offices at most major borders and cities across Europe as well. The VAT refund program doesn't apply to art or antiques.

SHOPPING BY AREA

Na příkopě and environs

Wide, colorful, varied and fun, Na příkopě i. Prague's favorite shopping street. Amid lots of mid-range international retailers, like Benetton and Marks & Spencer, you'll find plenty of independent shops and many places to break for a snack. Located between the Můstek and Náměstí Republiky Metro stations, the majority of Na příkopě is a pedestrian-only thoroughfare that has evolved into a daily parade of fashion.

On Železná, toward Old Town Square, you'll find a string of excellent fashion stores like Coccinelle and Sergio Rossi.

Václavské náměstí

This long rectangle in the heart of New Town *(Nové Město)* is packed with stores catering to both visitors and locals. Located between the Můstek and Muzeum Metro stations, the square is home to department stores, change offices, jewelry shops and casinos, and is well worth walking around.

Then take a walk down Vodičkova, where you'll find lots more of the same.

Pařížská & Environs

Pařížská, or "Paris" street, was laid-out at the beginning of the 20th century with an eye towards making it something of a local Champs-Elysées. Top-end international retailers like Ferragamo and Dior have taken the bait, turning this tree-lined thoroughfare into one of the swankiest stretches in town. Some surrounding streets, namely Široká, Maiselova, and V kolkovně, are also excellent shopping grounds. Pařížská runs between Old Town Square the river. The nearest Metro is Staroměstská.

…odní and environs

…dní, or "National" street, is a long … that runs southwest from Můstek, all … way to the river. There are several good galleries and fashion shops here, plus lots … interesting architecture along the way.

Between Old Town Square and Charles Bridge

Riddled with small, winding streets, this highly touristed area contains the city's highest concentration of shops. Stroll along Jilská, Liliová and Michalská, all the way down to Karolíny Světlé, and you'll discover dozens of shops that most visitors miss. The nearest metro is Staroměstská.

Between Old Town Square and Revoluční

Celetná, the main street connecting Old Town Square and náměstí Republiky is one of the most touristed strips in town. Accordingly, there are lots of stores here selling glass, trinkets and visitor-junk. There are also some good photo-processing places and the best gift-book shop in the city. The surrounding streets are smaller and quieter and great for strolling. There you will find some excellent specialty shops patronized by locals. The nearest Metro is Náměstí Republiky.

Malá Strana

There are no chain stores here, only locally-owned and operated shops selling everything from art and music to contemporary fashion. Mostecká, the Left Bank's main street, has lots of souvenir shops, eateries and an American Express office.

Other Neighborhoods

Although there are no outlying neighborhoods with better shopping than the city center, this chapter includes several slightly-out-of-the-way shops that are worthy of a special visit.

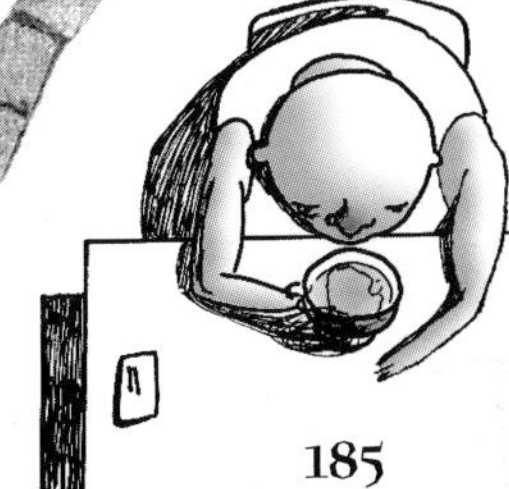

ShOPPING bY SUBJECT

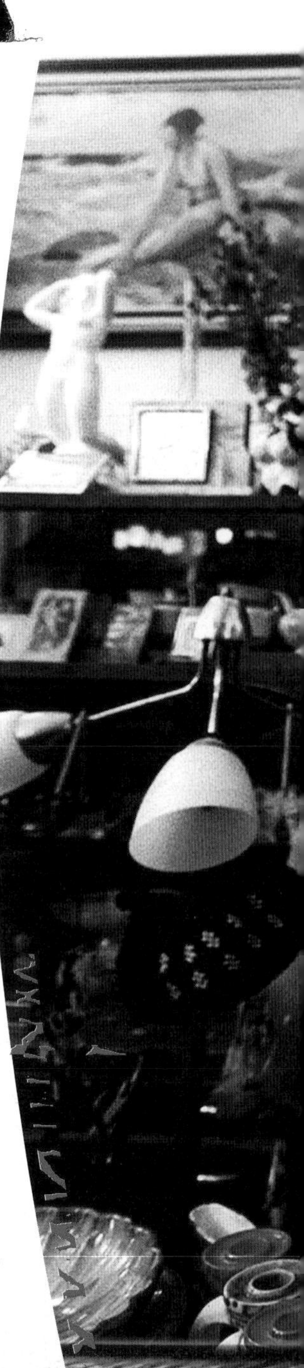

ART GALLERiES & ANTIQUES

Art Deco Galerie

Michalská 21, Praha 1 - Old Town. Tel. 2422-3076. Open daily 2-7pm.

Like the name says, this Old Town shop specializes in all manner of designs from the 1920s and 30s, including art glass, decorative clocks, ceramic lamps and even clothing. Everything is negotiable with the friendly owner, Miroslava Vávrová.

* 07 *
bUYiNG

Bric à Brac

Týnská 7, Praha 1 - Old Town. Tel. 232-6484. Open daily 11am-7pm.

One of the oddest and tiniest antique shops in the city, Bric a Brac offers a healthy mix of junk in a store cluttered with everything from ancient trombones and coal-fed irons to deco hats and silver cigarette cases. Tell owner Sonia Popovič we sent you.

Galerie Peithner-Lichenfels

Michalská 12, Praha 1 - Old Town. Tel. 2422-7680. Open daily 10am-7pm.

This is the best gallery in the city for top modern and contemporary Czech artists. Some of the biggest names in painting and sculpture are represented here, including Anderle, Brauer, Čapek, Crepaz, Hoffmeister, and Wagner.

Jiří Švestka Galerie

Jungmannova 30, Praha 1 - New Town. Tel. 9624-5024. Open Tues-Fri noon-6pm, Sat 11-6pm.

Founded by a former director of the National Gallery, this excellent art space deals in high-end works by well-known artists.

MXM Galerie

Nosticova 6, Praha 1 - Malá Strana. Tel. 531-564. Open Tues-Sun noon-6pm.

Hidden on a tiny Malá Strana backstreet, MXM has grown to become one of the most influential galleries in the country. Opened in 1990, it was one of the first post-Revolution art markets in Prague. It remains one of the best.

bEAUTY/BOdY

Body Basics

Koruna Palác, Václavské nám. 1, Praha 1 - Old Town. Tel. 2447-3072. Open Mon-Sat 930am-8pm, Sun 11am-7pm.

The Czech Republic's version of the UKs Body Shop is so good that its British rival has purchased a big stake in it. You can find natural everything here—from body lotion and bath oil to soaps and hair products. Excellent quality is matched by relatively low prices. We swear by their Aloe Vera moisturizing cream.

Branches: in Myslbek Pasáž, Na Příkopě 19 (tel. 2423-6800); in Vinohradský Pavilon, Vinohradská 50 (tel. 2209-7105); Celetná 17 (tel. 2481-1771); Ruzyně Airport (tel. 2011-3595).

Christian Dior

Pařížská 7, Praha 1 - Old Town. Tel. 0602/417698. Open Mon-Fri 10am-7pm, Sat 10am-2pm.

A stylish white cube, this corner Dior shop is heavy on the brand's cosmetics, perfumes, and lipsticks.

Estée Lauder

Železná 18, Praha 1 - Old Town. Tel. 2423-2023. Open Mon 9am-6pm, Tues-Fri 11am-7pm.

Prague's premiere pamperie sells house-brand cosmetics and perfumes in their fantastically stylish trademark containers. The extraordinarily friendly staff also offers manicures and pedicures.

JULIO
CORTÁZAR
HEAVY
WATER
MARTIN
AMIS
the
trial
of
god
MAN'S FATE
SAM SHEPARD
PRAGUE BUSINESS JOURNAL
CLINTON REMEMBERS
BABYLON
Praha

ßOOkS

Big Ben Bookshop

Malá Štupartská 5, Praha 1 - Old Town. Tel. 2482-6565. Open Mon-Fri 9am-630pm, Sat-Sun 10am-5pm.

This centrally-located Old Town shop has a well-chosen selection English-language classics, new fiction, travel guides and magazines. It's a great place to browse for everything from light train reading to Czech grammar books.

Branch: in the British Council building, Národní 10, Praha 1 (tel. 2199-1200).

The Globe

Pštrossova 6, Praha 1 - New Town. Tel. 2491-6264. Open Sun-Thurs 10am-midnight, Fri-Sat10am-1am.

Opened in 1993, and moved to this location in 2000, this English-language bookshop/cafe has long been a hub of American expat life. It offers a decent variety of new and used literature and non-fiction, and has the city's best English-language message board cluttered with announcements for jobs, flats and items for sale. The adjacent cafe serves good food (think club sandwiches and coffee-drinks) to poets and poseurs alike.

U Knihomola

(at the Bookworm) Mánesova 79, Praha 2 - Vinohrady. Tel. 627-7767. Open Mon-Fri 9am-9pm, Sat 2-9pm. M Jiřího z Poděbrad.
This extraordinarily pleasant bookstore and cafe stocks an extensive selection of English and foreign-language literature, guidebooks and artbooks. And the downstairs cafe is one of the most civilized meeting places in Vinohrady.

Knihkupectví U Černé Matky Boží

(Bookstore at the Black Madonna) Celetná 34, Praha 1 - Old Town. Tel. 2422-2349. Open Mon-Sat 9am-8pm, Sun 10am-8pm.
Located on the ground floor of the first Cubist building in Bohemia, this multi-lingual, tourist-oriented shop carries almost every Prague picturebook produced. There's a great selection of art books, art posters, and travel guides too. It's a great place for gifts.

CAMERAS & PhOTOGRAPhY

AZ Foto

Celetná 8, Praha 1 - Old Town. Tel. 2423-9170. Open Mon-Fri 9am-7pm, Sat 10am-3pm.
The largest photo chain in the city is *the* place to go for cameras, film and quality one-hour developing. They've got all the latest gadgets, plus some excellent used cameras, fine antiques and rare collectors' items from Voigtlander, Birnbaum, Moskva, Thowe, Kodak, Clack, and Langer.

Branches: in Světozor passage, Vodičkova 39, Praha 1; Senovážná 8, Praha 1.

Alfred Dunhill

Pařížská 14, Praha 1 - Old Town. Tel. 2481-7060. Open Mon-Fri 10am-7pm, Sat-Sun 11am-5pm.

Dunhill's classic men's clothes and accessories will always be in fashion. Think blue ties, and ribbed brown-knit sweaters.

Camomilla

Panská 1, Praha 1 - Old Town. Tel. 2423-2560. Open Mon-Fri 10am-6pm, Sat 10am-1pm.

Specializing in revealing, upscale fashions for the mid-thirties woman, Camomilla sells everything from T-shirts to flowing, feminine dresses that seem inspired by ancient Greece. It's an unusual store that's definitely worth a look.

Chez Parisienne

Pařížská 8, Praha 1 - Old Town. Tel. 2481-7786. Open Mon-Fri 10am-7pm, Sat-Sun 10am-6pm.

The underwear supplier to some of the best-undressed mistresses in Prague, Chez Parisienne is well known to high-powered executives and local diplomats. Silk panties, string bikinis, naughty marabou baby dolls... it's what the au pair will be wearing this summer. Men's PJs and robes too.

Coccinelle Accessories

Železná 22, Praha 1 - Old Town. Tel. 2422-8203. Open Mon noon-7pm, Tues-Sat 10am-7pm.

The whole range of Coccinelle's cool, Italian accessories are here, from fashionable handbags and wallets to chunky key chains and high-style sunglasses. Goods run from sassy to expensive, encompassing the brand's haute, bridge and sport lines.

Givenchy

Rybná 14, Praha 1 - Old Town. Tel. 2184-4004. Open Mon-Fri 10am-6pm.

Expensive women's suits by the French couturier are sold alongside branded accessories and Ysatis, the house perfume. Other brands sold here too.

Hermés

Pařížská 12, Praha 1 - Old Town. Tel. 2481-7545. Open Mon-Fri 10am-7pm, Sat-Sun 10am-6pm.

This small, traditional brand-store carries a choice selection of blankets, towels, perfumes, leather slippers, purses, bath robes, and trademark silk scarfs. There's always something fetching to be found in the store's comfortable wooden interior.

Kaygen.it

Pařížská 21, Praha 1 - Old Town. Tel. 2481-1234. Open Mon-Fri noon-7pm, Sat 11am-6pm, Sun noon-6pm.

This modern, all-purpose, designy high-ender features last season's hits by Fendi, Gucci, Miu Miu, Prada, and Paolo Pecora. It's mostly women's wear here, including shoes, suits, jackets, and business clothes.

Klára Nademlýnská

Dlouhá 7, Praha 1 - Old Town. Tel. 2481-8769. Open Mon-Fri 10am-7pm, Sat noon-6pm.

One of the Czech Republic's best-known young designers, Klára works and designs in Paris, but wows us here with her self-branded Prague shop. There's always something haute and beautiful; terrific evening gowns mostly, plus young spirited daywear displayed in the best-looking store in town.

Loisir and Oxette

Pařížská 15, Praha 1 - Old Town. Tel. 2481-7106. Open daily 930am-8pm.

This L&O company store is stocked with high-end accessories from watches, silver jewelry and charms, to rings, earrings, necklaces, and massive leather neck bands.

Louis Vuitton

Pařížská 11, Praha 1 - Old Town. Tel. 2481-2774. Open Mon-Fri 10am-7pm, Sat 10am-6pm.

Vuitton's Prague shop stocks the trademark beige-and-brown LV handbags, shoes, suitcases, planners, and other logo-covered leathergoods.

Marina Rinaldi

Železná 22, Praha 1 - Old Town. Tel. 2423-4643. Open Mon noon-7pm, Tues-Sat 10am-7pm.

Think Italian Liz Claiborne and you'll have a good sense of the skirts, suits and handbags carried by this down-to-business shop for women. Rinaldi designs everything from formless knee-length schoolmarm dresses to modest leather jackets, sold in a sterile, no-nonsense environment.

Max Mara

Havířská 1, Praha 1 - Old Town. Tel. 2421-2454. Open Mon-Fri 10am-7pm, Sat noon-6pm.

The Prague branch of this upscale luxury chain occupies its own fashion corner, just steps from Na příkopě.

M. Liška

Železná 1, Praha 1 - Old Town. Tel. 2422-1928. Open Mon-Fri 10am-6pm, Sat 10am-3pm.

When you want to see where the other half shop (read: wealthy ex-communist housewives), step into this stuffy world of conservative coats, many of which are collared and cuffed with the fur of grey rabbits and white foxes.

Nina Ricci

Pařížská 4, Praha 1 - Old Town. Tel. 2481-0905. Open Mon-Fri 11am-7pm, Sat 11am-4pm.

Nina Ricci is a tiny store known for perfume, cosmetics, and silk print scarfs. It's a romantic, dreamy, space with quality products and cheerful assistants.

Romantik

Karoliny Světlé 23, Praha 1 - Old Town. Tel. 2222-1632. Open Mon-Fri 10am-6pm, Sat 10am-4pm.

The perfect place for pre-ball shopping, Romantik stocks a large selection of cheap party dresses that can look like a million, if worn with bullet-proof confidence. Rentals too.

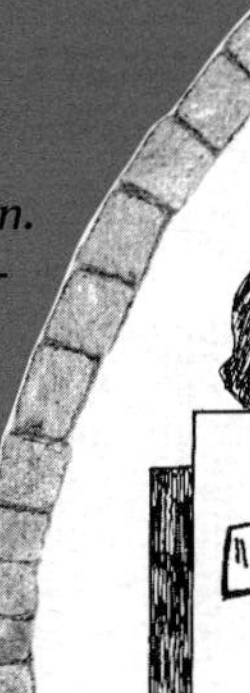

Salvatore Ferragamo

Pařížská 10, Praha 1 - Old Town. Tel. 2481-4779. Open Mon-Fri 1030am-7pm, Sat 1030am-6pm.

The 1980s seem to have never left this small geometric shop in which black-and-white suits and shoes front a short list of classic men's and women's clothes.

Sergio Rossi

Železná 5, Praha 1 - Old Town. Tel. 2421-6407. Open Mon-Sat 10am-7pm.

Known for expensive shoes with cool up-to-the-moment designs, Rossi's Prague shop specializes in sexy high-heels, handbags, and wallets, plus a small selection of men's shoes.

Strenesse

Pařížská 6, Praha 1 - Old Town. Tel. 232-4336. Open Mon-Sat 930am-7pm, Sun 11am-7pm.

At this small white boutique you'll find a pastiche of high-end brand-name goods for women that run the gamut from jackets and suits, to sexy pullovers and tight knitwear.

Taiza

Na příkopě 31, Praha 1 - New Town. Tel. 2161-3308. Open Mon-Sat 10am-8pm.

Cuban-born designer Osmany Laffita is known for extravagantly tailored women's wear and accessories. Designs run from sexy suits and full length coats to funky accessories and even turban head wraps. And the shop boasts some of the best-looking assistants around.

Timoure et Group

V Kolkovně 6, Praha 1 - Old Town. Tel. 232-7358. Open Mon-Fri 10am-7pm, Sat noon-6pm.

The contemporary clothes in this stylish shop are created by two Czech women who are known for minimalist business-style clothing with inspirational flourishes. Think very well-tailored suits, pants, jackets, and sweaters.

Wolford

V Celnici 10, Praha 1 - New Town. Tel. 2103-3103. Open Mon-Fri 10am-6pm.

Europe's best-dressed legs are caressed by Wolford's suitably expensive stockings and hosiery. Their extra-fine quality and refined designs extend to underwear, beachwear and body suits too.

CLOTHiNG–CASUAL

Benetton

Na příkopě 4, Praha 1 - New Town. No phone. Open Mon-Fri 930am-7pm, Sat 930am-8pm.

A huge selection of both men's and women's Benetton-branded clothes are sold in this landmark store. It's a great place for sweaters, in almost any color any style (polo, V, short, long), as well as T-shirts, sexy little backpacks, and a collection of clothes by Sissly.

Comtessa

Václavské náměstí. 20, Praha 1 - New Town. Tel. 2422-0142. Open Mon-Sat 10am-7pm.

Comtessa clothes are what young Czech execs wear at night. Fashions here are somewhere between sexy and feminine, made to last just one or two seasons. We often spot the store's gowns and coats in Prague's local fashion magazines.

Elisabeth

Pařížská 16, Praha 1 - Old Town. Tel. 231-0026. Open daily 10am-7pm.

Despite dark, wooden shelves and a moody interior, Elisabeth stocks a wide selection of contemporary jeans and jackets by trendy makers like Carlo Colucci and Diesel. Those in need of underwear can find designer smalls here too.

Gigasport

in the Myslbek Passage, Na příkopě 19, Praha 1 - New Town. Tel. 2423-7494. Open Mon-Sat 930am-7pm.

From the entrance, it's hard to tell how huge this sports megastore is. Three levels run the gamut from name-brand shoes and clothing to swimwear, tennis, diving and camping gear. Simply put, it's the best place for sporting goods in the city.

Jackpot

Železná 8, Praha 1 - Old Town. Tel. 2422-2380. Open daily 10am-7pm.

This Danish clothing store is heavy on young feminine fashions in earththone colors. The comfortable weekend and afterwork clothes include skimpy little knitwear, draw-string pants, long sleeve Ts, and heavy cotton and canvas waist jackets.

Kookai

in the Myslbek Passage, Na příkopě 19, Praha 1 - New Town. Tel. 2423-5734. Open Mon-Sat 10am-7pm.

France's best affordable-clothes exporter is known for tiny dresses and tight sweaters floating on steel hangers in a clean minimalist shop. Daring cuts and trendy colors extend to skirts, trousers and blouses for all occasions.

Marlboro Classics

in the Myslbek Passage, Na příkopě 19, Praha 1 - New Town. Tel. 2423-9550. Open Mon-Sat 10am-7pm.

You've smoked the cigarette, now live the hype; Classics sells all the clothes you'd expect the Marlboro Man and his dame to be wearing. Look for sturdy chaps, cowboy hats, flirtatious dresses, leather jackets, miniskirts and velvet body suits.

Pringle of Scotland

Pařížská 22, Praha 1 - Old Town. Tel. 231-5319. Open Mon-Fri 10am-7pm, Sat 10am-6pm, Sun 11am-5pm.

Known for conservative styles and classic Scottish patterns and materials, Pringle is tops for 100% cashmere clothes for men, women and children. Leisure and sport gear includes sweaters, scarves, wooly knee socks and even a wide selection of rain boots. They've got Rena Lange and Jil Sander brands too.

Reporter/Nový Svět

V kolkovně 5, Praha 1 - Old Town. Tel. 232-9823. Open Mon-Fri 10am-7pm, Sat 10am-530pm.

These two adjacent shops stock great looking contemporary Italian clothes for men and women, along with all the requisite accessories (including leather shoes, and even embroidered silk lingerie). It's a great place for young execs to blow their paychecks.

Stefanel

Železná 14, Praha 1 - Old Town. Tel. 2422-3500. Open daily 10am-7pm.

Although this youthful shop for hip chicks is not as good as Stefanel's other branches around the world, you can often find something nice amongst trendy seasonables in high-fashion colors. It's a spacious place full with everything from 3/4-sleeve shirts and jackets to hip huggers and Capri pants. Shoes and umbrellas too.

CLOThiNG–STREET & ViNTAGE

Black Market

Petrské náměstí 1, Praha 1 - New Town. Tel. 231-7033. Open Mon-Fri noon-7pm, Sat 10am-5pm. No cards.

The East Village comes to Prague in the form of this streetwear shop selling international skateware and sexy, tight pornwear. They've got international knock-offs and lots of their own-branded clothing. And DJs spin daily.

Devátá Vlna

Saská 3, Praha 1 - Malá Strana. Tel. 294-171. Open daily 11am-7pm. No cards.

This truly avant-garde shop is owned by a trio of young designers who produce the entire stock. There are plenty of tight tops, and lots of plasticwear, faux fur and other unusual materials. Quality is excellent and prices are low. We love this place.

Kenvelo

Václavské náměstí 1, Praha 1 - New Town. Tel. 2421-5904. Open Mon-Sat 9am-8pm, Sun 10am-8pm.

Famous citywide for cheap, teeny-bopping "disposable" clothing, Kenvelo has a lock on up-to-the-moment pants, vests, sweatshirts, skirts and jackets, all at unbeatable prices. This centrally-located store is perpetually packed with students playing hooky and foreigners looking to spend their leftover crowns before leaving the country.

Replay

Rytířská 23, Praha 1 - New Town. Tel. 2423-2531. Open Mon-Sat 930am-7pm.

Jeans, tank tops, midriff shirts, fly-away dresses... Replay is an American-themed style spot that reminds us of The Gap with an edge. Think of what a young and pretty executive might wear at a summer barbeque.

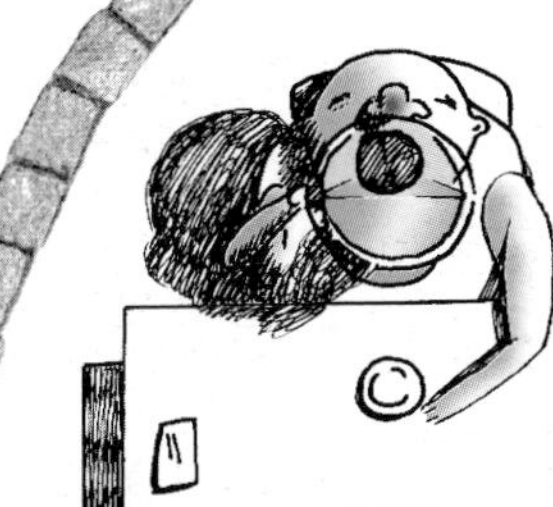

* 07 *
bUYiNG

Mýrnyx Týrnyx

Saská, Praha 1 - Malá Strana. Tel. 2492-3270 or 0603/460351. Open daily noon-7pm. No cards.

Even if it seems silly to be checking out second-hand clothing here in Prague, go visit American expat Maya Zhera Květný's pint-size shop to see what former Hollywood fashions she's stocking today. Ultra cool men's and women's clothes from the last fifty years are her specialty, along with a growing stock by cool young Czech designers. And tell Maya we sent you.

F()()TWEAR

Baťa

Václavské nám. 6, Praha 1 - New Town. Tel. 2421-8133. Open Mon-Fri 830am-7pm, Sat 9am-4pm, Sun 10am-6pm.

One of the best-known names in Czech retailing, Bat'a is essentially a family shoe store stocking a multitude of house brands on six floors. Detractors say this place is mid-everything (mid-quality, mid-class...) and its styles are far from the edge. But Bat'a is a classic and definitely worth a look.

Beltissimo

U prašné brány (Obecni dům), Praha 1 - Old Town. Tel. 2200-2320. Open Mon-Fri 10am-8pm, Sat 10am-6pm.

Although the selection is not big, there's usually something fetching in this beautiful shop. The high-heels here exude a mature, feminine elegance and are complimented by handbags and men's accessories (wallets, key chains, cigeratte holders).

Francesca Lecca

Staroměstské nám. 6, Praha 1 - Old Town. Tel. 2481-9467. Open daily 10am-7pm.

Hit or miss, we love this store for its always fashionable, and occasionally crazy shoes. Colors and shapes are always right on the money, and almost everything has quality leather soles. Both men's and women's shoes are sold here, along with some tasty handbags and scarves. Too bad about the rude assistants. **Branch:** Pařížská 14, Praha 1 (tel. 231-1030).

Leiser Shoes

U prašné brány 1, Praha 1 - Old Town. Tel. 2481-0431. Open Mon-Fri 10am-8pm, Sat 10am-6pm.

A shoe zoo that's not always in fashion, Leiser is known for everything from sandels to pumps, in restrained styles that are displayed just as conservatively—by size. That's not to say there's not some cool stuff; there is, but you have to dig. We like the old fashioned white Kangaroos with baby blue stripes. Handbags, accessories, sunglasses, wallets, and scarfs too.

Branch: Na přikopě 9, Praha 1 (tel. 2224-2973).

Salamander

Na příkopě 23, Praha 1 - New Town. Tel. 2210-1155. Open Mon-Fri 10am-8pm, Sat-Sun 10am-6pm.

Salamander specializes in elegant shoes for suits, plus good boots by makers like Hugo Boss, Llozd, and Magnanni. Nothing's shocking in either the men's or women's collections, but it's a good place to browse for comfortable walking shoes. Purses, briefcases, socks, and shoe-accessories too.

Branch: Na příkopě 16, Praha 1 (tel. 2421-0485).

Terra Nova

Revoluční 3, Praha 1 - New Town. Tel. 2180-3303. Open Mon-Fri 10am-7pm, Sat 10am-5pm.

This is a great place to shop for this month's fashion without worrying about breaking the bank. The trendy young shoes here are as low in quality as they are high in style; which means you might end up wearing your purchase just once. Some soles here are so high you'll need a parachute.

How To Buy Crystal

Crystal is any type of refined, high-quality glass. Like gasoline, it comes in two varieties, leaded and unleaded. Lead makes the glass softer and causes it to refract light. But some of the world's most elegant and expensive glass contains no lead. A lot of Czech glass is lead-free, including products from world-famous Moser, the country's most celebrated producer.

A truly top-notch piece of glass looks solid, feels good in the hand and has a rich luster. When examining cut glass, look for sharp, even cuts. Hold the piece up to the light and examine it from the bottom and other angles to see if the design elements conceal flaws or bubbles. Elaborate cuts are the most common way to hide flaws. You can check the quality of any crystal shop by administering the following test: Find an undecorated bowl or vase and examine it closely for impurities. Watch out for irregular swirls, bubbles, layers, nicks and rough or dull areas – these are indicators of impure raw materials. Check the way the bowl connects to the stem. A seam running down the length of a stem or an absolutely perfect joint means the piece was made by a machine. A slightly uneven joint or a stem that seems to flow into the bowl, are evidence that the glass is probably hand-blown.

* 07 *
bUYiNG

CRYSTAL & ChINA

Celetná Crystal

Celetná 15, Praha 1 - Old Town. Tel. 232-4022. Open daily 10am-8pm (later in summer).

If you just can't bear to leave Prague without something crystal, then dip into this two-story emporium that's sure to stock something for everyone, including stemware, vases, paperweights, and animals. Amber, garnets and porcelain too.

Moser

Na příkopě 12, Praha 1 - New Town. Tel. 2421-1293. Open Mon-Fri 9am-8pm, Sat-Sun 10am-6pm.

Founded in 1857, Moser is the greatest name in Czech glass, producing unparalleled stemware, vases and objects d'art. Nothing is cheap. The shop itself is one of the city's most beautiful sales spaces and definitely worth a look.

Branch: Malé nám. 11, Praha 1 (tel. 2161-1520).

Thun

Pařížská 2, Praha 1 - Old Town. Tel. 2481-1023. Open daily 9am-7pm.

If you've ever gone into a grandmother's house and wondered where she picked up that little blue-and-white seated harlequin, wonder no more. In addition to useless dust-collectors, this small and narrow shop sells some things you might actually like, including nice chandeliers, good etchings, and high-quality Karlovy Vary china. The shop is located at the northeast corner of Old Town Square.

dEPARTMENT STORES

Kotva

náměstí Republiky 8, Praha 1 - Old Town. Tel. 2480-1111. Open Mon-Fri 9am-8pm, Sat 9am-6pm, Sun 10am-6pm.

The best all-around department store in Prague is almost on par with its Western counterparts. From paper clips to pianos, anything you might need can probably be found at this one-stop shop.

Krone

Václavské náměstí 21, Praha 1 - New Town. Tel. 2423-0477. Open Mon-Fri 8am-7pm, Sat 8am-6pm, Sun 10am-6pm.

Boring displays and standard merchandise means that this is not a great place for strolling and browsing, but if you're looking for essentials it's good to know about this centrally-located store. Also, there's a large supermarket in the basement.

Tesco

Národní 26, Praha 1 - New Town. Tel. 2422-7971. Open Mon-Fri 8am-9pm, Sat 9am-7pm, Sun 10am-7pm.

The Prague branch of the familiar British middle-market department store is as good or better than its counterparts in London. It's one of the city's best places for toiletries and paper goods. There's an excellent supermarket in the basement and a fast-food Little Caesar's Pizza place on the ground floor. And few places in the city are better for girl-watching than Tesco's hair-dye department.

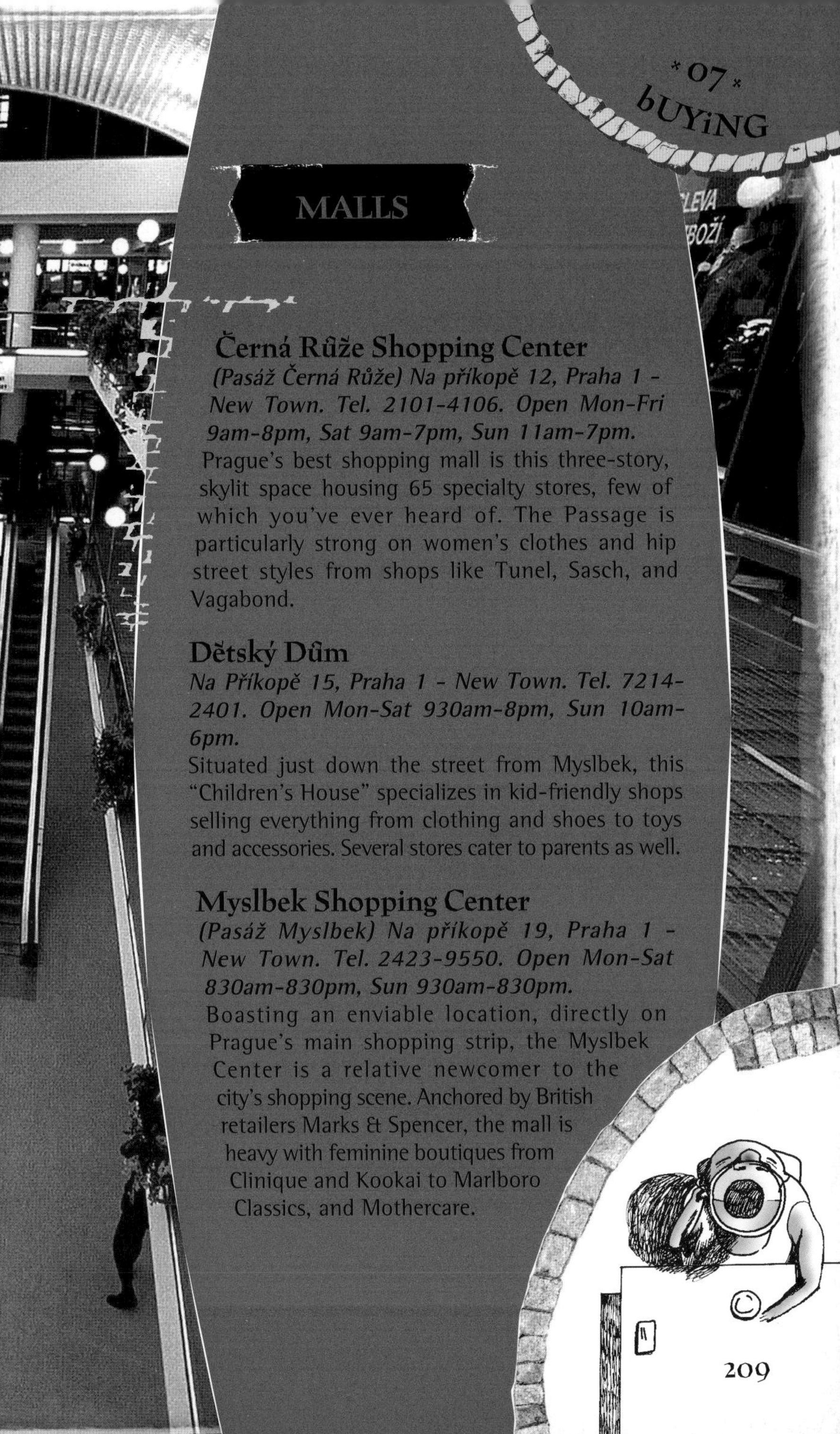

MALLS

Černá Růže Shopping Center

(Pasáž Černá Růže) Na příkopě 12, Praha 1 - New Town. Tel. 2101-4106. Open Mon-Fri 9am-8pm, Sat 9am-7pm, Sun 11am-7pm.

Prague's best shopping mall is this three-story, skylit space housing 65 specialty stores, few of which you've ever heard of. The Passage is particularly strong on women's clothes and hip street styles from shops like Tunel, Sasch, and Vagabond.

Dětský Dům

Na Příkopě 15, Praha 1 - New Town. Tel. 7214-2401. Open Mon-Sat 930am-8pm, Sun 10am-6pm.

Situated just down the street from Myslbek, this "Children's House" specializes in kid-friendly shops selling everything from clothing and shoes to toys and accessories. Several stores cater to parents as well.

Myslbek Shopping Center

(Pasáž Myslbek) Na příkopě 19, Praha 1 - New Town. Tel. 2423-9550. Open Mon-Sat 830am-830pm, Sun 930am-830pm.

Boasting an enviable location, directly on Prague's main shopping strip, the Myslbek Center is a relative newcomer to the city's shopping scene. Anchored by British retailers Marks & Spencer, the mall is heavy with feminine boutiques from Clinique and Kookai to Marlboro Classics, and Mothercare.

Eiffel Optic

Celetná 38, Praha 1 - Old Town. Tel. 2161-3301. Open Mon-Fri 8am-730pm, Sat 930am-7pm, Sun 10am-6pm.

Oakley, Fendi, Armani, Valentino, Moschino, Gucci... all the biggest names are here, at prices that feel far lower than those in the West. There's nothing much about the store itself, but with over 5000 frames to choose from, an in-house opthamoligist, and prescription-free contact lenses, Eiffel has all the bases covered.

Branches: Na příkopě 25, Praha 1 (tel. 2423-4966); Vodičkova 17, Praha 1 (tel. 9623-9020).

Fokus Optik

Hybernská 8, Praha 1 - New Town. Tel. 2421-5361. Open Mon-Sat 8am-730pm.

The largest chain of optitians in the Czech Republic is the best place to go for replacement contact lenses, saline solution, and emergency glasses.

Branches: Mostecká 3, Praha 1; Štěpánská 19 Praha 1; in pasáž Lucerna, Vodičkova 36, Praha 1; Na poříčí 33, Praha 1; Revoluční 5, Praha 1.

JEWELRY/GARNETS

Ametyst

Vodičkova 31, Praha 1 - New Town. Tel. 2422-6611. Open Mon-Fri 9am-7pm, Sat 930am-6pm.

Ametyst specializes in garnet jewelry and semiprecious stones. Because most of its business is from Czechs, prices are lower than they are just a few blocks away on the main tourist routes.

Český Granát

Celetná 4, Praha 1 - Old Town. Tel. 2422-8287 or 2421-1896. Open Nov-Mar, daily 10am-7pm; Apr-Oct 10am-8pm.

Quality garnets, well-designed settings and—despite this shop's very central location—reasonable prices. Pendants, bracelets and necklaces drip with garnets set in gold and silver. Most styles tend toward the traditional, and prices range from 1000 Kč to 50,000 Kč.

Branches: Celetná 15, Praha 1; Mostecká 3, Praha 1.

East Art Gallery

Václavské nám. 23, Praha 1 - New Town. Open Mon-Sat 10am-730pm, Sun 10am-6pm.

Excellent prices and funky designs make this the best amber shop in the city. Amber rings, pendants and earrings will set you back about 1000 Kč. The deco collection is slightly higher. You'll find lots of little gift items like letter openers and money clips.

Granát Turnov

Dlouhá 30, Praha 1 - Old Town. Tel. 231-5612. Open Mon-Fri 10am-6pm, Sat 10am-1pm.

If you want to see what all the fuss is about over Czech garnets, visit the retail headquarters of the largest domestic garnet producer. The store is chock-full of ruby-red stones in both traditional and modern settings. Prices are reasonable to excellent.

Halada

Na příkopě 16, Praha 1 - New Town. Tel. 2421-8643. Open daily 9-7pm.

This Prague-based jeweler produces and sells some beautiful wedding bands, engagement rings, necklaces, and watches, mostly in silver and gold. The house-made designs are modern and geometric.

Branch: Karlova 25, Praha 1 (tel. 2423-8928).

* 07 *
bUYiNG

Dr. Stuart's Botanicus

Havelská 20, Praha 1 - Old Town. Tel. 2422-9322. Open daily 930am-7pm.

The best smelling shop in the city is full of scented candles, organic jams, dried flowers, pure soaps and other hand crafted plant-based products. Almost everything is created from medieval recipes in the Botanicus village just outside Prague. This is an unusual place full of creative and beautifully-packaged goods that make excellent gifts.

Branches: Bílá Labuť, Na poříčí 23, Praha 1 (tel. 2170-5111, ext. 289); Lucerna, Stěpánská 61, Praha 1 (tel. 2422-1927); Michalská 2, Praha 1 (tel. 2421-2977); Mostecká 4, Praha 1 (tel. 5731-5089); Ungelt, Týn 1049, Praha 1 (tel. 2589-5446).

Le Patio

Pařížská 20, Praha 1 - Old Town. Tel. 232-0260. Open Mon-Sat 10am-7pm, Sun 11am-7pm.

Most of the wood and iron chairs, tables, cabinets, and other furnishings sold here are designed and created in-house. Some exotic pieces are imported from Southeast Asia, and many are antique. Other house-fillers include dishes, candle holders, and lamps.

Branches: Národní 22, Praha 1 (tel. 2491-8072); Ungelt 640, Praha 1 (tel. 2489-5773).

Sanu Babu

Michalská 20, Praha 1 - Old Town. Tel. 2163-2401. Open daily 930am-7pm.

Every city has it's hippy import shop, and in Prague it's this patchouli-infused space filled with wood and fabric from Nepal and India. Look for everything from clothes, leather goods and hemp products, to hand-made paper, ceramics, statuettes and masks.

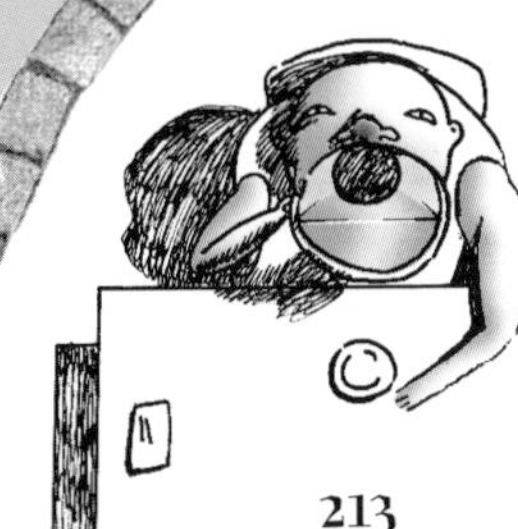

MUSiC

The cheapest CDs in the Czech Republic are sold online at the AlbumCity music site (www.albumcity.cz). After browsing for local music at the stores below, log on to this Prague-based Internet shop, place your order, and they'll deliver straight to your hotel. Average savings: 25%.

Bontonland Megastore

in Koruna Palac, Václavské nám. 1, Praha 1 New Town. Tel. 2422-6236. Open Mon-Sat 10am-8pm, Sun 10am-7pm.

The largest music shop in Prague is tiny compared to the London Virgin Megastore it's modeled on. Still, there's plenty here, including new European and Czech releases. CDs average about 700 Kč each.

Maximum Underground

Jilská 22, Praha 1 - Old Town. Tel. 0604/873558. Open Mon-Sat 11am-7pm, Sun 1-7pm. No cards.

This small shop, located in the corner of a funky clothing store, is popular with DJs and features hard-to-find European and local dance music on CD and vinyl.

Radost 234

Bělehradská 120, Praha 2 - Vinohrady. Tel. 2425-2741. Open Mon-Fri 930am-730pm, Sat 11am-4pm, Sun 1-5pm.

The best truly "alternative" music shop in the city stocks European dance music and electronica, as well as new-flava hip-hop, jazz, ambient and world music. 234 has become something of a contemporary music cultural center, attracting the country's top music producers, DJs and record execs.

Baker Street Praha

Celetná 38, Praha 1 - Old Town. Tel. 2161-3274. Open Mon-Fri 10am-8pm, Sat-Sun 10am-1230pm and 1-8pm.

The city center's best place for cigars, cigarillos, loose tobacco and papers, Baker Street also has Prague's finest selection of pipes and accessories, including racks, boxes, Zippos, knives, and liqueurs.

La Casa del Habano

in the Intercontinental Hotel, nám. Curieových 5, Praha 1 - Old Town. Tel. 2488-1544. Open Mon-Sat 9am-1245pm and 145-8pm; Sun 2-7pm.

This little shop stocks very fresh, authentic Cuban Cohibas, Julietas and other hard-to-find stogies in a variety of widths and lengths. A great place to stock up on gifts, it's worth a visit just for a whiff in their humidor.

Veronský dûm

Míšeňská 8, Praha 1 - Malá Strana. Tel. 0603/175368. Open Mon-Sat noon-7pm.

This small wine shop and tasting room on a Malá Strana backstreet has a small, but well-chosen selection of Czech reds and whites, most of which are available for tasting before you buy. The friendly owner, Martin Skora is usually on hand to let you in on his personal favorites.

Wine Shop Ungelt

Týnský dvůr 7, Praha 1 - Old Town. Tel. 2482-7501. Open daily 11am-11pm.

Hidden in the corner of a beautiful courtyard behind Old Town's Týn church, this excellent shop offers a well-chosen selection of local and foreign wines, including some excellent vintages from Bordeaux. The best wines are kept in the shop's vaulted 14th-century cellar, where you can sit with a glass and savor the unusual surroundings.

×08× ThE RESTAURANT SCENE

EATiNG

Alfredo
ESPRESSO

When *Prague Post* editor-in-chief Alan Levy dubbed this city the "Left Bank of the Nineties" he was certainly not thinking about gastronomy. One glance into a native kitchen, where families feast on deep-fried lard (*škvarky*) and horse-meat sausages (*koňský párky*), is all it takes to realize that, food-wise, Prague is no Paris.

If "you are what you eat," then Czechs are pigs, kraut and dumplings, the sum total of their most favorite meal. You can find that combo on almost every Czech menu. First and foremost, Czech chow is peasant chow. The best dishes will never be complicated, or influenced from anyplace farther than Poland, Austria or Germany. The cuisine relies on the fatty meats and cream sauces that American cardiologists banned long ago, and spices don't get much more adventurous than garlic and marjoram.

The first rule of Prague dining is: keep it simple. That's not to say that there isn't some seriously good food in Prague. There is. Wild game and smoked meats are the aces in Czech cuisine's proverbial hole. Duck, boar, goose and venison are some of the best in the world. Order any of these "exotics" and you'll rarely be disappointed. And, Czech chefs have never met pork or poultry they didn't like to smoke. Czechs are world champs of smoking everything from fish and tongue to pork and chicken. Every neighborhood in the nation has several great (and divvy) "smoked meat shops" (*uzeniny*) selling ready-to-eat meals (our favorite in Prague's center, Obchod Čerstvých Uzenin, is listed under Faster Food, below).

Like everything else in this communist-stunted country, restaurant appreciation remains forty years "behind" the West. It's unfathomable to most Czechs that any bistro can match the fine cooking of their mothers. And, for the most part, they're right. And when it comes to top restaurants, communism's effects still linger. The French guys still have the edge on the trattoria guys (as it was in America two generations ago), and far fewer than half of Prague's top twenty restaurants are wholly Czech-owned. Restaurants are now opening at a fast clip, and it's delicious watching it all unfold.

Local Wines

When faced with a Czech wine list, remember that local reds are light and thin and generally characterless, no matter how old or expensive they are. Frankovka, Rulandske and Vavřinecke are the three most popular varieties, with the last being fullest in body. When looking for complexity, you're always better off choosing the cheapest Italian, Spanish or Hungarian bottle than you are going native. Czech whites, on the other hand, can be light, fruity and exceedingly drinkable for not very much money. Mueller-Thurgau is the driest of the bunch.

The Reservations Game

Czechs start dinner early, say between 630 and 830pm. Reservations are not that hard to come by; you don't need to be *somebody* to snag a table, even in the city's top restaurants. But the good restaurants fill up nightly, especially from May to September, when the tourist season is in full swing. Booking is recommended at almost every establishment listed below. Anyway, it never hurts. The country code for the Czech Republic is 420; the city code for Prague is 02 (drop the 0 when phoning from abroad). From Great Britain dial 00-420-2 plus the local number; from the USA dial 011-420-2 plus the local number.

Tipping

In pubs and cheaper restaurants, servers only expect diners to round-up the total bill to the nearest few crowns. The waiter will add up your tab tableside, and stand around waiting for you to pay. Rather than leave a tip on the table, it's customary to round the bill up in your head and tell the waiter how much to keep. In fancier places checks are delivered on platters, change is returned, and 10% is the right amount to leave.

What's a Czech Crown worth today? Check out www.avantguide.com

Delivery Service

If you don't feel like getting out of bed but still want a taste of the city, phone **Delivery.cz** (tel. 2422-8538), a waiter-on-wheels service that delivers meals from a dozen local restaurants, from pub grub to pizza. Ask them to fax you their menu, or just tell them what you want. **Of course, you can check them out on the Web too** (www.delivery.cz).

Kibbles & Bits

With few very exceptions, Prague's top restaurants are far cheaper than comparable places in the West. This is a great city to pamper yourself with several fine dining experiences within the space of a few days.

- Prague eats early. Most restaurants are shut by 10 or 11pm.
- Round bills up by about 10%.
- You can drink the water. It tastes bad, but there's nothing in it that will kill you immediately.

Smoking

Go ahead, Fire up. Smoking is common in most restaurants and nicotine-fiends are allowed to get their fixes just about anywhere they please. Very few places have separate dining rooms for non-users, though some pubs ban smoking during lunch.

Our reviewers have no relationship to any establishment listed in this guidebook. All restaurant visits are anonymous, and expenses are paid by Avant-Guide.

Where To Dine When Dining Alone

Theoretically, you can eat solo in *any* restaurant. A good book or the *International Herald Tribune* can be far better companions than some human beings we've shared tables with. But when dining alone, we shy away from quiet places with stuffy service in favor of lively surroundings and bar chairs. In addition to all the cafes listed in this chapter, here's where to go when you're on your only.

Page	Restaurant
234	Barock
236	Dynamo
239	Kozička
239	Radost FX
241	Kogo
245	Bohemia Bagel
245	The Globe
245	Jáma
146	Modrá Zahrada
249	U Nováka
250	James Joyce Pub
253	Country Life
253	Govinda
254	Obchod Čerstvých Uzenin
254	Praha Tamura
254	U Bakaláře
256	Roma Due
256	U Zlatého Stromu

VIVRE

RESTAURANTS BY AREA, PRICE & CUISINE

The cost (*) reflects the average cost of a dinner with one drink and tip.

* = Under 150 Kč
** = 150–400 Kč
*** = 400–700 Kč
**** = 700–1000 Kč
***** = Over 1000 Kč

MALÁ STRANA

Page	Restaurant	Cuisine	Cost
245	Bohemia Bagel	American	**
226	Circle Line	Continental	*****
240	Faros	Greek	***
227	Kampa Park	Continental	*****
231	Nebozízek	Czech	***
232	Pálffy Palac	Continental	****
241	Pasha	Mediterranean	*****
228	U Modré Kachničky	Czech	****
233	Vinárna U Maltézských Rytířů	Czech	****

NEW TOWN

Page	Restaurant	Cuisine	Cost
236	Dynamo	Czech	***
259	Evropa Café	Czech	****
242	Gargoyles	American	***
245	The Globe	American	**
253	Govinda	Indian	*
255	Gyrossino	Gyros	*
262	Imperial Cafe	Czech	**
245	Jáma	American	**
245	Kogo	Italian	***
252	Novoměstský Pivovar	Czech	***
254	Obchod Čerstvých Uzenin	Czech	*
247	Pizza Coloseum	Italian	**
249	U Nováka	Czech	**
244	Universal	Continental	***
244	Velryba	Czech	**
247	Zlatá Ulička Pizzeria	Balkan	**

OLD TOWN

Page	Restaurant	Cuisine	Cost
240	Ambiente	Czech/American	***
234	Barock	International	*****
225	Bellevue	Continental	*****
245	Bohemia Bagel	American	**
253	Country Life	Healthist	**
250	James Joyce Pub	Irish	****
226	Jewel of India	Indian	****
246	Klub Architektů	Czech	**
241	Kogo	Italian	***
251	Kolkovna	Czech	**
236	Kozička	Czech	***
237	La Provence	French	****
246	Modrá Zahrada	Pizza	**
262	Obecní Dům Kavárna	Czech	**
232	Parnas	Continental	*****
254	Praha Tamura	Japanese	***
237	Pravda	International	*****
244	Rasoi	Indian	*****
256	Roma Due	Italian	**
228	Rybí trh	Continental	****
262	Slavia Café	Czech	**
254	U Bakaláře	Czech	*
252	U Medvídků	Czech	**
251	U Vejvodu	Czech	**
256	U Zlatého Stromu	Czech	**
230	Vinárna V Zátiší	Continental	*****

ELSEWHERE

Page	Restaurant	Cuisine	Cost
240	Ambiente	Czech/American	***
229	Ostroff	Italian	*****
239	Radost F/X	Vegetarian	**

Bellevue

Smetanovo nábřeží 18, Praha 1 – Old Town. Tel. 02/2222-1438. Reservations recommended. Kitchen open Mon-Sat noon-3pm and 530-11pm, Sun 11am-3pm and 7-11pm. Main courses 600-1000 Kč; fixed-price menu 900-1490 Kč. AE, MC, V. M Staroměstská

From the turreted brick exterior to the foie gras and caviar menu, everything about Bellevue screams Serious Restaurant! Maturely dressed with flowing draperies and elegantly laid tables, this is a "destination restaurant," meant to be the culmination of one's evening, not just a prelude to some other entertainment. Depending on whom you're dining with, Bellevue can feel either amorous or clubby—the atmosphere appeals to both corporate-card carriers and romantic couples in search of a quiet meal in beautiful surroundings. We've spied everyone here, from actress Whoopi Goldberg to a former President of Italy. Each guest is treated like a czar by a fawning waitstaff that never lets a glass become empty nor an emptied plate lie. And like the name says, there are beautiful views of the River Vltava and Prague Castle—for those who sit by the windows. In addition to goose liver and sturgeon eggs, most insiders begin with a pasta pocket packed with lobster and spinach. Entrees on the seasonally-modified menu usually include duck, beef, deer and fish selections. Even if it's not listed, you might ask for the restaurant's signature dish: rack of lamb, marinated in honey mustard. It's usually paired with garlicky spinach and pan-fried potatoes. Desserts, which are included in the three-course fixed-price menu, include chocolate mousse and crēme brulée, but the most popular ending is wild berries marinated in port and cognac on vanilla and walnut ice creams. Bellevue has one of the best-selected wine lists in town, and several good buys are amongst the offerings.

Circle Line

Malostranské nám. 12, Praha 1 – Malá Strana. Tel. 02/5753-0021. Reservations recommended. Kitchen open Mon-Fri noon-11pm, Sat-Sun 11am-11pm. Main courses 395-795 Kč; fixed-price menu 800-1200 Kč. AE, MC, V. M Malostranská

Circle Line serves great food. The restaurant is known for a freestyle Frenchish cuisine that plays to both meat lovers and shellfish-ionados. Regulars begin with ox tail ravioli tossed with a buttery shallot sauce; or little bay scallops, which are cooked in their shells with garlic, tomatoes and salt-cured ham. Entrees get high marks across the board, and may include French wild hare in a peppery game sauce; braised monkfish, served bouillabaisse style or spice bread-crusted sea bass infused with a hint of amaretto. The dining room is a nice, white-clothed affair set with comfortable chairs and well-spaced tables. The atmosphere can be a bit starchy at times, but that hardly matters to the foodies who come here to eat. Even willowy ballet star Mikhail Baryshnikov was caught here tearing into a steak, then lighting-up a cigar. During warm months, diners can eat alfresco, on the sidewalk overlooking busy Malá Strana Square and beautiful St. Nicholas Church.

Jewel of India

Pařížská 20, Praha 1 – Old Town. Tel. 02/2481-1010. Reservations recommended. Kitchen open daily noon-3pm and 530-11pm. Main courses 300-500 Kč; lunch 200-250 Kč. AE, MC, V. M Staroměstská

Easily the best Indian restaurant in Prague, and probably all of Eastern Europe, Jewel of India is an upscale, Old Town tandoori room cooking North Indian cuisine with spectacular results. The best entrees come from the 800-degree (427-degree Celsius) tandoor. Nan bread is perfectly speckled with char, and the chicken tikka masala–tender tandoori chicken bathed in a spicy, rich cream sauce–is absolutely dynamite. All the other curry house traditionals are here, including excellent Saag Paneer, made with homemade cheese and fresh spinach; and a truly gourmet black-bean dal. The restaurant's ground floor dining room is an intimate Raj-style space directly overlooking tony Pařížská. Service can seem hurried and a few tables are so close to each other it can feel like you're dining with strangers, but when the food arrives, all wrongs are righted.

Kampa Park

Na Kampě 8, Praha 1 – Malá Strana. Tel. 02/5753-2686. Reservations Required. Kitchen open daily 1130am–4pm and 6–11pm. Main courses 500–600 Kč. AE, MC, V. Ⓜ Malostranská

Kampa Park is best known for its outdoor terrace that, on sunny days, becomes the most coveted real estate in the city. Though only the briefest wisp of riverfront scenery is discernible from the majority of tables, thirty lucky people on the terrace's lower tier get up-close and personal with Charles Bridge and the banks of Old Town. For most mortals, a table on the lower level requires reservations up to a month in advance—and a prayer for clear skies. For others, it means swearing you're friends with owner Nils Jebens. In winter the terrace is glass-enclosed and other land disputes move inside, where the coziest tables are in the front room, beside an exhibition kitchen. On Thursday nights from November to March, the restaurant lays-out a huge fin- and shell-fish buffet that has become a winter institution. Food here is always very good, and sometimes even superlative. Meals are gloriously simple and artfully presented. Beef carpaccio, a dish that has made its way onto the menu at practically every expense-account restaurant in town, is a memorable appetizer that has become something of a signature dish here. Of entrees, standouts include venison in red wine, grilled salmon drizzled with creamy caper sauce, and tiger prawns with ginger butter. The latter was removed from the menu long ago, but the ingredients remain in stock for the many insiders who regularly order it. There is no bar scene here; indeed there is not even a bar. That keeps the restaurant sedate with businesspeople, diplomats and every star who has ever come to town, including Johnny Depp, Madaline Albright, Bruce Springstein, Sylvester Stalone... ad nauseum.

Rybí trh

(Fish Market) Týn 5, Praha 1 – Old Town. Tel. 02/2489 5447. Reservations recommended. Kitchen open daily 11am-midnight. Main Courses 300-450 Kč. AE, MC, V. M Staroměstská

This beautiful courtyard restaurant is revealing itself as the king of all things fishy. Good chefs and top ingredients converge daily in Rybí trh's hard-working kitchen where fresh ocean fish like halibut, cod, monkfish and tuna, are brought in each morning from Belgium and handled with utmost care. The freshwater catch—carp, trout, pike, sturgeon and eel—is also morning fresh, and chilled on crushed ice in front of an exhibition kitchen. Choose your *poisson* and have it cooked to your specifications: baked, boiled or grilled. You can match your selection with a complimentary sauce like horseradish-cream or lemon-and-ginger, but fish this fresh should land on your plate unmasked, except, perhaps, for a little bit of butter. As a rule, cognoscenti forgo appetizers here, which are overpriced and far from exceptional (the deep-fried smelt are some of the saltiest things we have ever put in our mouths). Sides, on the other hand, are as good as the main courses, and we usually order several. Try the potato gnocchi, garlic spinach, and roasted mushrooms seasoned with ground caraway. Rybí trh's crisp dining rooms are architectural showplaces, built with Renaissance vaults that have been stripped down to their original 16th-century stonework. On any given night, tables are occupied by local business people and well-heeled visitors. In summer, reserve a table outdoors, in one of the city's most bucolic courtyards.

U Modré Kachničky

(The Blue Duckling) Nebovidská 6, Praha 1 – Malá Strana. Tel. 02/5732-0308. Reservations recommended. Kitchen open daily noon–4pm and 630–1130pm. Main courses 280–450 Kč. AE. M Malostranská

U Modré Kachnicky dishes out Prague's best urban-rustic Czech cuisine, which is the closest thing there is to nouveau-Bohemian cooking. To accomplish this the chef whips really good ingredients into familiar recipes, thereby maintaining the spirit of each dish. The delicious result is Bohemian peasant food that is never completely incomprehensible to the Bohemian peasants in question. Wild game is the house specialty—if it's felled by gunshot, it's probably on the menu. Pheasant soup and boar goulash are usually available, but dishes like hare in cream and cranberries, and deer medallions in a cloyingly tangy brown sauce, are

only served during their respective hunting seasons. The restaurant is justifiably fabled for it's roast duck—succulent inside, but with a skin so crisp it crunches like a potato chip. Many regulars favor the "hunter's needle," a delicious barbecued skewer of rolled meats. The restaurant's trio of petite, vaulted dining rooms are full of busy fabrics, fabulous wall frescoes and antique furnishings set on Oriental carpets. The effect is so extraordinarily romantic, it feels like you're dining inside a Faberge egg. Dinners here are always lengthy multi-course affairs, often involving several bottles of wine. Over the years, almost everyone has eaten here, from heads of state and government officials to rock and film stars. Of course, there are plenty of mortals too. The large wine list includes several good Moravian archive selections.

Ostroff

Střelecký Ostrov 336, Praha 1. Tel. 02/2491-9235. Reservations recommended. Kitchen open Mon-Fri noon-2pm and 7-1030pm, Sat 7-1030pm, Sun 11am-3pm. Main courses 600-800 Kč. AE, MC, V. M Národní Třída

The best Italian restaurant in Prague occupies one of the most unusual spaces in town, isolated on a small island in the Vltava one span upstream from Charles Bridge. On warm summer days, dining is upstairs and al fresco, under an enormous canvass roof. When the weather turns, the action heads inside, to cavernous stone dining rooms that are dressed to the nines. Food here is very good, and often verges on excellent. The kitchen is equally comfortable dishing out meats and starches, from rack of lamb with potatoes Dauphinoise to perfectly-cooked risotto with breast of quail and rosemary sauce. Only brunch is served on Sundays. The lion's share of the restaurant is a woefully under-utilized cocktail bar that is one of the most beautiful drinking rooms in the city: a modern, swoony space with a long wall of windows that literally open onto unobstructed views of the National Theater reflected in the river.

V Zátiší

Liliová 1, Praha 1 – Old Town. Tel. 02/2222-1155. Reservations recommended. Kitchen open daily noon–3pm and 530–11pm. Main courses 400–800 Kč; fixed-price menu 770–1175 Kč. AE, MC, V. M Národní Třída/Staroměstská

A peaceful patch of culinary calm in the dark heart of Old Town, Vinarna V Zátiší is highly respected by locals and critics for its consistently good Continental cooking. Dishes served here are essentially the same as those served in their sister restaurant, Bellevue, but at distinctly lower prices. Pheasant consommé with quail eggs, and venison paté with cranberry sauce gives way to sturdy pastas, meats and fish. Herbed tagliatelle is tossed with mussels and shrimps, while veal medallions are juicy and tender, and cut far thicker than their price would indicate. Regulars swear by the marinated salmon with honeydew melon, beef Wellington and chocolate mousse, the only three menu items that have not changed since the restaurant opened, in July, 1991. An extensive wine selection includes several excellent buys from southern Moravia. The restaurant's understated, tan dining room is designed for commercial lunches and semi-formal dinners. Like the menu, nothing about the decor declares "Prague," but that's a plus in a city where, all too often, inferior food and dismal surroundings constantly remind you where you are. Boasting an absurdly-loyal business crowd following, this restaurant has matured into a cherished Prague institution. The combination of reliably good food, attentive service and cheerful surroundings adds up to a rave.

CLASSiC PRAGUE SPACES

Nebozízek

Petřínské sady 411, Praha 1 – Malá Strana. Tel. 02/537-905. Reservations required. Kitchen open daily 11am–1030pm. Main courses 200–350 Kč. AE, MC, V. Tram 12 or 22 to Újezd, then funicular up Petřín Hill

You should already realize that in Prague you're not going to find the best meal of your life. So, why not go for the view? That seems to be the logic of this fantastically-situated restaurant with unobstructed storybook vistas and the most mundane food imaginable. A large, lone building high up on Petřín Hill, Nebozízek has "romantic date" written all over it and it's the ideal place to take out-of-towners for a drink and dazzle them with the lights of Prague. In summer, the most coveted chairs are on a trellised patio. In winter, it's the window seats, of which there are precious few. Grilled meats are the restaurant's specialty—but stick to a simple steak or the most uncomplicated of their many chicken permutations. Keep it simple. Eschew ostrich in favor of duck, and choose venison over anything fishy. The garlic consommé is exceptional, but the potato soup with mushrooms has as much salt as it has heft. Nebozízek is accessible by foot or funicular (*see* Chapter 4/Petřín Hill).

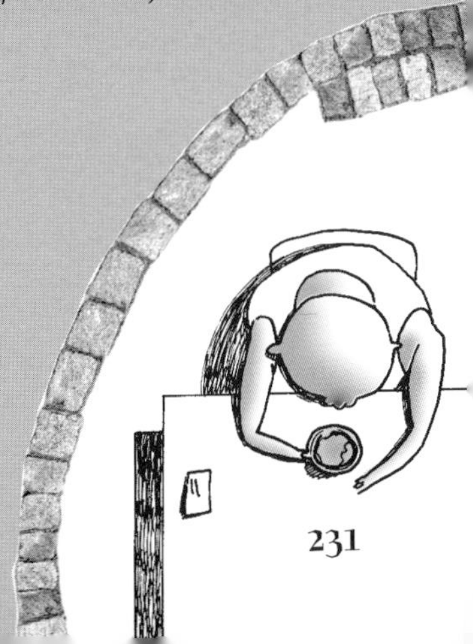

Pálffy Palac

Valdštejnská 14, Praha 1 – Malá Strana. Tel. 02/5753-1420. Reservations recommended. Kitchen open daily 11am-11pm. Main courses 275-400 Kč. MC, V. Ⓜ Malostranská

Half the fun at this oddly placed, shabby-chic joint is its novel location, on the second floor of an 18th-century aristocratic mansion in Malá Strana. Popular with governmentos at lunch, and a mixed business/young-casual crowd in the evening, the restaurant is a fading Baroque beauty that shares a decaying palace with one of the country's finest music conservatories. In summer, the best seats are on an open-air terrace, hemmed-in by the castle gardens. Crusty bread and a bulb of fresh-roasted garlic are served *gratis* while you study the menu—a short list that

Parnas

Smetanovo nábř. 2, Praha 1 – Old Town. Tel. 02/2427-8493. Kitchen open daily 6pm-midnight. Main courses 500-700 Kč. AE, MC, V. Ⓜ Staroměstská

Protected by the Architectural Landmarks Commission, Parnas is the most famous and beautiful high-rent dining room in the city. With yet another new chef, staff and management, Parnas can not be recommended for culinary consistency. But the ambiance is the main attraction here. Decidedly masculine, in a Ralph Lauren kind of way, the restaurant is built with inlaid woods, gentlemen's club lighting and large windows that entertain expansive river views. The kitchen compliments the surroundings with a Continental cuisine that is just Czech enough to give you a sense of place and refined enough to remind guests that they are, first and foremost, citizens of the Platinum Card. Wine-poached pike, crayfish cream soup and those deluxe-restaurant-requisites Sevruga caviar, fresh oysters and foie gras are all good. And that's just round one. Entrees include roasted perch with butter and hazel nuts, and ginger-infused duck breasts, slightly browned, then finished in the oven. There's a large selection of international wines, and baked Alaska is on the dessert menu.

Vinárna U Maltézských Rytířu

(The Knights of Malta), Prokopská 10, Praha 1 – Malá Strana. Tel. 02/5753-3666. Reservations recommended. Kitchen open daily 11am-11pm. Main courses 300-500 Kč. AE, MC,V. M Malostranská

Once the exclusive haunt of knowledgeable locals, Knights of Malta has long since been discovered by the masses. Whether you're a regular or a first-timer, owner Nadia Černiková will effusively welcome you like a friend and lead you to a table in the cozy whitewashed ground-floor dining room or vaulted, candle-lit cellar below. Gastronomically, The Knights of Malta is that rare and wonderful thing: a rigorously unambitious restaurant. The high-quality Czech cuisine served here is straightforward and perfect, and not nouveau or avant in any way. The menu is short and to the point: salmon steak with herb butter, lamb cutlets with spinach, steak with caper sauce, and one of the most tender chateaubriands we've ever put to tooth. With extraordinary consistency, meats are served perfectly grilled—seared on the outside and pink within. Order potato croquettes with everything, as they are the best homemade mashed-potato balls on the planet. Finally, end with Nadia's own apple strudel: a dense, fruity pie that's worth hanging around for.

changes almost daily, but always includes chicken, beef and fish dishes. Even if it's not listed, the kitchen is ready to prepare spinach crepes, a wonderfully garlicky signature starter. Chicken breast rolled around sun-dried tomatoes is typical of the Continental-nouveau entrees that may also include beef tenderloin with gorgonzola butter and an eggplant-based vegetarian lasagna. Cognoscenti order scalloped potatoes and spinach with everything. Plates are arty, as this kitchen is one of the precious few in town that concerns itself with "fooditecture." Rims are often dusted with colorful crushed spices and many dishes are garnished with edible flowers. Be forewarned that service here is infamously unhurried. Visit Pálffy Palac with good friends, and expect to stay a while.

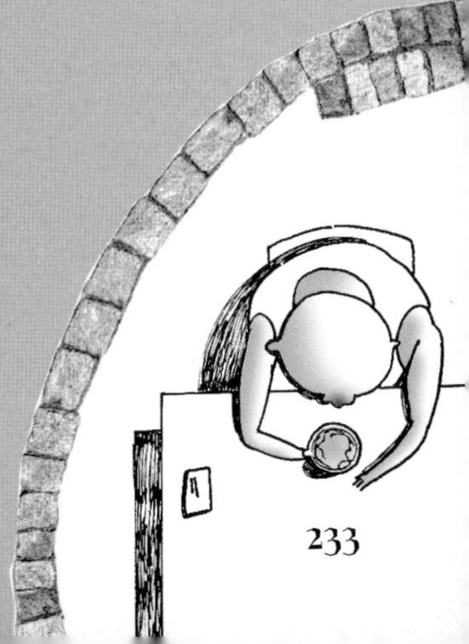

iN-STYLE SCENES

Barock

Pařížská 24, Praha 1 – Old Town. Tel. 02/232-9291. Reservations recommended. Kitchen open daily 1130am–11pm. Main courses 400-600 Kč. AE, MC, V. M Staroměstská. "Modelicious" photographs on the walls are first tip off to the atmosphere that Barock attempts to create: a scene-heavy cafe/restaurant that appeals to everyone from Euro-nobodies to genuine big shots from Andie MacDowell to Gérard Depardieu. Come summer, the small dining room almost doubles in size, when cafe tables spill onto the sidewalk and are filled by poseurs who hungrily eye passers-by. The multi-culti menu is all over the map, serving respectable starters like tuna tartar, grilled boneless quail with shitake and truffle sauce, and langoustine ravioli. Mains run the gamut from poached cod with coconut/ginger sauce to grilled duck breast marinated in soy and honey. And, surprisingly, Barock serves some of the best sushi in the city. Deserts are a strength here, and include triple chocolate terrine, and warm goat cheese with fig compote and cinnamon-honey syrup. The restaurant is also a good place for brunch, served on Saturdays and Sundays from 1130am-4pm.

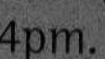

* 08 *
EATiNG

Dynamo

Pštrossova 29, Praha 1 – New Town. Tel. 02/2493-2020. Reservations recommended. Kitchen open daily 1130am–11pm. Main courses 150–300 Kč. AE, MC, V. M Národní Třída

Prague's most radically stylish restaurant is a modernist architectural masterpiece and a youth-magnet showplace. Hip would be the operative word here, where postmodernism rules everything from the mod logo and enigmatic wall clocks to the lighting and tableware. So why, then, is the food so archaic? Post-communist irony is the only explanation for a starchy kitchen that serves roast meats and chicken livers in heavy sauces; a throwback to the heavy old days that makes us feel as though the chef and the designer never got along. That's not to say the food is not good. It's just strangely incongruous. At least the bar manager got it right, stocking one of the finest single-malt scotch selections in town.

Kozička

(The Little Goat) Kozí 1, Praha 1 – Old Town. Tel. 02/2481-8308. Kitchen open Mon-Fri noon–115am, Sat-Sun 6pm–115am. Reservations recommended. Main courses 150–300 Kč. MC, V. M Staroměstská

Equal parts bar and restaurant, Kozička is a downstairs, downscale spot that's enormously popular with budget-minded students and other cheapskates with big appetites. The vibe is drunken, somewhat hip, and often studded with eye-candy. No matter where you sit (or stand), you can feel equally comfortable ordering steaks and sides or simply beer and Becherovka. If you do come for the food then grilled chicken and beef in various guises is the best way to go. Your entrance parade past the bar can be an eyeful and one that should be savored slowly. Reservations are recommended.

Pravda

Pařížská 17, Praha 1 - Old Town. Tel. 02/232-6203. Reservations recommended. Kitchen open daily 1130am-3pm and 6-11pm. Main courses 400-600 Kč. AE, MC, V. M Staroměstská

Situated beside the Old-New Synagogue on the city's most prestigious commercial street, Pravda is a self-consciously stylish space, designed with clean lines, white furnishings, and smartly-dressed waiters who are well-practiced at catering to their knowledgeable international clientele. Smart lighting, comfortable seating and a good sound system are all plusses. The restaurant's culinary hook—global cooking that brings together meals from all over the map—is riskier, and often ends up insulting several cuisines at once. Italy, Thailand, India and Japan are all represented, respectively as roasted scallops, grilled tiger prawns, chicken kebabs, and sushi. Food from a dozen other lands is whipped up too, and vegetarians are catered to with gratinated goat cheese and vegetables woked with noodles.

La Provence

Štupartská 9, Praha 1 - Old Town. Tel. 02/232-4801. Reservations recommended. Kitchen open daily noon-midnight. Main courses 300-700 Kč. AE, MC. M Náměstí Republiky

The closest that Prague comes to the youth-infected bistros of Paris and Lower Manhattan, La Provence appeals to the senses with exciting colors, funky sounds and the sort of low, flattering lighting that makes everyone look that much better. It's impossible to feel sad in this upbeat, downstairs dining room surrounded by pulsating dance music, kinte-cloth pillow coverings and an assortment of kaleidoscopic clutter. Once the Eurotrashiest place in Old Town (Brigit Nielson has partied here), the restaurant has matured into a respectable eatery with all the hallmarks of permanency. It's still a happening place: Good people-watching, large portions, and competent food (in that order) translate into long waits almost every night of the week. La Provence is a calorie-unconscious tip of the beret to French country cooking. Regular chef changes come with respective menu revisions, but the Franco-Czech staples that continue to draw regulars haven't budged an inch. The kitchen's winningest entrees are Barbary duck breast with honey and vegetables, escargots provencal, vegetable gratin, and a great coq au vin. Match your meal with a bottle from one of the city's longest list of expensive French wines.

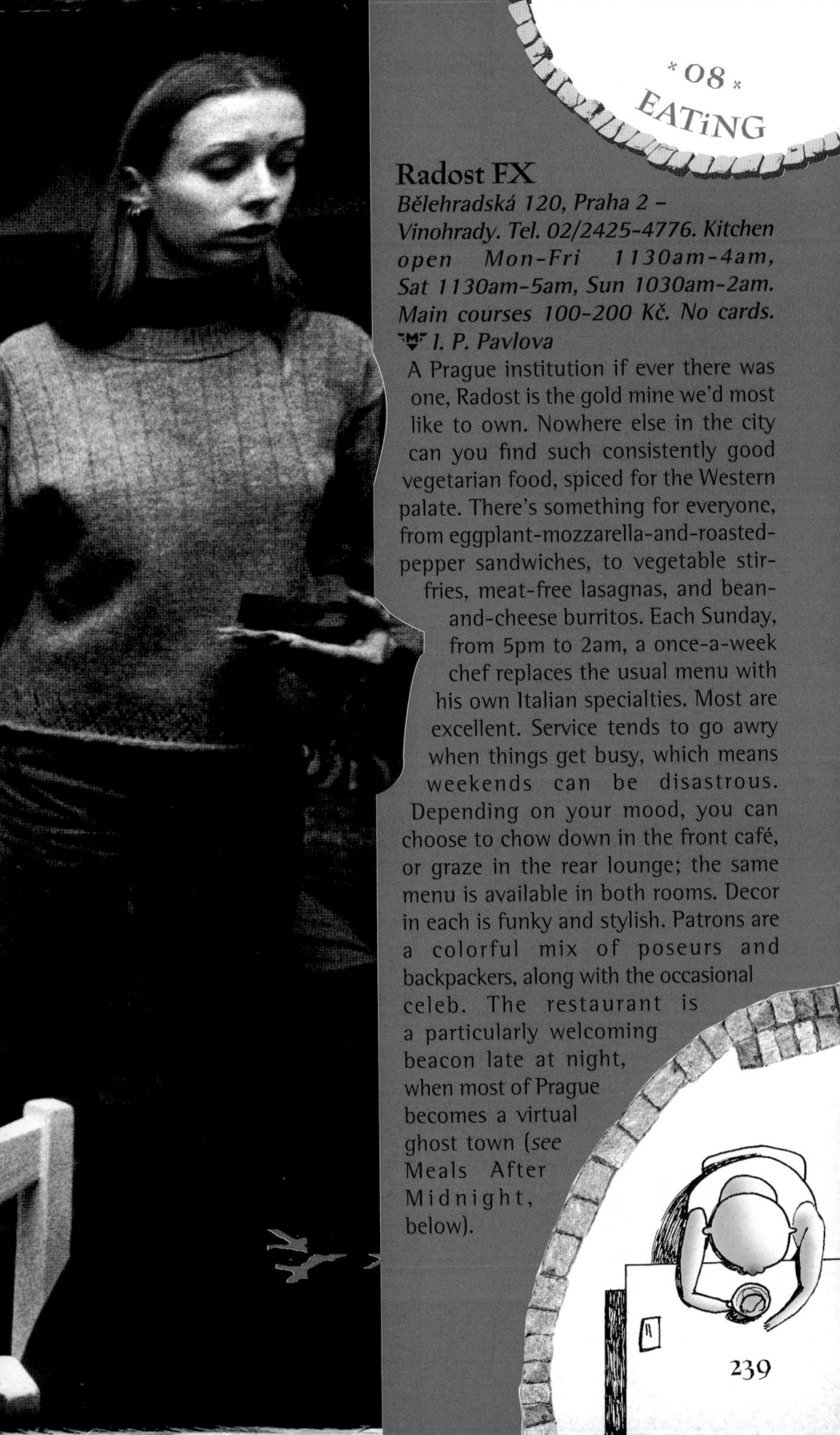

Radost FX

Bělehradská 120, Praha 2 – Vinohrady. Tel. 02/2425-4776. Kitchen open Mon-Fri 1130am-4am, Sat 1130am-5am, Sun 1030am-2am. Main courses 100-200 Kč. No cards. M I. P. Pavlova

A Prague institution if ever there was one, Radost is the gold mine we'd most like to own. Nowhere else in the city can you find such consistently good vegetarian food, spiced for the Western palate. There's something for everyone, from eggplant-mozzarella-and-roasted-pepper sandwiches, to vegetable stir-fries, meat-free lasagnas, and bean-and-cheese burritos. Each Sunday, from 5pm to 2am, a once-a-week chef replaces the usual menu with his own Italian specialties. Most are excellent. Service tends to go awry when things get busy, which means weekends can be disastrous. Depending on your mood, you can choose to chow down in the front café, or graze in the rear lounge; the same menu is available in both rooms. Decor in each is funky and stylish. Patrons are a colorful mix of poseurs and backpackers, along with the occasional celeb. The restaurant is a particularly welcoming beacon late at night, when most of Prague becomes a virtual ghost town (*see* Meals After Midnight, below).

ThE bEST Of ThE REST: OUR FAVORiTE RESTAURANTS

Ambiente

Mánesova 59, Praha 2 – Vinohrady. Tel. 02/627-5913. Reservations recommended. Kitchen open Mon-Fri 11am-1130pm, Sat-Sun 1-1130pm. Main courses 150-250 Kč. AE, MC, V. M Jiřího z Poděbrad

Prague's most successful wholly-Czech-owned restaurant is well-known for good food and friendly service that keeps regulars coming back for more. Located well off the tourist track, the restaurant caters to mainstream Czech sensibilities by toning-down both spices and prices. The restaurant's 18th-century cellar dining room is made contemporary with light-colored walls and a confusion of American kitsch. It can get aggressively noisy, especially if a large party is in the house. Ambiente whips up American cuisine from a Czech perspective—Yankee food with Teutonic undertones. Forgo the forgettable pastas in favor of real Argentinean angus steaks that are worthy of one's last meal. Also memorable are the tender beef ribs and spicy chicken wings, which are served with a trio of tangy sauces. When it comes to dessert, few calorie unconscious diners can resist the chocolate fondue, a large hot-pot served with sliced bananas and pineapples for dipping.

A second Ambiente in Old Town, at Celetná 11, Praha 1 (tel. 2423-0244), has an Italian menu, higher prices and more tourists.

Faros

Šporkova 5, Praha 1 – Malá Strana. Tel. 02/5753-3964. Reservations Recommended. Kitchen open daily noon-11pm. Main courses 165-330 Kč. AE, MC, V. M Malostranská

Hidden on one of the smallest streets in the Malá Strana foothills, this tiny Greek-Mediterranean find is an enjoyable alternative to the restaurants of Goulash Gulch, below. Don't expect line dances or plates being smashed on the floor. Do expect worthy Hellenic cooking. All the classics are here, including moussaka (a meat pie), souvlaki (skewered beef) and pasticcio (a pasta pie), which must be ordered 24-hours in advance. Grazing is our favorite way of eating here; making a meal of the terrific appetizers like tzaziki (yogurt with cucumber and garlic), taramosalata (cod roe salad), dolmas (meat- and rice-stuffed grape leaves), saganaki (feta cheese with tomatoes) and fried zucchini. You might want to visit (or avoid) Faros on Friday nights when there's live Greek music. In summer, a couple of tables are placed on the pocket-sized front patio.

?asha

.užického Semináře 23, Praha 1 – Malá Strana. Tel. 02/5753-2434. ?eservations recommended. Kitchen open Mon and Wed-Sat 1130am-11pm, Sun 1130am-10pm. Main courses 450-600 Kč. AE, MC, V. Ⓜ Malostranská

Draped in hues of crimson and scarlet and garnished with the same ntricately-patterned brass teapots and plates that decorate souks and harem dens throughout the Middle East, Pasha reigns as one of Malá Strana's most romantic restaurants. ust past the curtained entrance is a dimly-lit sexy space that's usually our top choice for a Valentines Day meal. The menu includes a substantial list of Lebanese and Turkish favorites like minced lamb kebabs, beef-stuffed eggplant and couscous. But we usually forego entrees in favor of a feast comprised of the largest selection of mezze in Prague. Favorites include marinated octopus, meatballs in a delicious spicy sauce, and meat-stuffed puff-pastries. The restaurant is situated ust a few steps from Malostranská Metro.

Kogo

in Slovanský dům, Na Příkopě 22, Praha 1 – New Town. Tel. 02/2145-1260. Reservations recommended. Kitchen open daily 11am-11pm. Main courses 150-250 Kč. MC, V. Ⓜ Můstek/Náměstí Republiky

If we had to eat dinner in just one Prague restaurant every night of the year, Kogo would be the one. First of all, the food is excellent. A huge menu of Italian favorites runs the gamut from steaks and seafood to well-made pastas and risotto. Salmon steaks, and everything else that comes from the wood-burning grill are fabulous. And even though they recently removed it from the menu, insiders still know to order tagliatelle with veal in cream sauce. Only the pizzas are disappointing. The beautiful dining room, most of which is under an enormous greenhouse, is modern, clean and exceedingly comfortable. And t's open-plan layout is perfect for eyeing other customers. Service is terrific. And to top it all off, prices are a third less then they could be. The restaurant is hidden in the very back of the Slovanský dům shopping mall.

PS: The original Kogo, located in Old Town at Havelská 27, Praha 1 (tel. 02/2421-4543) s just as terrific.

Gargoyles

Opatovická 5, Praha 1 – New Town. Tel. 02/2491-6047. Kitchen open Mon-Fri 11am-3pm and 6-11pm, Sat-Sun 6-11pm. Reservations recommended. Main courses 200-800 Kč; set menu 750 Kč (1450 Kč with wine). AE, MC, V. M Národní Třída

magine taking a very good San Francisco restaurant and setting it down in the center of Prague. The result is the city's best gourmet value. While the majority of Prague's other quality eateries are of the heavy, French variety, Chef Thomas Ponder's No-Cal kitchen whips up far lighter creations that don't rely on cream and fat to tantalize the palate. And Gargoyles is one of the precious few places in town that pays attention to "fooditecture." Meals run the gamut from beef carpaccio and duck "foie" gras to excellent Caesar salad, marinated vegetables, chicken in garlicky wine sauces, and coriander salmon. And the set-price, five course chef's feast must be one of the best culinary deals anywhere. Because there's not much to the basic interior, Gargoyles can hardly be called "upscale." But that's a plus to this restaurant's core fans: small groups and people on dates, for whom a meal here is often a prelude to a long night of partying.

* 08 *
EATiNG

Rasoi

Dlouhá 13, Praha 1 – Old Town. Tel. 232-8400. Reservations recommended. Kitchen open daily 11am-330pm and 6-1130pm. Main courses 400-600 Kč. AE, MC, V. Ⓜ Staroměstská/Náměstí Republiky

Unless you're from London or Delhi, you'll love this island of spice in Prague's otherwise bland foodscape. Centrally situated in the heart of Old Town, below the colonial-theme Bombay Cafe bar, Rasoi quickly attracted a loyal following with decent food, a comfortable atmosphere, and out-of-center prices. From masalas to vindaloos, all the curry house hits are here, moderated for local palates. Service is customarily friendly and the food is absolutely consistent. We always leave satisfied, feeling as though we got exactly the meal we bargained for.

Universal

V Jirchářích 6, Praha 1 – New Town. Tel. 02/2491-8182. Reservations recommended. Kitchen open Mon-Sat 1130am-11pm, Sun 1230-11pm. Main courses 150-350 Kč. No cards. Ⓜ Národní Třída.

Good food at reasonable prices make this restaurant's appeal, well, universal. The food, which is nominally Frenchish, includes a serviceable salad Nicoise, well-made chicken breast in tarragon sauce, and very good (and otherwise hard-to-find) lemon-and-vodka sorbet. Although it's situated on the ground floor, the twin dining rooms have the acoustics of a cellar, and the seating is strictly hardwood. Not surprisingly, the crowd trends young, creating something of a college vibe. The eclectic menu and no-nonsense atmosphere makes this place perfect for small groups with dissimilar tastes. It's also a great standby when your simply confused about where else to go.

Bohemia Bagel

Újezd 16, Praha 1 – Malá Strana. Tel. 02/531-002. Kitchen open Mon-Fri 7am-midnight, Sat-Sun 8am-midnight. Sandwiches 90-140 Kč. Tram 9, 12 or 22 to Újezd

It's amazing but true: The bagels served at this successful little Malá Strana eatery are on a par with Brooklyn's finest. These are dense breads that are boiled, not steamed, then smothered in toppings that range from orthodox to reform. Though the main focus is overstuffed bagel sandwiches (which run the gamut from lox-and-tomato to ham-and-cheese) the bagels are good enough to stand alone, lightly toasted or with a schmeer of cream cheese. Add the *International Herald Tribune* and it's the perfect morning meal. Tables are increasingly hard to snag at breakfast, when arty sorts are lingering over bottomless cups of joe.

A second Bohemia Bagel is located in Old Town at Masná 2, Praha 1 (tel. 2482-2560).

The Globe

Pštrosova 6, Praha 1 – New Town. Tel. 02/2491-6264. Kitchen open daily 10am-10pm. Main courses 95-150 Kč. AE, MC, V. M Národní třída

Wondering where to get a large green salad? Where to pick-up a good novel? Where all the Americans are? While The Globe is no longer the only bookstore/café in town, it has successfully taken-on all comers and remains a cultural and culinary champ. It's still hard to find a chair at lunch, when semester-abroad students and American English teachers are chomping on well-made salads, sandwiches and vegetable soups. Brunch is served on weekends until 3pm.

Jáma

(The Hallow) V jámě 7, Praha 1 – New Town. Tel. 02/2422-2383. Kitchen open daily 11am-1am. Main courses 100-190 Kč. AE, MC, V. M Můstek/Muzeum

Largely Mexican-American in flavor, Jáma dishes out overstuffed tacos, fajitas and burritos, along with a variety of hamburgers and several vegetarian dishes. The pollo quesadilla—chicken, cheese, green pepper, rice and beans rolled into a flour tortilla—is the restaurant's most popular meal. Loud rock and music posters attract a youngish, CzEnglish clientele, most of whom are here to drink. Jáma's condensed late-night menu, available after 10pm, reads like a greatest hits of their daylight offerings. And there's major sports on satellite TV on Sunday nights.

Klub Architektů

(Architect's Club) Betlémské nám. 5a, Praha 1 – Old Town. Tel. 02/2440-1214. Reservations recommended. Kitchen open daily 1130am–11pm. Main courses 90–130 Kč. AE, MC, V. M Národní Třída

Klub Architektů's exceptionally veiled entrance—through a church gate then down a short hallway and a flight of steps—makes one's arrival in the stone-vaulted cellar a particularly dramatic event. Everyone who walks into this restaurant for the first time feels honored to have made such an extraordinary discovery, an effect that's heightened by the walk past an open kitchen and shadowy lighting in the dining rooms. Food here is, let's say, "interesting." Typical are beef strips with apples in cream sauce, and chicken steak with ham and pineapple—two meals from a cuisine that might be labeled "bachelor-pad experimentation." And a surprisingly good wine selection confirms this playboy point. Ask for the oldest Czech vintage in their cellar, and you'll get something nice for under $10. Oh, and whatever you do, stay away from the deep-fried celery burgers.

Modrá Zahrada

(Blue Garden) Pařížká 14 (entrance on Široká) – Old Town. Tel. 02/232-7171. Reservations accepted. Kitchen open daily 11am–1130pm. Main courses 75–100 Kč. No cards. M Staroměstská

Of the numerous pizzerias that have sprouted up around Prague, Modrá Zahrada bakes one of the best. There are about two dozen wood-fired pies to choose from, the most popular of which is Capriciosa, a ham and mushroom pizza that, like most others, is topped with tangy tomato sauce and locally-produced edam cheese. Lots of people come here because this is one of the few places in town that serves large green salads, many of which are variations on the meat-and-cheese chef. Beer and wine are served.

Pizza Coloseum

Vodičova 32, Praha 1 – New Town. Tel. 02/2421-4914. Reservations recommended. Kitchen open daily 1130am-1130pm. Main courses 100-150 Kč. AE, MC, V. M Můstek/Muzeum

Hidden in a passage, a half-block from Wenceslas Square, Pizza Coloseum remains a locals kind of place that is well-known to shopkeepers and college students. The large U-shaped dining room is a boisterous space, where both couples and groups easily integrate. The crisp, thin-crusted pizzas and above-average pastas are well-spiced and well-priced. Spinach tagliatelle with ham and mushrooms is typical of the arms-length list of pastas. Equally pizza-intensive, the menu covers all the hits and is augmented by a particularly good selection of local wines.

Zlatá Ulička Pizzeria

(Golden Lane) Petrská 21, Praha 1 – New Town. Tel. 02/231-7015. Kitchen open Mon-Fri 830am-1045pm, Sat-Sun 11am-1045pm. Main courses 100-250 Kč. No cards. M Náměstí Republiky/Florenc

Nine-to-fivers from the adjacent Prague Business Center are still this bistro's bread and butter. But this place has also become a hip diners' hangout on summer evenings, and weekends year-round. It's the windows that do it; gloriously large sliding glass panels that open onto a cobbled sidewalk and a beautiful ancient square. The food, basic Yugo-Italian, is also bright, featuring smart pizzas, a couple of steaks and a dozen pastas tossed with meats and vegetables. And the price is light. There's a full bar and a small selection of Moravian and Italian wines.

Knedlíky Culture

Dumplings (*Knedlíky*), the culinary glue that binds all Czechs, come in several varieties. Most common is the **flour dumpling** (*houskový knedlík*). Dough is loafed into the shape of a small baguette, boiled, and sliced into patties. The result is a tasteless white bread that's used to soak up soups and gravy at almost every meal. The typical plate of roast pork and cabbage is accompanied by four of these fluffy patties.

Dangerously dense, **potato dumplings** (*bramborový knedlík*) are only marginally more flavorful then their bland white bread cousins. You can often request these instead of flour dumplings, or order them půl na půl (half and half).

Harder to find is the **bacon-fat dumpling** (*špekový knedlík*), a puck of mid-viscosity that's flecked with bits of brown pork.

Occasionally you may come across a menu announcing **fruit dumplings** (*ovocný knedlík*). These rare treats are small, round fruit-filled balls that are usually only made at home. The proper way to eat them is under an avalanche of powdered sugar.

4 PORCE

PUb FOOd

Czech pub fare, the nation's soul food, includes roast pork, grilled trout and baked duck, plus the ubiquitous dumplings and cabbage. It's not gourmet; it's the food of the people. And compared to what's served in most European pubs, it's some of the best beer-ballast going.

At the most genuine places, a simple meal will be under 150 Kč, and a half liter of beer will rarely top 25 Kč. Outside the city center prices drop 20% to 25%. If you're not up for a full meal, check-out the beer snacks, which usually include pickled sausages (*utopenci*), pickled fish (*zavináč*), head cheese (*tlačenka*), and a very stinky cheese known simply as "beer cheese" (*pivní sýr*).

The pubs listed below are especially known for their food.

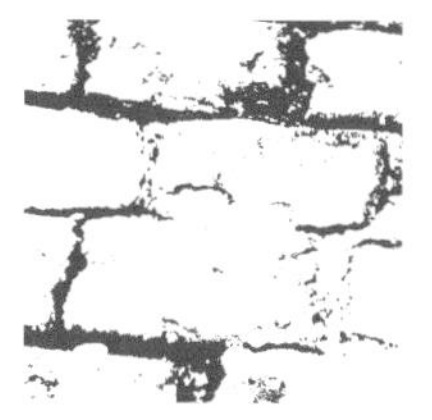

U Nováka

V Jirchárích 2, Praha 1 – New Town. No phone. Kitchen open Mon-Fri 11am-11pm, Sat noon-1030pm, Sun noon-9pm. Main courses 75-100 Kč. No cards. *Ⓜ Národní Třída*

U Nováka is a sanitized, almost Disneyfied, version of an authentic Czech pub. Owned by TV Nova, the tavern is meant to resemble a pub that was the star of the network's sitcom "Hospoda" (Pub). A kind of Peach Pit for adults, U Nováka serves excellent beer and tasty food at exceptionally low prices. The goulash with fried diced potatoes (*Templářský flamendr s cmundou*), and cheese-stuffed chicken breast (*Kuřecí prsíčka plněná*) are hands-down favorites. So what if it's cheerful, clean and relatively smokeless? This pub doesn't suck.

James Joyce Pub

Liliová 10, Praha 1 – Old Town. Tel. 02/2424-8793. Kitchen open daily 930am–11pm. Reservations not accepted. Main Courses 250–300 Kč. AE, MC, V. Wheelchair access. M Staroměstská

A dead-ringer for any number of pubs in Belfast, James Joyce doubles as the embassy to Eire, packed with Irish daily-breaders, here to loosen their chokers in this little bit of all right. Actor Dennis Hopper made this place his regular haunt when he was in town, and our spies also cornered Liam Neeson here. The food's so good that visiting Irish complain it isn't authentic. Irish stew, the pub's signature dish, is chunked-out with beef, onions, carrots and potatoes and served with plenty of fresh bread. The menu boasts that their steak is the "best fillet in Prague," and it's not far from the truth. Cut thick and paired with a robust sauce, it makes a memorable meal. Irish breakfasts, served all day, lard up the plate with sausages, fried eggs and black toast. Draught Guinness and whiskey are the drinks of choice but, like most offerings here, they are prohibitively expensive for most Czechs.

U Vejvodů

Jilská 4, Praha 1 – Old Town. Tel. 2421-9205. Reservations recommended. Open Sun–Thurs 11am–midnight, Fri–Sat 11am–2am, Sun 11am–midnight; kitchen closes one hour earlier. Main courses 100–200 Kč. No cards. M Národní Třída

After languishing for years under an arcade of scaffolding, this ancient pub received a complete makeover and has become a terrific Pilsner Urquell beer hall. Walk past the wood-and-brass front bar and descend the stairs into an enormous rear drinking room that's reminiscent of a Hollywood film set; a high-volume space in which waiters laden with half-liters dodge between tightly packed tables. Between the top-of-the-line beer and a full menu of Czech favorites, only the price is light.

Kolkovna

V Kolkovně 8, Praha 1 – Old Town. Tel. 2481-9701. Reservations recommended. Open Sun–Thurs 11am–midnight, Fri–Sat 11am–2am, Sun 11am–midnight; kitchen closes one hour earlier. Main courses 100–250 Kč. MC, V. M Staroměstská

One of our favorite places in Old Town, Kolkovna is a great-looking pub/restaurant that's nice enough to take a date. While most other beer halls are smoky, manly affairs, this light and bright space heralds a new breed of drinkery. In addition to beer they offer a full bar that even includes cocktails and blender drinks. And the food, which ranges from salads to steaks, duck and ribs is both delicious and plentiful. Kolkovna is a Pilsner Urquell pub, which means that special attention is paid to the beer, which is some of the best in the land, served at terrific prices. With so much going for it, reservations are definitely recommended.

Novoměstský Pivovar

(New Town Brewery) Vodičkova 20, Praha 1 – New Town. Tel. 02/2223-2448. Reservations recommended. Kitchen open Mon-Sat 1130am-1130pm, Sun noon-10pm. Main courses 130-250 Kč. AE, MC, V. M Můstek

Novoměstský Pivovar is a foreigner's perfect dream of Prague: a boisterous, labyrinthine cellar, decorated with Czech kitsch, and populated with happy-looking blue-collar workers and wide-eyed foreigners. When friends from abroad come to Prague we often find ourselves entertaining them here, lapping up huge portions of Czech comfort food and massive quantities of home-brewed beer. Not only is Novoměstský Pivovar one of only two microbreweries in the city center (the other is U Fleků), it's also one of the finest restaurants of the genre, serving up all the Bohemian hits in a festive pub atmosphere. Nothing on the menu can be mistaken for "fusion" or "nouvelle." It's just excellent straight-forward food from various parts of the Old Country. The kitchen has created several combination plates that literally give you a taste of Bohemia or Moravia, with mixtures of roast duck, smoked meats, sausages and, of course, dumplings. *Koleno*—pork knee—is the specialty of the house. Served on a cutting board and stabbed with a steak knife, the dish's appearance is just one step removed from caveman. Carve through the fat, and you'll experience some of the most sublimely tender meat you've ever tasted. The Pivovar's light and dark lagers are excellent, and waiters will automatically replenish your glasses, until you say "ne."

U Medvídků

(The Bear Cubs) Na Perštýně 7, Praha 1 – Old Town. Tel. 02/2421-1916. Reservations recommended for large groups. Kitchen open Mon-Sat 1130am-11pm, Sun noon-10pm. Main courses 90-250 Kč. AE, MC, V. M Národní Třída

Great food, a central location, long hours and plenty of chairs puts this place high on our list of recommendations. A beer hall since the 15th century, U Medvídků is known for excellent Budvar on tap and fine meaty meals at almost pre-Revolution prices. The best of a long list of entrees are venison in a thick fruity brown sauce, wild duck legs with red cabbage and dumplings, and beef in gravy atop a large potato pancake. As in most pubs, seating is at large wooden tables that are meant to be shared with other guests. One of these—the one closest to the beer taps—is reserved for regulars: graying members of the Old School who wouldn't think of diluting their alcohol with food. Many locals avoid weekends, when the pub swells with foreigners and an accordionist plays. After entering the pub's front door, turn right, into the larger pub space that's both more jovial and less expensive than the restaurant to your left.

fASTER fOOD

Country Life

Melantrichova 15, Praha 1 – Old Town. Tel. 2421-3366. Kitchen Open Sun 11am-830pm, Mon-Thurs 9am-830pm, Fri 9am-4pm. Closed Sat. Main courses 70-150 Kč. No cards. Ⓜ Můstek

This Seventh-Day Adventist answer to Krishna-run Govinda (*see* below) sells meatless, cholesterol-free stews, bakes and stir-frys, as well as sandwiches, thick soups and thin pizzas to either eat-in or take away. Cheap and fresh are the twin attractions that make this self-service buffet one of the most popular lunch spots in the neighborhood. Tofu goulash anyone? No matter that most of the meals have the same consistency and a uniform shade of brown.

Govinda

Soukenická 27, Praha 1 – New Town. Tel. 02/2481-6631. Kitchen open Mon-Sat 11am-5pm. Complete meal 70 Kč. No cards. Ⓜ Náměstí Republiky

What luck for us that Hare Krishnas believe it's such a *mitzvah* to serve good, nutritional and cheap food to the unbelieving masses. Popular with journalists from nearby *MF Dnes* newspaper and stingy working people everywhere, Govinda's tasty vegetarian buffet is an all-you-can-eat Indian affair that includes vegetables in curry sauce, rice, lentil soup, salad and chutney, all of which, thank Krishna, is dished without religious dogma. Most of the food is grown on the Krishna's organic farm in eastern Bohemia. A ground-floor tea shop sells juice, tea, decaffeinated coffee and two-dozen kinds of peculiar homemade sweets. Lines can be long at lunch time, but Govinda is great after 2 or 3pm.

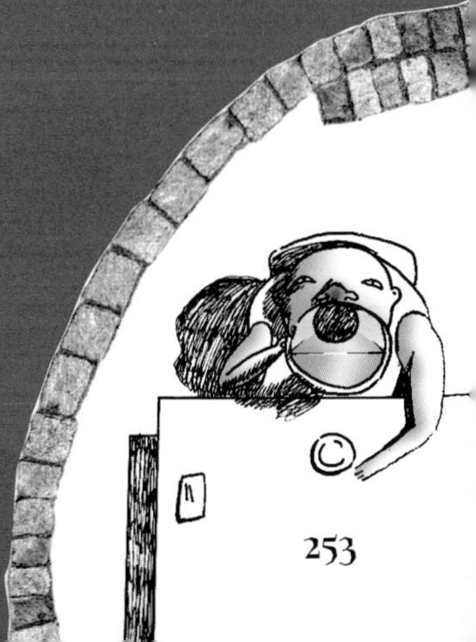

Obchod Čerstvých Uzenin

(Fresh Smoked-Meat Store) Václavské nám. 36, Praha 1 – New Town. Tel. 02/2422-7439. Kitchen open daily 7am-7pm. Main courses 30-70 Kč. No cards. Můstek

Plunge into Czech carnivore culture at this high temple of beef, pork, poultry and lard. A traditional stand-up buffet, this meatery is a palace for the people, serving the freshest cuts of cooked meat, sliced to order onto single-serving plates. Servers in grease-stained whites, who have seen much and forgotten little, dish out boiled, roasted and smoked meats to a strange mix of construction workers and street urchins. And there are usually several types of goulash on offer. If you're lucky you can get the world's leanest, tastiest cow tongue sided with dollops of mustard and horseradish. You may also find some of the juiciest, most aromatic smoked chicken. Of course, Pilsner beer is in the cooler at all times.

Praha Tamura

Havelská 6, Praha 1 – Old Town. Tel. 02/2423-2056. Kitchen open Mon-Sat 11am-11pm. Main courses 100-500 Kč. AE, MC, V. Můstek

A dead-ringer for any number of noodle shops in Tokyo, Tamura is a quirky little place decorated with matte black tables and chairs, white walls and plastic reproductions of every dish on the menu. A loyal clientele fills the small bright dining room with noodle slurps and chopstick clacks. *Udon* (thick wheat noodles) and *soba* (narrow buckwheat linguine) are the main choices here. Both are served either hot or cold in a variety of soups and sauces that veteran noodle-slurpers might find too bland and too thin. A variety of tempuras is also available and it all seems oh so Japanese—except for the prices.

U Bakaláře

(At the Baccalaureate) Celetná 13, Praha 1 – Old Town. No Phone. Kitchen open Mon-Fri 9am-7pm, Sat-Sun 11am-7pm. Open-face sandwiches (chlebíčky) 10-15 Kč; crepes (palačinky) 30 Kč. No cards. Náměstí Republiky

When your stomach is empty and your wallet is not far behind, U Bakaláře comes to the rescue with an excellent selection of little open-face sandwiches (*chlebíčky*) and spinach crepes (*palačinky*), displayed under refrigerated glass. Famous for low prices, bullet service and a thoroughly frills-free atmosphere, this student buffet, hidden in plain sight on the ground floor of a Charles University building, is a culinary kindergarten of simple local foods like potato pancakes (*bramboráčky*) and fried cheese (*smaženy sýr*). Few meals ever top 50 Kč. Order at the counter, then fend for a seat.

MEALS AfTER MidNIGHT

In general, there aren't a whole lot of places to relieve late-night munchies. Several restaurants listed above keep their kitchens open after midnight. Many others claim they do, but often close early when customers are few. Check-out **Jáma** (1am), **Kozička** (115am) and **Radost FX** (2–5am). Other restaurants open very late, or 24/seven, are listed below.

Gyrossino
Spálená 47, Praha 1 – New Town. No phone. Open Mon-Sat 10am-5am. Gyros 50 Kč. No cards. M Národní Třída
Almost literally a hole in the wall, this divvy take-away is a regular late-night stop for clubbers and other bleary-eyed night crawlers. Conveniently located across from Tesco, at the night-tram locus, this place does brisk business throughout the wee hours. Their stock-in-trade are super-cheap, tasty, overstuffed gyros sandwiches, cut from a huge spit of chicken, not lamb. They've got awful deep-fried chicken wings too, and vegetarian drunkards love their doughy pizzas. You'll hate yourself in the morning.

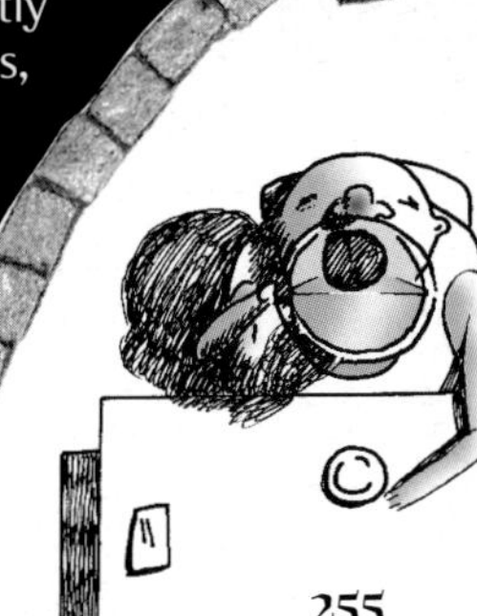

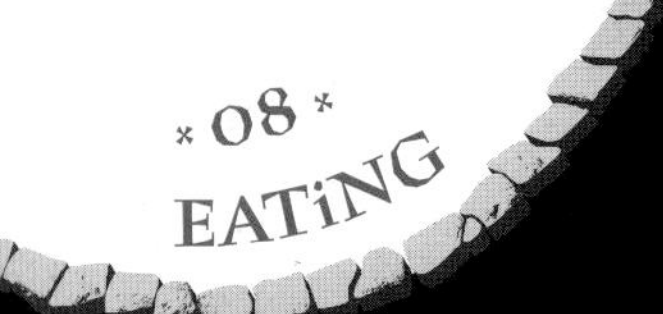

U Zlatého Stromu

(At the Golden Tree) Karlova 6, Praha 1 – Old Town. Tel. 02/2222-0441. Kitchen open nonstop. Main courses 100–200 Kč. AE, MC, V. M Staroměstská

Because it's the only place in the center serving full Czech meals all night long, U Zlatého Stromu is the best place in Old Town for vampire dining. The actual dinners look very little like the photographs printed on the menu, but the selection is extensive, the prices are right and the food is fine. All the late-night glitterati have sat on this restaurant's padded chairs and benches, including Italian tenor Luciano Pavarotti, who stopped by for an after-concert munch. Our tip: the cheese-filled pork pocket "Jan Hus" and other roast meat dishes are far better than the pasty pastas.

Roma Due

Liliová 18, Praha 1 – Old Town. Tel. 02/0606-287943. Kitchen open nonstop. Main courses 100–150 Kč. No cards. M Staroměstská

A good place for a late-nite snack, this woody pizzeria serves very decent pies and sub-par pastas all the way to sunrise. Never crowded, but always full, Roma Due is the perfect place for an after-hours chill-out. Fitted with mismatched wooden tables gleaned from second-hand shops, the low-key ground-floor dining room is augmented by a larger cellar space that accommodates the overflow.

BREAkfAST & BRUNCh

Unless it's Saturday or Sunday, finding breakfast in Prague can be a problem. So few Czechs eat the "most important meal of the day" that even the local Golden Arches refuses to stock McMuffins (though you can get a Big Mac and a beer at 7am!).

Most of the hotels listed in this book include some kind of morning bite with their rates, though it's seldom more than the roll and coffee that French and Germans mistake as a meal.

Several of the city's top restaurants, all of which are detailed above, serve excellent weekend brunches, often accompanied by live music:

Bellevue offers an extensive all-you-can eat buffet (Saturday and Sunday 11am to 330pm) matched with all-you-can-drink sparkling wine and mimosas. They charge around 800 Kč per person.

On warm weekend mornings (11am to 3pm) there is no better place for a leisurely brunch than the outdoor terrace at **Pálffy Palác**. The 350 Kč menus tend towards light-and-healthful with fruit and croissants followed by smoked salmon with dill, spinach-filled crepes and rosemary roasted potatoes.

Radost FX's quintessential American brunch (Saturday 1130am-3pm and Sunday 1030am-3pm) includes omelets, huevos rancheros, waffles, French toast and bagels. The a la carte menu runs from 80 Kč to 150 Kč. Unless you arrive very early or very late, it can be hard to find a seat.

The **Globe** also serves a special weekend menu (from 10am to 4pm) that includes poached egg dishes, pancakes, musli and crispy hash browns.

Obecní Dům Kavárna (*see* Cafés & Tea Rooms, below) has become one of the best breakfast places in town (daily 730am to 10am). There's a choice of several set morning meals: the Milk Breakfast includes cornflakes with milk, yogurt, honey and fruit salad; the Czech Breakfast is made of meats and cheeses; and the Breakfast "Flamendr" involves pickled sausage slices, marinated fish, and a glass of Pilsner beer.

If you want a really big brunch during the week (daily 6am to 1030am), head for the **Hilton Hotel Buffet**, at the Hilton Atrium Hotel, Pobřezní 1, Praha 8 (tel. 2484-1111). The drill is simple: you pay about 600 Kč per person, heap-on lots of goodies from the buffet, grab a table and eat till you burst. It's a true test of willpower.

Everyone knows that Prague is a pub land, but there are also plenty of leaf-and-bean places to choose from. About half of Prague's cafés are created in the Viennese mold, with little on the menu except for coffee and cakes. The others are more bohemian (with a small "b"), catering to brooding young artists and intellectuals with full bars and simple meals.

Most places don't brew American-style coffee, and most waiters never heard of decaf. Espresso and Cappuccino are the primary drinks of choice, along with Turkish coffee (*Turecká Káva*), which has muddy grounds on the bottom, and Viennese Coffee (*Vídeňská Káva*), which has a thick head of cream on top.

Archa Café

Na poříčí 26, Praha 1 – New Town. Tel. 02/232-4149. Kitchen open Mon-Fri 9am-1030pm, Sat 10am-10pm, Sun 1-10pm. No cards. M Florenc

Archa's contemporary design, built with giant windows and lots of chrome, reflects the avant character of the theater it's attached to. A popular pre-concert meeting place for black-clad youth, the café has also attracted the likes of John Cale, Min Tanaka and the members of The Residents, who spent several months rehearsing a show in Prague. The house drink, Kava Archa, is spiked with Galliano. Other coffees are also available, along with teas, juices and a full bar.

Blatouch

(Marsh Marigold) Vězeňská 4, Praha 1 – Old Town. Tel. 02/232-8643. Open Mon-Fri noon-1am, Sat 2pm-2am, Sun 2pm-midnight. No cards. M Staroměstská

This cozy Old Town coffeehouse appeals to film school students and other earnest youngsters who sit here for hours carousing with friends over hot mulled wine and tequila sunrises. From the street, the view inside is obscured by an easel shouldering a large Classicist painting and the reflections of a case full of books. Inside, there's jazz music, and tiny latte tables on two levels. Snag a seat upstairs if you can. The frightful food is literally for starving artists only.

Caffe Nuovo

Staroměstské náměstí 5, Praha 1 – Old Town. Tel. 02/2481-0512. Open daily 830-midnight. M Staroměstská

This cafe's ground-zero location, directly behind the Jan Hus statue on Old Town Square, makes one suspect this is a tourist trap. To be sure, there are plenty of tourists here, but Caffe Nuovo is great anyway. It's a sexy and stylish place, set with Philippe Starke chairs on steely stone floors. The coffee is strong, tea is served in small pots, and their toasted mozzarella-and-tomato focaccia sandwiches are the best in town. Grab one of the complimentary newspapers hanging on the rear rack and watch Old Town Square pass by.

Evropa Café

Václavské nám. 25, Praha 1 – New Town. Tel. 02/2422-8117. Kitchen open daily 7am-11pm. Main Courses 285-320 Kč. AE, MC, V. M Můstek

Hailing from the beginning of the last century, the Evropa Café remains beautifully unrestored and inelegantly run by a management and staff that hasn't changed much since the communist era. Built in 1906, Prague's finest art nouveau café now boasts a faded elegance evocative of Mucha murals and turn-of-the-century cruise liners. The tea dance atmosphere is particularly popular with gays, though the casual visitor might never notice. The pianist is awful and service is worse, but both seem integral to this particular cultural experience. There's a small music charge after 3pm.

Chez Marcel

Haštalská 12, Praha 1 – Old Town. Tel. 02/231-5676. Kitchen open Mon-Fri 11am-11pm, Sat-Sun 11am-11pm. Main Courses 100-300 Kč. No cards. M Staroměstská

The perfect place to order Pernod, smoke a Gauloise and eat a hard-boiled egg, Chez Marcel attracts a young French embassy crowd and the occasional Francophile, like Václav Havel or Sigourney Weaver. The Chez is a comfortable place to linger with a newspaper in front of broad plate glass windows overlooking a quiet Old Town square. Both a café and a bistro, Chez Marcel is equally at home serving a simple café au lait or a feast that includes quiche Lorraine and steak frites And their hand-cut, flash fried potatoes are some of the best in town.

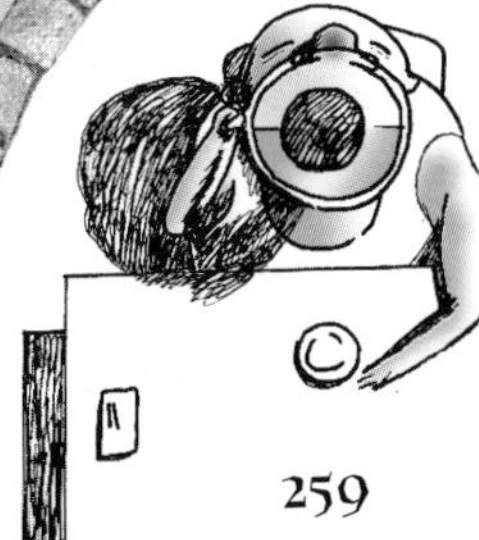

Dobrá Čajovna

(The Good Teahouse) Boršov 2, Praha 1 – Old Town. Tel. 02/2222-1324. Open daily 2pm-midnight. Teas 30-80 Kč. No cards. M Národní Třída

Tea is not just a drink, it's a way of life in this exceedingly genteel space, where patrons sit on pillows and soft-spoken waiters are summoned with little table bells. Recklessly low lighting and ethereal New Age music complete an overall experience that is very much a journey to an alternative reality. Dozens of teas are served, including several hard-to-find varieties. Darjeeling, the house specialty, is available as the sweeter "young-cut," and the bolder "second-cut." Gyokuro, a Japanese green, and Jynan Mao Feng, a Chinese black, are the most popular choices. Pull the doorbell chain and wait patiently to be admitted.

Branch: Václavské nám. 14, Praha 1 (tel. 2423-1480). Open Mon-Sat 10am-9pm, Sun 3-9pm. No cards. M Můstek

× 08 ×
EATiNG

Imperial Cafe

Na Poříčí 15, Praha 1 – New Town. Tel. 02/231-6012. Reservations accepted. Kitchen open Mon-Thurs 9am-11pm, Fri-Sat 9am-midnight, Sun 9am-10pm. Main courses 100-200 Kč. No cards. M Náměstí Republiky

Shabby-chic without the chic, the Imperial is a dingy Art Nouveau extravaganza that wows us for its throwback atmosphere, socialist-era service and impossibly mediocre kitchen. Don't eat here. Instead, stop in for tea or beer, admire the faded tile-wrapped interior, have a philosophical debate, catch up on some Kafka, and pray they never reconstruct this place and jack up the prices.

Obecní Dům Kavárna

(The Municipal House) nám. Republiky 5, Praha 1 – Old Town. Tel. 02/2200-2763. Open daily 730am-11pm. Small meals 100-230 Kč; fixed-price breakfast 170 Kč. AE, MC, V. M Náměstí Republiky

Obecni Dům reopened in 1997 after an enormous reconstruction that returned every gilded lantern, carved statue and inlaid chair to museum-quality art deco decadence. The result is a jewel of architectural "flamboasting." The starched atmosphere plays especially well to visiting Viennese, and the bright lighting deters couples on covert escapades. But the room is unique and the coffee is good, as are the little sandwiches and few simple warm meals that are offered. Ask to see the Tortes Trolley, full of Austrian-style cakes and pastries, wheeled around by vested waiters in lieu of menus. For more about the Municipal House, see Chapter 4/The Top Sights.

Slavia Café

Smetanovo nábř. 2, Praha 1 – Old Town. Tel. 02/2421-8493. Kitchen open daily 9am-11pm. Small main courses 90-110 Kč. AE, MC, V. M Národni Třída

Once known as a café where dissidents congregated, Slavia is so closely linked with the Velvet Revolutionaries that its post-communist reconstruction was an important political and social event. And the café's late-1997 re-opening, after a controversial five-year closure, made international news. Situated on a window-wrapped corner, across from the National Theater, the new Slavia is once again a great place to waste time, linger over coffee, juice or tea, and pick-up a light meal. Their goulash is particularly excellent, and, like the rest of the short menu, is created by the same chef who heads the fancy kitchens of Parnas next door. There's a full bar and nobody minds if you wile away an entire day over a single glass of Becherovka. Absinthe, which is also on the menu at all times, is celebrated with a famous "green fairy" oil painting on the back wall. The adjacent Slavia Bar is a swoony place for a tryst, with comfortable booths, bedroom lighting, and a well-stocked bar.

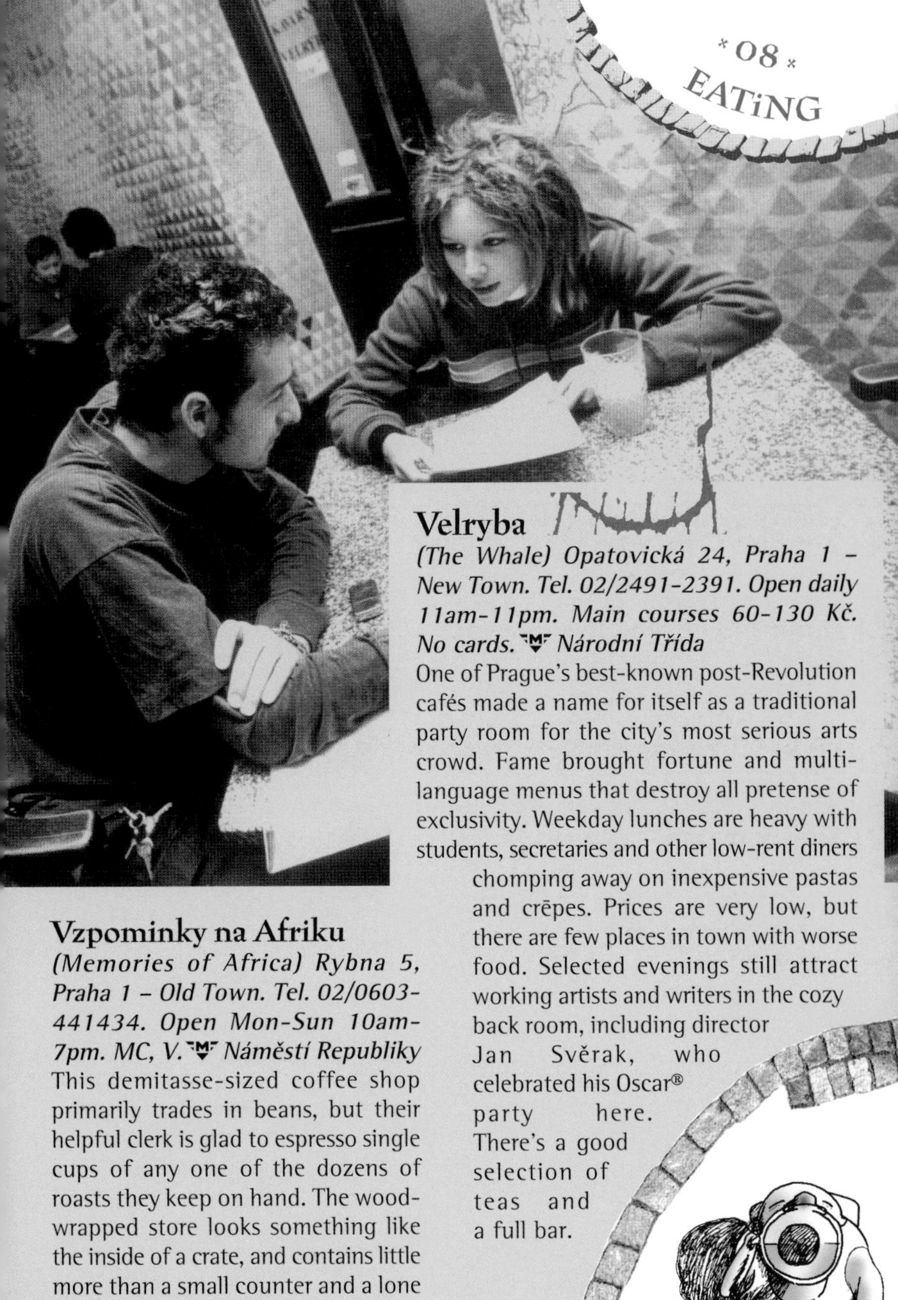

Velryba

(The Whale) Opatovická 24, Praha 1 – New Town. Tel. 02/2491-2391. Open daily 11am–11pm. Main courses 60–130 Kč. No cards. Ⓜ Národní Třída

One of Prague's best-known post-Revolution cafés made a name for itself as a traditional party room for the city's most serious arts crowd. Fame brought fortune and multi-language menus that destroy all pretense of exclusivity. Weekday lunches are heavy with students, secretaries and other low-rent diners chomping away on inexpensive pastas and crēpes. Prices are very low, but there are few places in town with worse food. Selected evenings still attract working artists and writers in the cozy back room, including director Jan Svěrak, who celebrated his Oscar® party here. There's a good selection of teas and a full bar.

Vzpominky na Afriku

(Memories of Africa) Rybna 5, Praha 1 – Old Town. Tel. 02/0603-441434. Open Mon–Sun 10am–7pm. MC, V. Ⓜ Náměstí Republiky

This demitasse-sized coffee shop primarily trades in beans, but their helpful clerk is glad to espresso single cups of any one of the dozens of roasts they keep on hand. The wood-wrapped store looks something like the inside of a crate, and contains little more than a small counter and a lone table with four chairs and a sugar bowl. It's not the easiest place to find an empty seat, but this place has the best coffee in town.

bAkERiES & food MARkETS

Bakeshop Praha

V kolkovně 2, Praha 1 – Old Town. Tel. 02/231-6823. Open daily 7am-7pm. No cards. Staroměstská

We can only talk about this upscale Old Town bakery in superlatives. The very best breads, cakes, croissants and quiches in Prague consistently emerge from this top take-away shop with a few counter stools. From designer-tomato salad and focaccia sandwiches to decadent brownies and cakes-by-the-slice, this is a gourmet's paradise. Yet, prices are so low they make you wish you lived nearby.

Fruits de France

Jindrišská 9, Praha 1 – New Town. Tel. 02/2422-0304. Open Mon-Wed and Fri 930am-630pm, Thurs 1130am-630pm, Sat 930am-1pm. No cards. Můstek

After the Revolution, Fruits de France became the first store in Prague to import Western European-quality fruits and vegetables. A veritable *tre colore* salad in this land of root vegetables, this little shop has endeared itself to the hearts and homes of expat pioneers. The store remains a great place for top-quality produce, cheese and wine.

Havelský trh

Havelská, Praha 1 – Old Town. No phone. Open Mon-Fri 8am-6pm, Sat 7am-6pm. No cards. Staroměstská

After the fall of communism, the excellent Havelský trh produce market reopened adjacent to one of Old Town's busiest pedestrian thoroughfares. This ancient farmers market is full of stalls selling the best fruits and vegetables from the Czech countryside and beyond. On Sundays the street becomes a tourist-oriented souvenir strip.

Paneria Pekařství

Valentinská (at Kaprova St), Praha 1 – Old Town. Tel. 02/2482-7912. Open daily 7am-10pm. Sandwiches 30-100 Kč; cakes, marmalades, jams, 50-150 Kč. No cards. M Staroměstská

Although it can't hold a candle to the American-owned Bakeshop Praha, the quickly-expanding Paneria chain is one of the best Czech bakers around. People pop in here for everything from fresh-baked loaves of bread to freshly-made sandwiches, sausage rolls and pizza squares. Increasingly, Paneria is finding its niche as a fast-food snack shop; a great place for a spinach-and-cheese pastry that will hold you until the next dumpling dinner.

Branches: Bělohorská 25, Praha 6 (tel. 3335-2960); Seifertova 39, Praha 3 (tel. 2271-3424); Vítězná 15 (Újezd), Praha 5 (tel. 533-401); Bělehradská 71, Praha 2 (tel. 2251-9140); Křížovnická 12, Praha 1 (tel. 2481-8941).

Tesco

Národní třída 26, Praha 1 – New Town. Tel. 02/2422-7971. Open Mon-Fri 8am-9pm, Sat-Sun 9am-8pm. AE, MC, V. M Národní Třída

The basement level of this multi-story department store houses the best supermarket in town. There's nothing really special about it, except that its got a full range of foods that almost guarantees you'll find what you're looking for. For fruits and vegetables, head to the open-air produce market located behind the store.

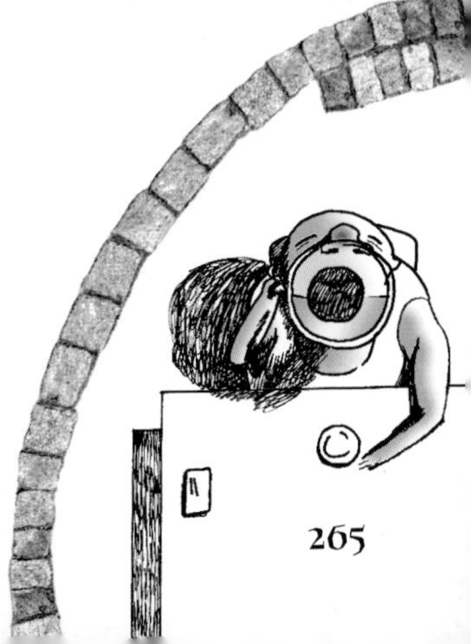

×09× ENTERTAiNiNG
NiGhTLIfE

They say that size matters, and it does: being small has everything to do with this city's great nightlife. Beer is served by the half-liter, but that's the only thing about pint-sized Prague that's larger than London, New York or LA. As far as bars and clubs are concerned, there aren't an awful lot of places to choose from, but most are so close to one another that you can easily floss in and out of several in a single night—standard practice for local cluberati. Prague is a sexy place after dark, and stumbling along lamp-lit, cobbled streets from one boozer to the next can be as fun and wonderful as arriving there.

Prague's pubs are as old as the cobblestones, but bars and lounges are distinctly post-Revolution phenomena. Opened in 1992, Jo's in Malá Strana was the first. Now there are dozens of beer bars and cocktail clubs, though that's still far too few for a city of 1.2 million. The limited number of party places has the positive effect of making Prague's nightlife a relatively intimate affair. Even those who are here for a short stay will see familiar faces after making the rounds a few nights in a row.

With few exceptions, Prague's pubs and bars don't accept credit cards. But, in a city where a big beer is so cheap it's almost free, cards hardly seem to matter. And, yeah, we know we say some nasty things about some of the places below, but we like something about every establishment included here. Really.

As for "serious" music and dance, we can't think of any other small city in the world that supports so many superb companies. In Prague there are two grand operas, three major orchestras and even a decent ballet. And almost a dozen chamber orchestras perform nightly in churches and other venues all around town. Sure, the most famous players have vacated their chairs to pursue bigger bucks elsewhere, but while Prague is short on star power, the benches are incredibly deep with talent.

To find out what's happening before you get to town, check-out avantguide.com. Once you arrive, head to a newsstand for the current week's *Prague Post*, which always has good mainstream listings. *Culture in Prague*, a pocket-sized monthly sold in bookshops, is even more comprehensive. For the best alternative happenings, find a free copy of the monthly magazine *Think* at Jo's, Glenn's, Casa Blů or many of the other bars listed below. Other good gig guides are *Fan*, a large, bi-weekly poster that's plastered onto public street columns, and the bilingual *Doměsta (Downtown)*, a cinema, theater and club guide available free at most bars and movie houses.

Banana Cafe

Štupartská, Praha 1 – Old Town. Tel. 232-4801. Open daily 8pm-2am. Ⓜ Staroměstská/Náměstí Republiky

Banana Cafe, located above La Provence restaurant, is a fun, colorful and thoroughly canned pick-up bar with paid bar-top dancers and occasional drag shows (ohmygod!). There are few tables which encourages mingling. Most nights it's standing-room-only with nouveau riche Italians and the platinum-blond, Wonderbra-wearing Czech girls who love them. Physically, Banana Cafe is a nice place, with a beautiful bar, decent tapas and an unbeatable location two blocks east of Old Town Square. While women won't necessarily find Mr. Right here, they can surely smile themselves into a drink from any number of Euroboys. Be forewarned: Some regulars say this bar is so incestuous that having sex with someone you meet here is like fucking yourself—twice.

Barock

Pařížská 24, Praha 1 – Old Town. Tel. 232-9221. Open Mon-Wed 830am-1am, Thurs-Fri 830am-2am, Sat-Sun 10am-2am. Ⓜ Staroměstská

Opened by the same Scandihooligans who started the excellent Kampa Park restaurant, this outstanding cafe/bar is a popular poseur joint for celebutants and the cell phone set who come here to eat, drink and be very. In Stockholm there are dozens of places like this; in Prague, it's one of the best-looking games in town. Barock is a fairly small place, and excellent sightlines mean that you can see everyone else from almost every seat in the house. In summer, the entire glass front folds open and tables sprawl onto the sidewalk. The pan-Asian menu includes Thai soups, Peking-style duck and even sushi.

Blue Light

Josefská 1, Praha 1 – Malá Strana. Tel. 5753-3126. Open daily 6pm-3am. Ⓜ Malostranská

One of the best bars in Malá Strana, Blue Light is a clubby two-room space that's almost entirely patronized by locals. Although it's situated on the ground floor, the cavern-like interior does it's best to mimic a basement. The jazz posters which cling to these aged walls allude to the genre of live music that's performed here on Tuesdays and Thursdays from 730pm-10pm. At other times the tunes are all over the map, emanating from a terrific sound system that never overpowers the conversationalists. We love this place.

Bugsy's

Pařížská 10 (entrance on Kostečná), Praha 1 – Old Town. Tel. 232-9943. Open daily 7pm-2am. Ⓜ Staroměstská

Bugsy's was one of the first upscale watering holes in Prague, and it remains one of the few in this genre. It's packed nightly with Versace-wearing locals who don't seem to realize that in any other city this bar would be struggling for customers. The hook here is a cocktail menu as thick as *War and Peace*, offering everything from Pink Ladies to Prairie Oysters, a ghastly liquid sushi spiced with Tabasco and garnished with a raw quail egg. For foreigners, Bugsy's provides a terrific cultural study: a front row chair to the nouveau riche beginnings of post-communist civilization. The seating is awkward, the music is all wrong, and the kaleidoscopic cocktails epitomize style over substance. Enjoy a drink, ogle and move on.

Érra

Konviktská 11, Praha 1 – Old Town. Tel. 2222-0568. Open daily 10am-midnight. Ⓜ Národní Třída

Érra is located on a small Old Town backstreet that, until 1989, was occupied by the StB or *Státní bezpečnost*, the hated secret police. It's a common assumption that a few StB officers still work around here but it's unlikely that any agents hang-out in this quirky, gay-friendly lounge; a funky bi-level space with Brady Bunch-on-acid decor that borrows liberally from the worst stylistic excesses of the 1970s. Warhol would have loved the amoeba-shaped tables and chairs that are painted the colors of the Partridge Family bus. Because you're disco clothes will match the decor perfectly, Érra is the perfect pre-club meeting place.

The Last Resort

Dlouhá 7, Praha 1 – Old Town. Tel. 2481-8320. Open Mon-Thurs 11am-midnight, Fri 11am-1am, Sat noon-1am, Sun noon-midnight. AE, MC, V. Ⓜ Staroměstská

The Last Resort is what a Czech pub would look like if it weren't owned by Czechs: quality wood furnishings, clean and un-smoky, all with excellent local beer on tap. There's even above-average bar food, served until 11pm. Occupying a great window-wrapped corner in Old Town, you can easily scope out the action inside before committing yourself to walk through the door. And despite its name, nobody we know ends their night here. Quite to the contrary; The Last Resort is a great place to start your journey when trolling around Prague on a night of intemperance.

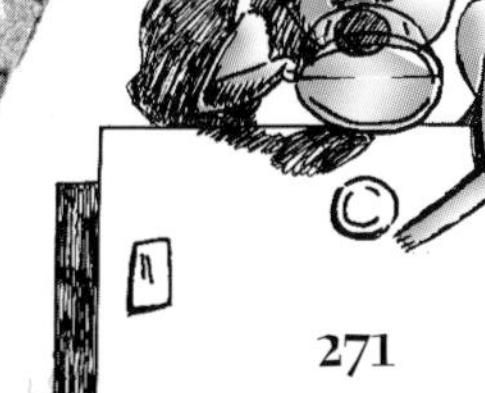

The Red Room

Křemencova 17, Praha 1 – New Town. Tel. 2491-6047. Open Mon-Sat 11am-3am, Sun 11am-midnight. MC, V. Národní Třída/Karlovo náměstí

Inspired by the lounge of the same name in San Francisco, this burgundy bar is known for good cocktails, excellent vodka infusions, a tasty bar menu, fine tunes, and one of the best bar staffs in the city. The wooden tables and chairs are not quite cozy enough to install yourself for an entire night, but they are the perfect place to wile away a few hours with friends. The adjacent bar scene is best during special events; like Ladies Night, when the risk of attending a sausage fest is minimized. Situated in a bustling nightlife neighborhood behind the National Theater, The Red Room is a great stop to add to your crawl.

Le Clan

Balbínova 23. – Vinohrady. No phone. Open Sun-Wed 10pm-5am, Thurs-Sat 10pm-10am.

You've got to know about this after-hours club that just gets going at 3am and stays open until long past sunrise. It's really best on Fridays and Saturdays, but something's often happening here on other nights as well, especially if there was a huge rave or party somewhere else in the city earlier in the evening. Don't worry if you don't see anyone hanging out at the ground floor bar; the party is downstairs, where you'll find a second bar plus a lounge space and dance floor. Despite the hour, most of the revelers here are just too amped to go home. Never a cover and no velvet ropes, this is a great place to extend your trip.

Zvonařká

(The Bellmaker) Šafaříkova 1, Praha 2 – Vinohrady. Tel. 2425-1990. Open Mon-Sat 11am-2am, Sun 11am-midnight. M IP Pavlova

Bathed in soft blue lighting, this self-consciously hip bar is a locals-only style spot, situated just out of the center at the top of the Nusle Steps. The single, large room is set with a centerpiece bar and, when busy, is as good for a cozy cocktail as it is for people-watching and partying. Unfortunately, the crowd here can be hit or miss; and when this place is empty it feels as vacant as an airplane hanger. Come summer, the action spills onto one of the biggest terraces in Prague, where private parties are often held and DJs sometimes spin into the wee hours. There's decent food here too. Zvonařká can be hard to find. Consult a good map before heading out.

St. Nicholas Café

Tržiště 10, Praha 1 – Malá Strana. Tel. 5753-0204. Open Mon-Fri noon-1am, Sat-Sun 3pm-1am. M Malostranská

French café meets Jesuit cloister in this impressive semi-subterranean Malá Strana lounge. An ancient cavernous cellar is far from unorthodox for Prague, but an expert design that warms the rosy walls to intimate temperatures makes this cafe one-of-a-kind. St. Nicholas is a very comfortable place to linger, at one of a dozen candle-lit tables or a half-dozen bar stools. The staff is excellent, and the bartenders know how to mix a drink. St. Nick's crowd largely consists of unpretentious creatives and others in their 20s, 30s and 40s, joined by staff from the US and German embassies, both of which are located just up the street.

Tretter's Cocktail Bar

V kolkovně 3, Praha 1 – Old Town. Tel. 2481-1165. Open daily 7pm-3am. M Staroměstská

A knock-off of any number of cocktail bars in Vienna, Tretter's is kind of a swanky place for Prague. From the sophisticated lettering on curtained plate-glass windows, to the suspender-wearing bartenders who shake colorful drinks into Y-shaped glasses, the whole package is designed to look like a cocktail bar is *supposed* to look. Tretter's is as good a spot to take a date as it is to find one. There's usually a few couples who look like they're having a tryst. And the bar scene usually includes several girls in their late-20s waiting to ignore some guy who tries to pick them up. The bottle-spinning bartenders look like they've seen Tom Cruise in Cocktail way too many times, but they pride themselves on knowing how to make almost any drink.

TOP DIVES & EXPAT BARS

La Casa Blu

Kozí 15, Praha 1 – Old Town. Tel. 2481-8270. Open daily 2pm-midnight. Ⓜ Staroměstská

A hidden, downscale retreat for the young and the trendless, Casa Blu is a slightly grungy wood-and-fern bar, minus the ferns. It's a fun, locals kind of place popular with Czechs, Euroyanks, visitors and the occasional movie star. Uma Thurman and Liam Neeson were regulars here when they were in town filming "Les Miserables." There are lots of tables and a small bar scene too. If you arrive after midnight the bar looks like it's shut tight. Ring the bell to the left of the door and someone will let you in.

Le Chateau

Jakubská 2, Praha 1 – Old Town. Tel. 231-6328. Open Mon-Fri noon-3am, Sat 4pm-4am, Sun 4pm-2am. Ⓜ Staroměstská

More than just a stinky bar with crimson walls, Le Chateau is an institution sporting a good sound-system and some of the best lighting in Prague. Now experiencing something of a renaissance, everyone floats through here at some point during the week, making this one of the best late-night scenes in town. It's a colorful fishbowl, containing every skin color and every length of hair—the unifying factor seems to be a desire to get liquored up and lucky. Skunk smokers roll up early to meet with their "travel agents." Later it's workers from other bars and horny locals dropping lines on random tourists who regularly swim by. Beer is the drink of choice, though the bartenders are just capable enough to make simple mixed drinks too. Chateau is best after midnight or 1am.

Jo's Bar

Malostranské nám. 7, Praha 1 – Malá Strana. Tel. 0602/987635. Open daily 11am-4am. Ⓜ Malostranská

Jo's claim to fame is that it was the first North American bar to brave post-Soviet Eastern Europe. The bar extended its proverbial fifteen minutes of celebrity by opening Jo's Garage, a small-but-lively cellar bar/disco that recast this place into one of Malá Strana's best late-night dives. Now under new ownership, Jo's is attracting a bigger mix of locals with discount beer and a foosball table. The crowd, when there is one, is usually relatively sedate. But a good night here can still be a blast.

Marquis De Sade

Templova 8, Praha 1 – Old Town. Tel. 2481-7505. Open daily noon–2am. Staroměstská/Náměstí Republiky

Dig if you will a picture of a 1980s off-campus college bar fitted with lots of functional tables and the most rudimentary trimmings. Beer is cheap, talk is loud, and it's so well located that you can easily stumble home. Much less debauched than its name would imply, the Marquis De Sade is a good place to visit if you actually want to sit down and be with the ones you're with. Because you can easily gun across the single large room, this would be the perfect space for seeing and being seen, if only there were anything worthwhile to look at. When you get booted at closing time, they will kindly give you a plastic cup in which to take the rest of your beer.

U Malého Glena

(At Little Glenn's) Karmelitská 23, Praha 1 – Malá Strana. Tel. 535-8115. Open daily 10am–2am. Malostranská

Publican-turned-bagelmeister Glenn Spicker is an American expat-for-life with a penchant for strong coffee and cool jazz. His Malá Strana pub is one of Prague's best-loved Left Bank institutions, known for good beer, friendly conversation and decent soups, salads and sandwiches, all of which are served until late. Downstairs is a second bar in a diminutive jazz cellar which hosts live bands almost nightly. Glenn sometimes even sits in on the drums.

Zoo Bar

Jilská 18, Praha 1 – Old Town. Tel. 0604/231684. Open daily 6pm–4am. Staroměstská

Visit Zoo Bar to get FUBAR; that's what the owners like to say. But it must be true because every time we descend the steep wooden staircase into this Gothic cellar drinkery we have trouble getting back up again. The Zoo is a simple two-room affair, with a bar up front and a cavernous lounge in back. And the location, between Charles Bridge and Old Town Square, can't be beat. Say "hi" to Aran for us.

DJ BARS

DeLux

Václavské náměstí 4, Praha 1 – New Town. Tel. 9632-5314. Open Mon-Fri 11am-2am, Sat-Sun 6pm-2am. Kitchen open Sun-Thurs 11am-1130pm, Fri-Sat 11am-1am. AE, MC, V. M Můstek

Glenn Spicker's beautiful Thai restaurant/Salsa club is a thoroughly cool Old World space hidden beneath a painstakingly communist building at the foot of Václavské náměstí. Although it's open throughout the week, DeLux rocks hardest on weekends. Designed as a Deco-era dinner club, with padded booths that horse-shoe around a stage and dance floor, DeLux has thoroughly embraced the Latin dance craze that has swept through Prague. Nights here can be sultry affairs. The food is good too, with main courses ranging from 200-500 Kč. Reservations are recommended on Friday and Saturday nights.

Bazaar

Nerudova 40, Praha 1 – Malá Strana. Tel. 9005-4510. Open daily noon-midnight. AE, MC, V. M Malostranská

Opened by the people who brought us La Provence restaurant in Old Town, this Euro-style restaurant/nightspot is one of the most provoking spaces in Prague. Physically, Bazaar is, well, bizarre. A warren of rooms is centered around a main dining room in which seating is on various levels. Sightlines are good, due to strategically placed mirrors angled off the walls, but the food is hardly as memorable as the atmosphere. That's why you should come here for drinks; either in the downstairs bar, with tabletop dancers and thumping pop music, or on the far more romantic and sedate terrace, which is accessed via a giant, stone circular staircase that leads to a large garden just beneath Prague Castle. There's something different happening most every night of the week: singles party on Tuesdays, striptease on Wednesdays and transvestite shows on Thursdays.

* 09 * NiGhTLIfE

Akropolis Bar

Kubelíkova 27, Praha 3 – Žižkov. Tel. 2271-2287. Open daily 7pm-3am. Jiřího z Poděbrad

Bar meets pub in this off-the-beaten-tourist-track hang catering to a healthy mix of tobacco-addicted Czechs and foreigners. The small downstairs techno bar is crammed almost nightly with drinkers and tokers who come here to meet friends and dance to some of the best DJs in the city.

Solidní Nejistota

(Solid Uncertainty) Pštrossova 21, Praha 1 – New Town. Tel. 2491-0593. Open Mon-Fri noon-3am, Sat-Sun 6pm-6am. No cards. Národní Třída

OK, here's the rap: This is a good-looking, red-wrapped bar with bad music that's become a major meat market for locals who listen to the radio station that owns it. Because the big bar stands in the middle of the room, it's easy to catch the eyes of cute customers standing across it. Then there's a small dance floor where soused Czech mates boogie. There are few tourists here. The bartenders serve cheap drinks. And Mondays and Fridays there's usually live music from 730-9pm, after which a DJ spins. Admission is free and reservations are necessary on weekends if you want to get a table. The bar's name, Solid Uncertainty, could refer to any number of things: whether you'll get in the door on weekends, whether you'll ever get served at the sluggish bar, whether that blonde on the dance floor will go home with you....

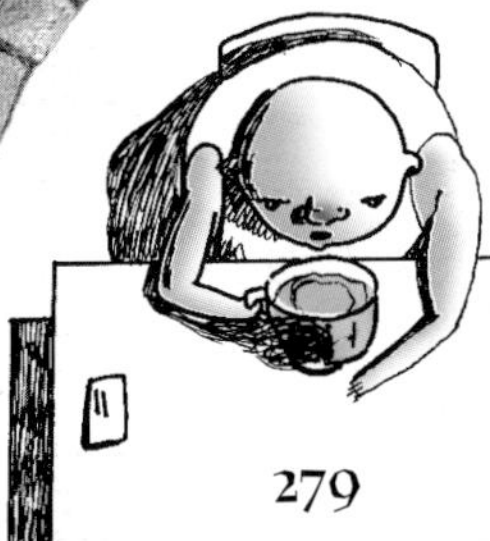

ThE bEST PUBS

What makes a pub "traditional?" In the Czech Republic that title seems to mean minimalist decor, cheap beer and nothing on the walls except white paint and smoke stains. The most authentic are filled with old Bolsheviks sporting white combed-back hair, pudgy bellies and big Breznev eyebrows. Vehemently anti-German, the old workers talk a lot about World War II and the pros and cons of life in the communist state. Surprisingly, quite a few of these guys speak English and will be most friendly and open with you, as long as you're polite and don't say idiotic things like "You must have really suffered under communism."

When clinking glasses, remember to always stare into your companions' eyes; it's a sign of trustworthiness and a willingness to abide by drunken oaths.

Traditional pub food includes *Utopence* (literally, "drowned men"), frankfurter-type sausages, pickled in vinegar and served with bread and pickled onions. *Matesy* are pickled herring and *pivní sýr* (beer cheese) is a stinky Limburger type served with butter, mustard, salt, pepper and chopped onion and pickle. Season with all of the above, mush with a fork and spread on bread.

You certainly don't need a guidebook to point you in the direction of a pub; at least one exists on most every street in Prague. But the selections below are particularly special.

Letenský Zámeček

(Little Castle) Letensky sady 341, Praha 7.
Tel. 3337-8200. Open June-Sept, daily 10am-10pm.

On hot summer afternoons, there's no better place to quench your thirst then at this leafy outdoor pub high above the city. The whole shebang is little more than a small, self-service snack bar that sells Gambrinus beer in plastic cups for about 20 Kč. The draw is the location, atop Letna Hill, under shade trees, overlooking the entire city below. Take your brew to a shared picnic table and get drunk with the locals. Just behind, with no view, is a table-service restaurant with decent food.

JJ Murphy's

Tržiště 4, Praha 1 – Malá Strana. Tel. 5753-0018. Open daily 11am-3am. M *Malostranská*

Malá Strana's best Irish pub is a friendly, woody place with very good food, Guinness, Murphy's and local brews on tap and a penchant for bands playing on weekends. There's fewer than a dozen tables and a handful of bar stools. The second-floor bar is usually closed but, if you're on a date, nobody minds if you take your drinks to the comfy couch upstairs. The crowd is heavily Anglo; popular at lunch with local expats, and later with Marines from the nearby US Embassy.

Molly Malone's

U Obecniho Dvora 4, Praha 1 – Old Town. Tel 2481-8851. Open Sun-Thurs 11am-1am, Fri-Sat 11am-2am. M *Staroměstská*

With floors, furniture and food that feel more Irish than a drunk potato, Molly's is the place in Prague where those in the brogue turn when in need of a pint and sympathy. Winter or summer, the pub's two wood-wrapped rooms are some of the most cozy wombs in town. Molly's attracts a good mix of Czechs and expats, ranging in age from almost wed to almost dead. Pub meals are served, but if you're hankering for a taste of Eire, the James Joyce across town is a far better choice.

U Fleků

Křemencova 11, Praha 1 – New Town. Tel. 2491-5118. Open daily 10am-midnight. M *Národní Trída*

U Fleků is one of only two brewpubs in the city center (the other is Novoměstsky Pivovar). Begun as a brewery in 1459, this famous old beer hall is a multi-room Bavarian-style extravaganza, fitted with long tables under timbered ceilings. Oom-pah is in the air at all times. It's Prague's version of Munich's Hofbrau House, perpetually packed with octogenarian German tour groups gumming their goulash by the busload. It's a fun place if you're with a group, and U Fleků's special dark beer is truly excellent. But relatively high prices, horrible food and the über-tourist atmosphere keep locals away like a bad case of German measles.

U Krále Jiřího

(At King George's) Liliová 10, Praha 1 – Old Town. Tel. 2222-0925. Open daily 4pm-1am.
Staroměstská

Famous for being one of the cheapest pubs in the center, U Krále Jiřího (At King George's) is a smelly cellar catering to a diverse band of crown-pinching barley cats. The doors open at 10am to older men who have called this place their "local" for longer than any of them can remember. As the hours advance, the crowd becomes progressively younger, so that by midnight it's unusual to find anyone here over thirty. There is no menu, and if there was one it would contain just a single item: Platan beer. The pub is a good place to meet typical Czechs and refresh in totally authentic surroundings. U Krále Jiríha is located at the end of the hall, in the same building as the James Joyce Pub.

U Rudolfina

Křížovnická 10, Praha 1 – Old Town. Tel. 232-8758. Open daily 11am-11pm; kitchen open daily 11am-10pm. Main courses 70-150 Kč. No cards. Ⓜ *Staroměstská*

Hands down the best "real" Czech pub in Old Town, U Rudolfina is a cavernous cellar space set with archetypical heavy wooden tables and hosted by career waiters. Despite its traditional ambience, this pub is actually a relative newcomer that has quickly become a favorite of everyone from factory workers and students to musicians from the nearby Rudolfinum concert hall. There's a terrific, traditional menu too and low-priced Pilsner Urquell is on tap at all times. Don't be fooled by the small storefront entrance; the action is hidden downstairs.

U Zpěváčku

Na struze 7, Praha 1 – New Town. Tel. 291-563. Open nonstop. Ⓜ *Národní Třída*

The motley crew that calls this pub their own came of age after the 1968 Soviet invasion of Czechoslovakia and became united with each other as anti-establishment rockers. They lost their collective *reason d'ètre* when communism collapsed, and now they just seem to drink a lot. These ex-dissidents have long hair and beards, listen to a lot of AC/DC and Nazareth, and wear tight jeans and jean jackets twelve months a year. Acutely cynical about all political systems, they wear mullet hair-do's, love ice hockey and football, and are busting with Russian and communist jokes. They can carry on for hours and will spend their last crown on a beer for a friend. They're also the biggest group of drinkers we've ever run across.

U Zlatého Tygra

(At the Golden Tiger) Husova 17, Praha 1 – Old Town. Tel. 2222-1111. Open daily 3-11pm. Ⓜ *Staroměstská*

The late Bohumil Hrabal, one of the most revered Czech writers of all time, wrote a lot about U Zlatého Tygra, his most favorite watering hole. The pub, now legendary, is perhaps the most famous room in all of Bohemia; even Václav Havel hosted former President Clinton here for a brew and some dumplings. Although this pub is about as centrally located as you can get, it's full of old regulars marinating their livers, and precious few tourists. Out-of-towners are frowned upon here, but that's just as well, because few foreigners can stand the intense smoke. When you master the phrase "pivo, prosim," muster up some bravery, pop in for a drink and know that it doesn't get any more genuine than this.

CZECh BEER FiRSTS

Where do you go when the Germans or the Russians occupy your country? You go to the pub, that's where. Bohemia is Beer Central. Hops were cultivated here as far back as 859, and were being exported as early as 903. To this day, barley pop remains the region's national drink. Per capita, the Czech Republic is the world's biggest beer-drinking nation.

Beer (*pivo* in the vernacular) is an intrinsic part of Czech culture, as essential as air and water.

In The Bartered Bride, Bedrich Smetana's famous opera celebrating Czech identity, the first act opens with a stage full of peasants singing about drinking beer and making merry.

Václav Havel, who used to work in a brewery, wrote many plays in which beer is an integral element. In the course of one play, the protagonist downs eight beers before the curtain comes down.

And it's a common joke that the Czech National Anthem "Where is My Home?" is about getting absent-mindedly drunk at the pub.

Some wags have suggested that perhaps the reason why Czechs drink so much because it's the only way they can force down such dreadful food.

Broadly speaking, there are only two beers served here: pale and dark lager. Dark *(černé)* beer is sweet and fruity, and considered by locals to be a wimpy, girly drink. Beers are referred to by their strength in "degrees;" a measurement that refers to the sugars in the wort before fermentation. In most pubs, the choice is usually between 10- and 12-degree (*desítku* and *dvanáctku*). Degrees are not necessarily related to alcoholic content. For example, Pilsner Urquell (12%) contains 4.4% alcohol, whereas Bernard (10%) is 4.5% alcohol.

Pilsner Urquell and Gambrinus, both brewed in Plzeň, are considered to be the country's best beers. Budvar (the original Budweiser), brewed in Českě Budějovice, is also highly respected and widely available. The best Prague-brewed beers are Braník, Měšťan and Staropramen.

When entering a pub, look at the beer tap. It usually has a little plaque hung on it announcing what brand of beer is being sold and how much it costs. The standard measures are 0.5l and 0.3l; if you don't specify which you want, the waiter will assume that you want the larger one.

Waiters mark each delivery with a shaky line on a tab of paper that's glued to the table with a spot of spilled beer.

- First • in per-capita beer consumption
- First • beer museum
- First • Budweiser
- First • beer brewing textbook
- First • President to have written an absurdist play based on his experiences working in a brewery.

Many locals argue that pubs were better in the Bad Old Days. But don't despair. You can still rub elbows with workers in blue and orange overalls at 6am in pubs that are so smoky you can get a 7-day nicotine fix just by walking in the door. You just have to go farther from Old Town Square to find them.

During socialist days, every pub in the same class charged exactly the same prices. Now there are huge differences, but most places still charge less than $1 per half-liter, which is cheap even for Czechs. Many of the most historic pubs are now tourist-oriented traps, charging far more than any self-respecting Czech is willing or able to pay. If you are paying over 35 Kč for a 1/2 liter of beer, you can be sure that you are drinking in a restaurant or bar with precious few, if any, locals.

Most pubs open at either 10am or 11am and close 12 hours later. Some pubs in the center are keeping longer hours — several even stay open 24/seven.

GAY & LESBIAN NIGHTLIFE

Prior to 1989, when the brotherhood of socialism was in full swing, the entire country seemed to operate under an unofficial don't ask/don't tell rule that effectively placed gays and lesbians at the margins of society. Since that time the scene has percolated, and Prague is increasingly becoming something of a Central European focus for the pink triangle set. Don't be misled: Prague doesn't come close to London, New York or San Francisco. But there are now many excellent bars and clubs catering to an almost exclusively gay clientele. Many other places, including the Evropa Hotel tea room, Pálffy Palace restaurant and Érra Cafe are gay-friendly while being more egalitarian. Like most of the rest of the world, the Prague scene is very male oriented. Local grrrrls just don't get out that much, we guess. Check out avant-guide.com for a great list of local gay links. SOHO, the largest national gay and lesbian organization, publishes the monthly Czech-language journal, *Revue*, which contains lots of listings, advertisements and a brief English-language summary. It's available at most of the places listed below, as well many newsstands in the city center.

A-Club

Milíčova 32, Praha 3 – Žižkov. Tel. 2278-1623. Open daily 7pm-6am. Admission free-50 Kč. Tram 5, 9, 26 to Lipanská

The city's only lesbian club is an intimate two-room affair, with a pocket-size dance floor, a half-dozen tables and a small bar with cheap drinks. It's usually seventy-five percent butch, with more lipstick on the weekends. Men are permitted everyday but Friday.

Alcatraz

Borivojova 58, Praha 3 – Žižkov. Tel. 2271-14 58. Open daily 930pm-4am. Admission free-130 Kč. Tram 5, 9, 26 to Lipanská

Prague's most happening club for uniforms, rubber and leather, Alcatraz can get wild on weekends. Czech guys are often trolling for foreigners, and English conversation is not hard to find. They're best-known for naked and underwear parties the first and third Saturdays of each month.

Drake's

Petřínská 5 (at Zborovská), Praha 5 – Smichov. No phone. Open nonstop. Admission 500 Kč Tram: 6, 9, 12, to Vítězná

Full of smoke, sleaze and German businessmen, Drake's is where you'll find good-looking rent boys who perform naked lap dances and share video cabinets. After paying the high admission fee, you'll find a bar with strip performances most nights at 9 and 11pm. Go through the stage door and downstairs to a dark sex cellar with glory holes.

Friends

Náprstkova 1, Praha 1 – Old Town. Tel. 2163-5408. Open daily 4pm-3am. Admission free. M Staroměstská

Situated a cobblestone's throw from Charles Bridge, Friends is a, well, friendly cellar music bar that's popular with both visitors and locals from nearby Charles University. There's Internet access daily from 4-8pm.

Tom's Bar

Pernerova 4, Praha 8 – Karlín. Tel. 2481-3802. Open Sun-Thurs 6pm-2am, Fri-Sat 6pm-4am. Admission 50 Kč. M Křižíkova

Tom's is a mid-sized bar and dance floor that's popular with thirtysomething locals and foreigners who live here. A second chill-out room contains a video screen, and the inner sanctum is dark. Thursdays and Saturdays are best.

Gejzee..r

Vinohradská 40, Praha 2 – Vinohrady. Tel. 2251-6036. Open Thurs 6pm-5am, Fri-Sat 9pm-5am. Admission free-150 Kč. M Náměsti Miru

The biggest gay dance club in Prague is a cavernous and sweaty venue. It's also a great place to dance, hang out, get liquored up and lucky. There's a big dance floor, twin bars, and darkrooms downstairs. Entrance includes a free drink on weekends. Thursdays are free, and drinks are 2-4-1.

Tunel

Plzeňská 41, Praha 5 – Smichov. No phone. Open Mon-Thurs 10pm-4am, Fri-Sat 10pm-5am. No cover; 50-80 Kč minimum. M Anděl.

Tunel is uniform and leather oriented, but the dress code is not strict. You can arrive wearing anything, check out the scene, and change in the cloak room. But make no mistake: people come here for action. There are beds in the dark room and the Naked Fuck Party the last Sunday of each month leaves nothing to the imagination.

U Střelce

(At the Shooter)

Karoliny Svetlé 12, Praha 1 – Old Town. Tel. 2423-8278. Open Wed and Fri-Sat 930pm-5am. Admission 100-150 Kč. M Národní třída.

Gay, straight... it doesn't matter, U Střelce is one of the most fun weekend nights in Prague. On Fridays and Saturdays it's a nonstop six-hour drag show, where a rotation of about eight performers keep changing costumes and lip-synching everything from tearful Whitney Houston anthems and exuberant Czech pop songs to hilarious Russian folk ballads. Fifty customers is a crowd in the tiny showroom where entire tables are often reserved by sparkling-wine-sipping local boys. This is not the best place to make new friends, but there is a small bar scene, and long stares across the room are common.

DANCE & TECHNO

Prague has an excellent dance club culture. Top DJs regularly come in from London, Amsterdam and Berlin, and some homegrown spinners really know how to mix. In summer, there is a giant party somewhere almost every weekend, and several recent events have attracted over two thousand revelers each. Ecstasy remains the drug of choice and other brain ticklers are widely available. The promoter Roxydust is currently throwing Prague's most Caligula parties, but Planet Alfa, On Strike and other energetic sound systems are also pushing limits. For the most up-to-date information on what's happening in (and out of) clubs pick-up a free copy of *Think* magazine from many of the bars listed above. Keep your eyes peeled for street posters touting upcoming events and check-out the party links on avantguide.com.

Disco Letná

Veletržní 61, Praha 7. Tel. 3337-1855. Open daily 9pm-6am. Admission 50 Kč.

Disco Letná is a large Italian-Euroclub clone with an excellent sound system, advanced lighting technology and plenty of dark-haired guys leaning around like Towers of Pisa. It's a huge electronic dance emporium with Neanderthal doormen and nonstop Europop spun by the worst DJs in Prague. So why do we love this place? It's where Prague's finest young prostitutes go when they finish work, which means that this place starts at midnight and gets a second wind around 3am. Bleached blondes are so commonplace here that spotting the girl you just hit on at the bar can be more difficult than finding Waldo.

Lávka

Novotného lávka 1, Praha 1 – Old Town. Tel. 2222-2156. Open daily 9pm-5am. Admission 50-100 Kč Ⓜ Staroměstská

Restaurant/bar by day, pop discotheque by night, Lávka is a club for the masses. Loud club hits and Eurobeat trash from strategically-placed speakers practically lifts foreigners off Charles Bridge and tractor-beams them in. Czechs are here too; at least the women are. The dancefloor is way too small for the space and is plagued by a low ceiling and horrible black-lighting. But the later it gets, the less anyone seems to care. The club is best on warm summer nights, when speakers are stacked in the rear garden and you can dance under the gaze of the disapproving saints on Charles Bridge.

Lucerna Music Bar

in the Lucerna Passage, Vodičkova 36, Praha 1 – New Town. Tel. 2421-7108. Open daily 9pm-4am. Admission 60-600 Kč Ⓜ Muzeum/Můstek

Tuesdays at Lucerna have become legendary. On a night when most other places are hurting, Lucerna is absolutely hopping with virtuous young Czechs in their twenties bopping to homegrown hits from the '60s. It's quite a scene. Karel Gott, the most famous crooner from the genre, is in heavy rotation on the club's turntables. Part Esquivel, part Sinatra and part The Monkey's, he is typical of what you can expect here. Every third tune usually riles the crowd into a frenzy and re-fills the dancefloor to overflowing. Lucerna on Tuesday is a guaranteed cultural experience for foreigners looking for the real Czech McCoy. Quality is variable on all other nights, when live bands belt out classic rock, blues or jazz.

Mecca

U Průhonu 3, Praha 7 – Holešovice. Tel. 8387-0522. Open Fri-Sat and special club nights 10pm-6am. AE, MC, V. Ⓜ Vltavská

Mecca is one of the best techno clubs in Prague. It's also feast or famine, which means that it can be an epic night or dull as a board. When a good DJ is spinning and the glitterati turn out, both of which happen often, there is no better place to be. A spacious, industrial lounge gives way to an even larger dance space, built with a clean sound system, good lighting package, and an excellent dance floor lorded over by a DJ stage. And there's a large chill-out room in the basement. You'll need to take a cab.

Radost F/X

Bělehradská 120, Praha 2 – Vinohrady. Tel. 251-210. Open Mon-Sat 9pm-4am. Admission 70-200 Kč M IP Pavlova

When it comes to stylish urban club scenes, Radost remains on top of its game. The longest-running techno club in Prague sports an intensively-designed basement with good sound levels and a thoughtful layout that keeps traffic flowing. In-house DJs are supplemented with regular imports from London and Amsterdam. And the avant black-clad crowd is a healthy mix of good-looking straights, better-looking gays and more than a few college-aged LUGs (Lesbians Until Graduation). The upstairs cafe, also accessible to non-clubbers, functions as the discotheque's de facto chill-out space and serves munchies until 5am (see Chapter 8/Eating). Radost is best on weekends, and when guest DJs are in the house.

Roxy

Dlouhá 33, Praha 1 – Old Town. Tel. 2482-6390. Open Mon-Fri 9pm-5am. Admission 50-200 Kč M Náměstí Republiky

There's nothing false or pretentious about this gutted underground art deco theater: authentic grunge is what makes this someplace special. Funk and techno-oriented DJs are often preceded by live theater or musical performances that run the gamut from frightening to fantastic. Weekends are best, but a great Friday or Saturday night at Roxy is not guaranteed; when there's nothing special on the program, it can really be a snooze. But, when a big DJ is in town, or when a special event is going on—both of which are frequent—this place becomes the best frolic pad in town. Time your night to arrive here around midnight.

Karlovy Lázně

(The Charles Baths) Novotného lávka, Praha 1 – Old Town. Tel. 2222-0502. Open daily 9pm-5am. Admission 100 Kč; special DJs 300 Kč. M Staroměstská

When floating across Charles Bridge at night you'll undoubtedly be brought back to the ground by the enormously garish neon sign for the "Largest Club in Central Europe." The signage alone should give you a good idea of what this place is all about: a teen-tourist club on four floors meant to attract those who don't know anyplace better to go.

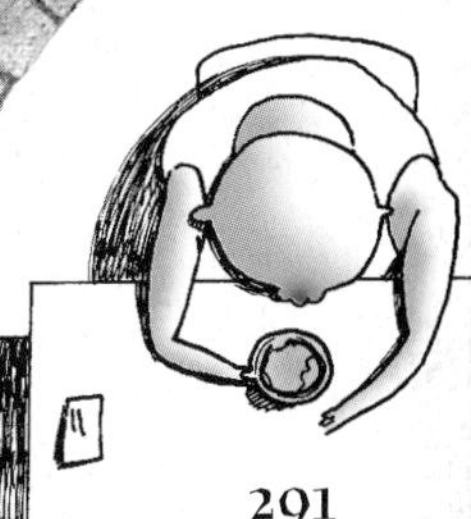

LIVE ROCK

The overwhelming majority of local rockers are screamers and guitar thrashers doing passable imitations of their counterparts in London and Los Angeles. The best of the high-energy bands are Dunaj, Lucie, Support Lesbians, Laura and her Tigers, and Už jsme doma. Slightly tamer is classic rock diva Lucie Bila and the band Buty. Iva Bittová, the best of the art-rock stars, strokes here violin while singing and shrieking through emotion-filled songs. If Czech Gramy award-winning Colorfactory is playing while you're in town, don't hesitate to snap-up a ticket to one of their mellow, acoustic-heavy shows. Prague has also become a regular stop for major bands on European tours, and concerts are widely publicized. Check the listings publications for the latest. The most important venues for local talent are listed below. Most charge between 70 Kč and 300 Kč, depending on what's on. For the latest happenings, check the local listings magazines or the links on avantguide.com.

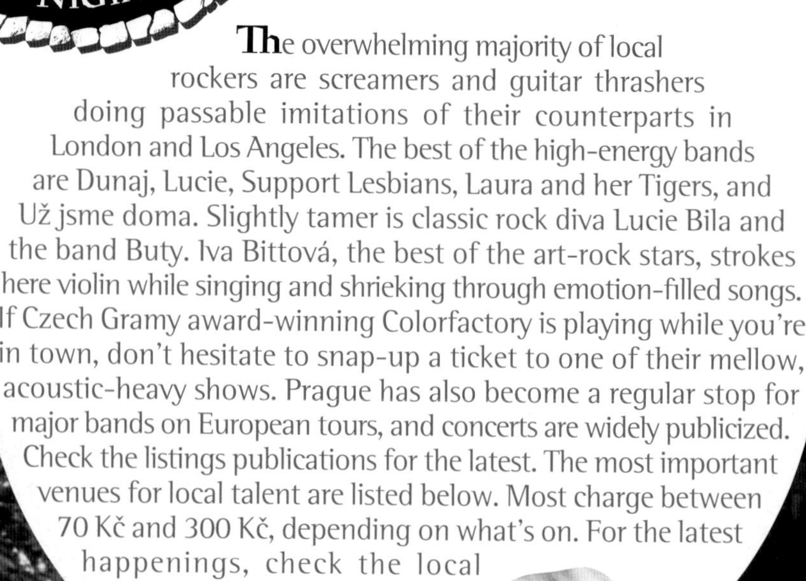

Delta

Vlastina 887, Praha 6. Tel. 3331-2443.

Delta is one of those rare spaces that emits a full-house worth of energy even when the room is half empty. Perhaps that's why so many local bands like this barn-like theater best. The club is located on the way to the airport, about 15-minutes by cab from the city center.

Malostranská Beseda

Malostranské náměstí 21, Praha 1 – Malá Strana. Tel. 5753-2092. Music daily 830pm–2am. M Malostranská

The Beseda, or meeting house, is one of the few clubs left from socialist days. That is the only plausible explanation for its incredible location, on Malá Strana Square blasting towards the offices of the Czech Parliament. Something's happening here almost every night, usually something leaning towards jazzy-flavored rock.

Palác Akropolis

Kubelíkova 27, Praha 3 – Žižkov. Tel. 2271-2287. M Jiřího z Poděbrad

An excellent booking policy means lots of interesting art-rock, world-beat, techno and alternative bands play in this excellent venue. Acoustically and atmospherically, this is one of the best places in Prague to hear a band work.

Rock Café

Národní 20, Praha 1 – New Town. Tel. 2491-4416. Music Mon-Fri 10am-3am, Sat-Sun 7pm-3am. M Národní třída

Featuring lots of local bands, sometimes served by the half-dozen, Rock Café puts you in the trenches of the city's garage rock scene. This is a serious rocker crowd, attracting Möterheads in Ozzy eye-liner. There's something happening here almost every night of the week.

LiVE jAZZ

In Prague it's unlikely that you'll hear anyone you've ever heard of, but the quality of the local talent is generally very high and the home-grown musicians can jam 'til they're beat to the socks. Most musicians have their favorite rooms. But in order to play frequently, everyone seems to gig around to all the major clubs. Once regarded here as a subtle form of protest against the communist government, America's most distinctive musical export has arm-stronged its way into Prague's clubs, featuring everything from Dixieland and boogie-woogie to swing, be-bop and modern electric jazz. Top players to look out for include flautist Jiří Stivin and saxophonist Karel Růžička. Because it's usually impossible to know what the sound will be from a name in a program, telephone the clubs beforehand to find out what's on. Most will speak enough English. Admission usually ranges from free to about 200 Kč.

Jazz Club Železná

Železná 16, Praha 1 – Old Town. Tel. 2423-9697. Open Sun-Wed 3pm-1230am, Thurs-Sat 3pm-2am. Shows from 9pm. Admission 100 Kč Můstek/Staroměstská

This pint-size gothic cave just might be the world's oldest jazz cellar. Each of the club's forty-odd seats is a good one and, although volume is high, conversationalists can retreat to the bar.

Reduta Jazz Club

Národní 20, Praha 1 – New Town. Tel. 2491-2246. Open daily 9pm-midnight. Admission 100-200 Kč. Národní třída

Everybody plays in this famous pre-Revolutionary jazz joint. Even Bill Clinton blew horns with Václav Havel here. For musicians, this smoky cellar is the best-known, but not the best-loved, room in town. The environment is friendlier elsewhere.

U Staré Paní

(At the Old Maid) Michalská 9, Praha 1 – Old Town. Tel. 2422-8090 or 2422-6659. Open daily 9pm-midnight. Admission 160 Kč. Můstek/Staroměstská

U Staré Paní is soon-to-be sax legend Karel Růžička's favorite club. It's also an uncharacteristically clean space with terrific sightlines and excellent acoustics.

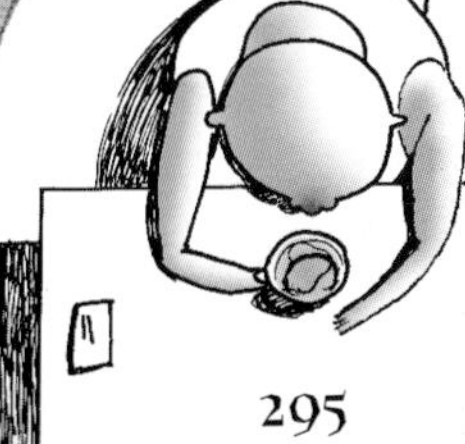

CLASSICAL MUSIC, OPERA & DANCE

Classical music knows no season in Prague, and major and minor symphonies and soloists are performing every night of the year. Beethoven, Paganini and Chopin have all tickled the ivories or waved their batons here. So have Mozart and Vivaldi, both of whom liked Prague so much they dug in for extended stays. They, along with native sons Dvořák and Smetana, remain local favorites. Concert prices remain extremely low; too low, some say, to stage operas and ballets that are truly world-class. Some of Prague's best concerts are the nightly chamber affairs that take place in many churches around town. The *Prague Post* has good classical music, opera and dance listings. Tickets usually cost between 100 Kč and 700 Kč and are best purchased in advance from theater box offices or from **Prague Tourist Center**, Rytířská 12, Praha 1 – Old Town (tel. 2423-6047), **TicketPro**, Salvátorská 10, Praha 1 – Old Town (tel. 14051), or **Bohemia Ticket International** Na příkopě 16, Praha 1 – New Town (tel. 2422-7832 or 2421-5031). If a performance you want to see is sold out, just show up at curtain time and ask the *ticket-taker* if you can "buy" some available seats ;).

Classical Music

When the Iron Curtain was raised many of the most talented players fled the country to chase big money in the West. Yet Prague's three major orchestras are awash with ability, and quality remains extremely high.

The **Czech Philharmonic Orchestra** enjoys an international reputation and attracts famous guest conductors with regularity. The most obvious effect of the free market has been on the musical programs themselves, which appeal to the lowest common denominator with plenty of popular, time-tested works by the best-known composers. The Czech Philharmonic plays at the Rudolfinum (*see* Major Concert Halls, below). The less tradition-bound **Prague Symphony Orchestra** takes chances with newer works and almost always tosses some 20th-century music into their programs. The emphasis is often on Czech composers. The PSO plays in the recently renovated Smetana Hall in the Municipal House *(Obecní dům)*, a fantastic space that would be worth visiting even if Pauley Shore were performing.

Although it spends the majority of its time recording, the **Prague Radio Symphony Orchestra** also makes regular concert appearances. It rivals the Prague Symphony Orchestra in both quality and content, offering programs of historical and contemporary works to generally favorable reviews.

The best Church Concerts

With religion on the outs and tourism in full-swing, many churches have turned to classical music as a way of attracting crowds and money. When walking around the city center you'll undoubtedly be besieged with flyers advertising these shows. No matter where you go, the repertoire will consist of the best-known baroque and classical hits by Bach, Handel, Beethoven and Mozart. And because you probably won't know any of the players, it's best to choose a concert by program and venue.

The **Chapel of Mirrors**, in the Klementinum, Karlova, Praha 1 – Old Town (tel. 2166-3200), is widely considered to have the best acoustics of any church in the city. It's a small space with only about 100 chairs surrounded by amazing gold baroquetry reflected in dozens of mirrors. The **Basilica of St. George**, in Prague Castle, is also well-known for sound quality, said to be ideal for chamber music concerts. The **Church of St. Nicholas** *(Kostel sv. Mikuláše)*, on Old Town Square (no phone), is a larger space specializing in organ recitals.

Major musical events, including large chorales and symphonies, are sometimes held in Prague Castle's **St. Vitus Cathedral**. These are don't-miss events. Likewise, if a concert is happening in Prague Castle's **Spanish Hall** *(Španělský sál)*, don't waste any time counting lucky stars. Just score a ticket as fast as you can.

Tickets for all shows range in price from about 100-500 Kč and can be purchased at the door.

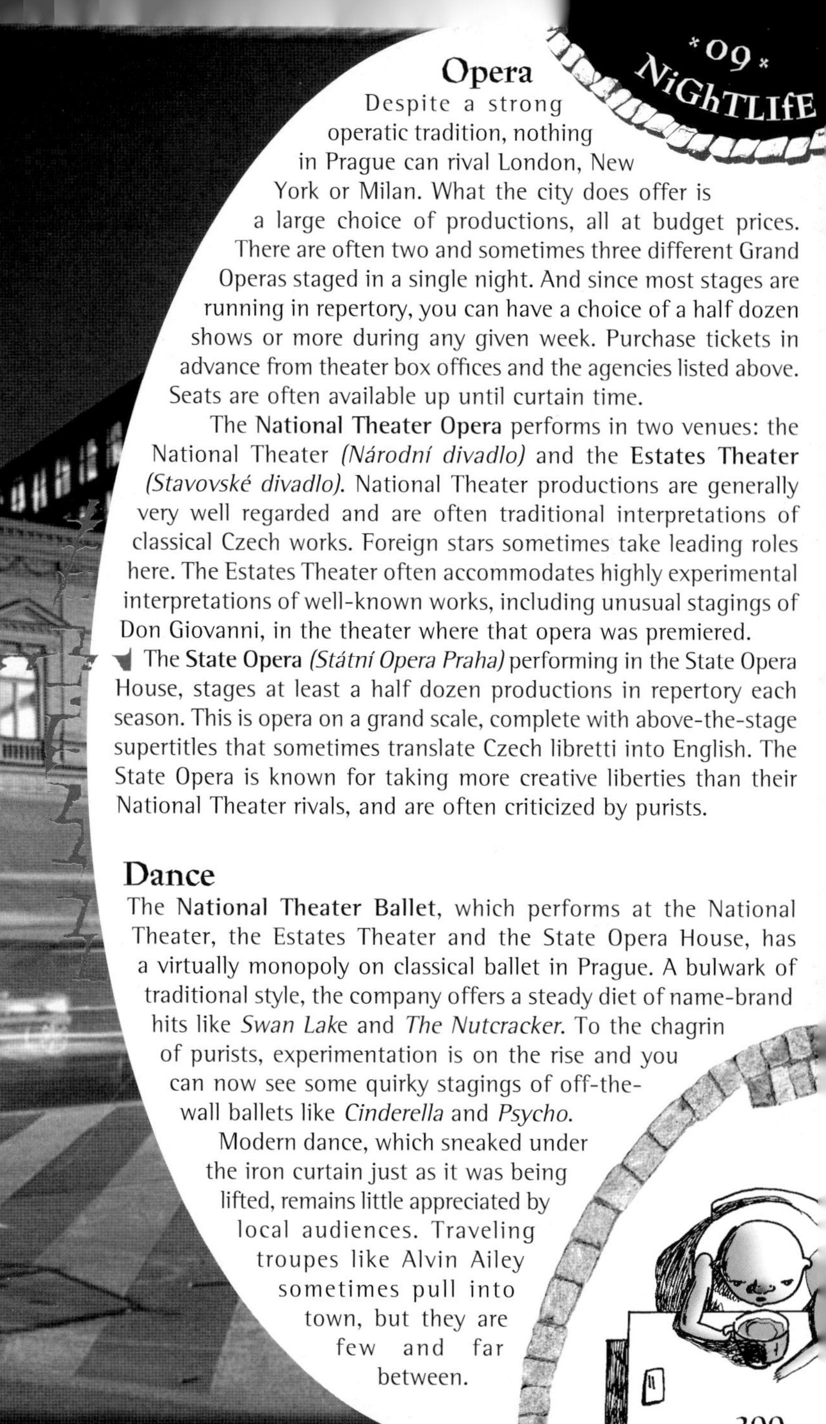

Opera

Despite a strong operatic tradition, nothing in Prague can rival London, New York or Milan. What the city does offer is a large choice of productions, all at budget prices. There are often two and sometimes three different Grand Operas staged in a single night. And since most stages are running in repertory, you can have a choice of a half dozen shows or more during any given week. Purchase tickets in advance from theater box offices and the agencies listed above. Seats are often available up until curtain time.

The **National Theater Opera** performs in two venues: the National Theater *(Národní divadlo)* and the **Estates Theater** *(Stavovské divadlo)*. National Theater productions are generally very well regarded and are often traditional interpretations of classical Czech works. Foreign stars sometimes take leading roles here. The Estates Theater often accommodates highly experimental interpretations of well-known works, including unusual stagings of Don Giovanni, in the theater where that opera was premiered.

The **State Opera** *(Státní Opera Praha)* performing in the State Opera House, stages at least a half dozen productions in repertory each season. This is opera on a grand scale, complete with above-the-stage supertitles that sometimes translate Czech libretti into English. The State Opera is known for taking more creative liberties than their National Theater rivals, and are often criticized by purists.

Dance

The **National Theater Ballet**, which performs at the National Theater, the Estates Theater and the State Opera House, has a virtually monopoly on classical ballet in Prague. A bulwark of traditional style, the company offers a steady diet of name-brand hits like *Swan Lake* and *The Nutcracker*. To the chagrin of purists, experimentation is on the rise and you can now see some quirky stagings of off-the-wall ballets like *Cinderella* and *Psycho*.

Modern dance, which sneaked under the iron curtain just as it was being lifted, remains little appreciated by local audiences. Traveling troupes like Alvin Ailey sometimes pull into town, but they are few and far between.

MAJOR STAGES & CONCERT HALLS

Estates Theater

(Stavovské divadlo), Ovocný třída 6, Praha 1 – Old Town. Tel. 2421-5001. Ⓜ *Můstek*

Everyone in Prague seems to know that this is the theater where Don Giovanni premiered, conducted by the Mozart himself. If you've seen the movie "Amadeus" then you've seen the remarkable blue and gold interior of this relentlessly ornate 18th-century gem, a space so beautiful that it almost doesn't matter what's happening on stage. Most of the programming here is serious theater, accompanied by simultaneous English translation, transmitted via headphone. Opera is regularly on the calendar too, with Mozart leading the way.

National Theater

(Národní divadlo), Národní 2, Praha 1 – New Town. Tel. 2491-3437. Ⓜ *Národní třída*

Widely considered to be the top Czech stage, the gold-crowned National Theater is lit most every night with a revolving repertoire of theater, opera and ballet. Financed by public donations, the building was completed in 1881 as part of the Czech National Revival—a nationalistic cultural uprising that peaked at the end of the 19th Century. Its opening was celebrated with the premiere of Bedřich Smetana's opera Libuše. The composer then conducted the theater's orchestra until 1874, when deafness forced him to retire.

Rudolfinum

nám. Jana Palacha, Praha 1 – Old Town. Tel. 2489-3352. Ⓜ *Staroměstská*

There are two music halls here. The fittingly named Little Hall is well suited for chamber concerts, while the main Dvořák Hall is home to the Czech Philharmonic Orchestra. This is also the main stage of the annual Prague Spring festival.

Smetana Hall

(Smetanova sín) in the Municipal House (Obecní dům), nám. Republiky 5, Praha 1 – Old Town. Ⓜ *Náměstí Republiky*

Smetana Hall occupies the entire central section of Prague's Municipal House, one of the most distinctive art nouveau buildings in the world. Designed as a multi-purpose space, it is now home to the Prague Symphony Orchestra.

State Opera House

(Státní Opera Praha), Wilsonova 4, Praha 2 – New Town. Tel. 2422-7693. M Muzeum

Opened in 1887 as the German Theater, this Baroque music box filled with huge dimpled cupids has hosted many great names, including Wagner, Strauss and Mahler, whose Seventh Symphony had its premiere here. Operas are performed here almost every night of the year. They are mostly of the Italian variety, though German, Russian, French and Czech works have recently been finding their way into the programs.

THEATER & PERFORMANCE ART

Per capita, there are probably more theaters in Prague than in any other major city in the world. Perhaps that could be expected from a country that elected a playwright to the presidency. Theater has long played an unusually important role in the Czech lands. Drama reigns supreme, though mammoth musicals like "Hair" and "Jesus Christ Superstar" have appeared post-revolutionarily. On any given night you can find a good selection that includes time-tested international hits, experimental performances, and works by local authors. Czech theater utilizes the skills of some of the world's best set and costume designers, which alone can make a trip to foreign-language theaterland worthwhile. The most admired and innovative theaters are **Archa**, Na poříčí 26, Praha 1 – New Town (tel. 232-8800); **The National Theater** *(Národní divadlo)* Národní 2, Praha 1 – New Town (tel. 2490-1448); **Theater on the Balustrade** *(Divadlo na zábradlí)*, Anenské nám. 5, Praha 1 – Old Town (tel. 2222-2026); and **Vinohrady Theater** *(Divadlo na Vinohradech)*, náměstí Míru 7, Praha 2 – Vinohrady (tel. 257041). Check *Culture in Prague* for the most up-to-date theater listings.

Globe '99, Výstaviště, Praha 7 (tel. 2010-3204), is copy of Shakespeare's famous theater in London (the current one of which is, itself, a copy of the Elizabethan playhouse). Because it is open at the top, productions here are warm weather events. Phone or check the *Prague Post* for showtimes.

There are a couple of somewhat permanent English-language theater troupes in Prague, but we'd be hard-pressed to recommend them. Wait until London or New York.

Tickets usually cost between 300 Kč and 800 Kč and should be purchased in advance from theater box offices or a ticket agency. Try **TicketPro**, Celetná 13, Praha 1 – Old Town (tel. 2481-1817), or **Bohemia Ticket International** Na příkopě 16, Praha 1 – Old Town (tel. 2421-5031 or 2422-7832).

Literary Readings

You were suckered here by all that "Left Bank of the 90s" bull. So where are all those goatee-slinging, beret-wearing, clove-smoking expat boho writers and poets anyway? If truth be told, they're gone. But if you want to see a vestige of how it used to be, circa 1994, check out **Beefstew**, an ultra civil poetry thud (it's not quite a slam) held each Sunday from 6pm at **Radost F/X**, Bělehradská 120, Praha 2 – Vinohrady (tel. 251210). Last time we dropped by there were about a dozen attendees (three of whom were indeed wearing hats) plus one dog. There's no booing and everyone politely claps after each performance, even if it's a complete yawn. There are, however, usually some gems hiding in the rough. Best of all, it's free. M: IP Pavlova

Marionette Theater

In Bohemia, puppet theater is not just child's play, it's a centuries-old tradition that has been raised to the highest levels of art. Even the prestigious Charles University offers a degree in Puppet Theater Direction. Puppets, or more accurately, marionettes, are so popular that, until their owners started offering them up for hard currency, they could be found in practically every home in the land. There is a brand of puppet theater for every taste: Surrealist, soap opera, grand opera, comedy—it's even rumored there are porno puppets, though we've never seen them. Humor and music are trademarks of the genre, producing scenes like the one where a naked Don Giovanni sings an aria in a bathtub while getting his back scrubbed by a wooden Leporello.

The **National Marionette Theater** *(Národní divadlo marionet)*, Žatecká 1, Praha 1 – Old Town (tel. 2481-9322), is particularly recommendable. Bring good humor or good drugs to have an unforgettable time. Because there are no reserved seats and front rows are best, we suggest you arrive early. Shows usually take place nightly and tickets cost 500 Kč. The box office is open daily from 10am-8pm. M Staroměstská.

Blacklight Theater

Blacklight theater is a strangely popular phenomenon that has become something of a trademark of Prague's tourist nightscape. There are at least five houses featuring these colorful non-verbal shows, all of which rely on the same single neon joke. It's fun for about fifteen minutes, after which it becomes an alternative to Nyquil. **Ta Fantastika**, Karlova 8, Praha 1 – Old Town (tel. 2222-1369 or 2222-0389) is the best of the lot. Tickets cost 200-300 Kč.

Laterna Magika, Národní třída 4, Praha 1 – New Town (tel. 2491-4129), a multi-media show with healthy doses of blacklight antics, has been the staple fare of the National Theater's "new" wing for over forty years. That's about thirty-five years too long for anyone who can remember the rudimentary special effects in the movies "The Poseidon Adventure" or "Airport '75." Less cynical observers think Laterna Magika produces visually stunning avant-garde performance pieces. And they may be right, considering how difficult it can be to score tickets. Either way, it will cost you about 600 Kč to find out.

CASiNOS

Casinos, like seemingly everything else in this country, are legal in the Czech Republic. All relatively small, the game rooms are often full of Chinese betting the 50 Kč minimums and Russians pushing the 5000 Kč limits. Blackjack and roulette are the main games, played in both crowns and dollars. House rules vary from place to place, but they are usually similar to those in Vegas. **Casino Palais Savarin**, Na příkopé 10, Praha 1 – New Town (tel. 2422-1636), on the second floor of an amazing rococo palace, has a James Bondian sense of style and is the city's prettiest gameroom. But a recent policy change that limits free drinks has soured us on this place. it's open daily from 1pm to about 4am. M Můstek).

Millennium Casino, in the Prague Marriott Hotel, V Celnici 8, Praha 1 – New Town (tel. 2103-3401) is our new game room of choice. It's very contemporary, the staff is friendly, drinks are free, and they serve food all night. It's open daily from 4pm to 4am. M Náměstí Republiky.

VIP Casino at the Ambassador Hotel, Václavské nám. 5, Praha 1 – New Town (tel. 2419-3111), gets mention here because it is centrally located and is open nonstop. There are usually just a couple of tables working after 5am.

SEX

Sexually speaking, Czechs are very liberal people. Whether you're gay or straight or anything in-between you'll have no trouble getting what you need. Newsstands are littered with locally-produced porn, prostitution and gay sex is legal, condoms are sold from machines in Metro stations, and the age of consent is just fifteen.

For in-depth information on the best sex shops, escorts and brothels, pick-up a copy of the colorful Prague Sex Guide, which is sold at the Můstek newsstands at the foot of Wenceslas Square.

Strip Clubs

At **Goldfingers**, Václavské nám. 5, Praha 1 – New Town (tel. 2419-3856), some of the region's most gorgeous girls get buck naked in one of the most beautiful show rooms in the city. Although it's unrelated to the venerable US strip-club chain of the same name, this Goldfingers is very much in the American mold. When the girls are not taking their clothes off on stage, they're offering private lap and table dances. The club is open daily from 9pm to 4am.

Brothels & Escorts

You can tell a lot about a culture by it's language. In England "Public House" is a pub. In Czech, *Veřejný dům* (public house) refers to a brothel. There are dozens of sex clubs in Prague, and dozens more private apartments where you can pop in for an hour. Prostitutes advertise themselves on the back pages of *Annonce (Volný Čas edition)*, as well as on www.escort.cz, a weighty website packed with working girls and boys.

Hanka Servis, Bulharská 10, Praha 10 (tel. 734-011) is a tiny brothel and escort service that's jam-packed with girls—up to two-dozen at any one time. There's a full bar and a small swimming pool. It's open nonstop.

K5 Relax, Korunní 5, Praha 2 – Vinohrady (tel. 2425-0505; www.k5relax.com), is a safe upstairs bar with lots of girls and a half-dozen mirror-wrapped rooms. They do not pay commission to taxi drivers. It's open daily from 4pm-4am.

Marthy Club, Seifertova 35, Praha 3 (tel. 627-8013), is another small basement club with a truly laid-back lounge room, about a half-dozen girls, and music that's kept at conversational levels. The club's discrete entrance is squeezed between a row of storefronts. It's open daily from 2pm-2am.

Although it looks like a gay nightclub, **Escape**, V Jámě 8, Praha 1 – New Town (tel. 0602/403744) is really a male escort emporium where patrons can find rent boys while downing a drink or two. Pretty much everyone here under the age of 25 is working, and 3000 Kč an hour is the going rate for just about anything. Continuous strip shows grease the wheels from 10pm. It's open daily 10pm-5am. Admission 100 Kč. M Muzeum.

fiLM

Most of Prague's movie houses are grand old cinemas with lots of seats, big balconies and huge screens. These are great places to see films, especially when the average ticket price is a mere 130 Kč. Many of the city's biggest theaters are located on Václavské náměstí (Wenceslas Square). The city's cinemaniacs love Hollywood's flash and trash which, like all foreign films, is usually screened in the original language with Czech subtitles. Most American films seem to hit Prague's movie screens about the same time they are released to the airlines. Although they are few and far between, some of the most popular Czech-language releases appear in cinemas sporting English subtitles.

The Ster Century multiplex in Slovanský Dům, Na příkopé 22, Praha 1 – New Town (tel. 2145-1214), is the newest theater complex in the city center. Dolby sound, luxury seating, and perfect sightlines make it a welcome addition to the city's cinemascape. It's also one of the only places where you can catch a film after 9pm. Check The *Prague Post* or *Culture in Prague* for current show times.

×10× DAY TRIPS & SLEEP AWAYS

TRIPPING

VCS
BEN

If you already know your destination and which mode of transport you'll be using, you can go directly to the appropriate station *(nádraží)* and belly up to the ticket window. Alternatively, visit **Čedok**, Na příkopě 18, Praha 1 (tel. 2419-7111), the country's largest travel agent, for information, tickets and schedules. They're open Monday to Friday from 9am to 7pm.

ThE bEST DAY TRiPS

KARLŠTEJN

The romantic, but tourist-ridden village of Karlštejn and its Castle is the most visited attraction outside of Prague. The Castle tour is a dud, but come prepared for a short hike in the woods and a visit to Karlštejn becomes a wonderful, quick introduction to the Czech countryside and life outside the Big City. Insider tip: the best part is the Castle's **Chapel of the Holy Rood**, which has walls encrusted with over 2000 semi-precious stones. But only ten visitors are allowed in per hour; phone in advance for tour tickets (tel. 02/74008154).

Getting There: Karlštejn is 20 miles (32 km) southwest of Prague. Trains depart hourly from Smíchov Station *(Smíchovské nádraží)*. The trip takes about 40 minutes, then it's an easy, 20-minute walk from the train station to the Castle.

KUTNÁ HORA

Most visitors come to Kutná Hora to see the **Ossuary** *(kostnice)*, in which tens of thousands of human skeletons were made into sculptures by a 19th century wood carver. See urns made of thigh bones, an anchor from femurs and spectacular chandeliers that are each said to incorporate every bone in the human body. Other sights in town include the **Cathedral of St. Barbara**, which is a masterpiece of Gothic design and one of the most beautiful churches anywhere. And in the **Museum of Medieval Mining** *(Muzeum a středověké důlní dílo)* Barborská 28 (tel. 0327/512159), you can actually tour ancient mining tunnels.

Getting There: Kutná Hora is 50 miles (80 km) east of Prague. Trains leave from Prague's Main Train Station *(Hlavní nádraží)* and take about an hour.

TEREZÍN (THERESIENSTADT)

In 1940 this 18th-century fortress was transformed into a concentration camp for the express purpose of imprisoning Jews, Gypsies and other "genetically undesirable" people. Terezín was not a "death camp," but rather a massive holding pen that functioned as a way station to the gas chambers further east. The Germans also used Terezín as a show camp, to counter rumors of mass gassings, and fool the world into thinking that their concentration camps weren't so bad after all. Out of 140,000 people who passed through Terezín, 84,000 were subsequently murdered in death camps. Thirty-four thousand people died in Terezín itself, primarily from starvation and disease. You can walk around the town and see the crematorium and cemetery, both of which are located on the other side of disused railway tracks, which were built by the inmates. Info: Tel: 0416/782225 or 0416/782442.

Getting There: Terezín is located 30 miles (48 km) northwest of Prague. Buses 17 and 20 depart from Prague's Florenc station five times daily, and take about an hour.

ThE BEST OVERNiGhT EXCURSiONS

ČESKÝ KRUMLOV

This southern town is simply a place of dream-like beauty that feels frozen in time and is ranked second (after Venice) on UNESCOs World Heritage List. The town has a wonderful castle and has perfectly preserved its unique Medieval character with narrow alleys, underground taverns and cobblestone streets. The best restaurants are Eggenberg Brewery and Cikánská Jizba. Our favorite place to stay is **Pension Barbakán**, Horní 26 (tel. 0337/717017), a beautiful 18-room hotel perched on a rock across from the town's theater. Doubles run between 1200-1800 Kč in summer, and 1000-1500 Kč in winter, breakfast included. The best cheap-sleep is **Travellers' Hostel**, Soukenická 43 (tel. 0337/711-345; fax 02/2482-6665; www.travellers.cz).

Getting There: Český Krumlov is 100 miles (161 km) south of Prague. Trains from Prague's Main Train Station *(Hlavní nádrazi)* take about five hours, including a change at České Buděvice.

KARLOVY VARY (CARLSBAD)

Nestled in a narrow valley, Karlovy Varya cheerful and romantic place, with graceful architecture surrounded by gentle tree-covered hills. In its center is a single, lengthy strip of grand colonnades built with Belle Epoch filigree atop twelve natural hot springs to which Europeans have been making pilgrimages for centuries. The **Grandhotel Pupp**, Mírové nám. (tel. 017/310-9111; fax 017/322-4032; main@pupp.kpgroup.cz) is one of the finest hotels in the Czech Republic. At about a third the price, **Penzion Elefant**, Stará Louka 30 (tel. 017/322-8122), is excellent too.

Getting There: Karlovy Vary is 75 miles (121 km) west of Prague. Buses depart from Prague's Florenc station almost hourly and take about two-and-a-half hours. There is no convenient train service from Prague.

× 11 ×

BEfORE YOU G() ESSENTiALS

PLANNiNG

iNfORMATION & WEAThER

The *www.avantguide.com* CyberSupplement™ is the best source for happenings in Prague during your stay. Visit for updates and links to info on current cultural events and other happenings.

See Chapter 2 for a list of information sources in Prague.

For information and entry requirements, duty-free limits and other concerns, see Essential 411, below.

For Travelers With Disabilities

Prague's cobblestone streets and sidewalks are not very hospitable to wheelchair-bound travelers. Moreover, most buildings are ramped, few restaurants and hotels are accessible, and public transport makes almost no accommodation for wheelchairs. It is, however, common in Prague for theaters, nightclubs and attractions to offer discounts to people with disabilities. Ask for these before paying full-price.

Climate

Average monthly temperatures are listed below. Check avantguide.com. for current weather conditions.

	°Celsius	°Fahrenheit
January	2	36
February	3	37
March	8	46
April	14	58
May	19	66
June	22	72
July	24	75
August	23	73
September	20	68
October	13	55
November	8	46
December	3	37

SAViNG MONEY GETTiNG THERE

Frankly, we don't trust most travel agents to really dig for the lowest fare. They get paid a small percentage of the price of each ticket, so it doesn't benefit them to spend *more* time trying to make *less* money. We usually make reservations ourselves, directly with the airlines, then visit our travel agent for ticketing. Here's the secret to getting the best deal: If you don't know airline jargon, don't use it. Just ask for the lowest fare. If you're flexible with dates and times, tell the sales agent. Ask him or her to hunt a bit.

Budget Airlines & Consolidators

Recently we have been buying airplane tickets almost exclusively from consolidators. Also known as "bucket shops," consolidators are travel agents that buy airline seats in bulk, in return for deep discounts. This business has become so sophisticated that most of them now buy their tickets from even larger wholesalers. To find the best fare at any given time, check the travel sections of *The New York Times*, the *Los Angeles Times* or any other big-city newspaper. Bucket shop ads are usually very small, and list a lot of destinations. The US-based consolidators we use to get to Prague are **Cheap Tickets** (tel. 212/570-1179 or 800/377-1000); **Air Brokers** (tel. 800/883-3273); **Cheap Seats** (tel. 800/451-7200); **Travel Link** (tel. 213/441-3030); and **Travel Abroad** (tel. 212/564-8989).

Several cut-rate, **UK-based budget airlines** offer service to Prague, including **Go** (www.go-fly.co.uk) and **Virgin** (01293/747747).

The Major Airlines

Airline	US Telephone	UK Telephone	Czech Telephone
Air France	800/237-2747	0345/581393	02/2011-3737
Alitalia	800/223-5730	0870/544-8259	02/2011-4504
American Airlines	800/433-7300	0345/789789	02/2422-1556
Austrian Airlines	800/843 0002	0207/439-0741	02/2011-4324
ČSA Czech Airlines	877/293-4225	020/7255-1898	02/2010-4111
British Airways	800/247 9297	0345/222111	02/2011-4421
KLM	800/225-2525	0208/750-9000	02/2011-4148
Lufthansa	800/645-3880	0345/737747	02/2011-3655
SAS	800/221-2350	0207/734-4020	02/2011-4456
Swissair	800/221-4750	0207/439-4144	02/2481-2111

Packages vs. Tours

When it comes to travel lingo, most people confuse *packages* and *tours*. In the industry, a **tour** usually refers to a group that travels together, follows a flag-toting leader and is herded on and off busses. Obviously we seldom recommend this kind of tourism.

A **package**, on the other hand, is a travel deal in which several components of a trip—transportation, accommodation, airport transfers and the like—are bundled together for sale to independent, unescorted travelers. Many independent travelers purchase complete vacations from travel agents without ever knowing that they're buying a package. That's O.K.—packages can offer great values. Package companies buy in bulk and are often able to sell complete vacations for less than you'd pay for buying each component individually.

CARS & dRiViNG

You don't need a car in Prague and it's a hassle to have one. Anyway, public transport and taxis can get you almost everywhere. Traffic crawls along at a snail's pace, street parking is difficult and a garage will set you back several hundred crowns per day.

Some rules: All passengers must wear seat belts (though few actually do), foreign drivers are supposed to carry an International Drivers License and proof of insurance (a green card that comes with rental papers), and drivers must stop for pedestrians in zebra-crossings.

If you drive your own Porsche to Prague, be sure to pack your car's registration and insurance documents. American and British automobile associations don't have reciprocal arrangements with their Czech counterpart. You can buy breakdown insurance in the UK from **Europe Assistance** (UK tel. 01444/442 211).

Prague is the hub from which the country's major roadways radiate, like spokes on a wheel. The highway to Brno is the only six-lane freeway in the land. All the other "major" thoroughfares are bumpkin roads by comparison.

Be forewarned that Czech police are some of the country's worst criminals. They stop cars indiscriminately, then hunt for infractions for which they can extract cash penalties. Expect to pay a 500 Kč bribe for a broken headlight or speeding, and 2000 Kč or more for driving drunk. Before getting behind the wheel, make like you will be walking through a bad neighborhood in New York—distribute your cash amongst several different pockets so the criminals won't see your wad.

Auto Rentals

As is usual, the big international car-rental firms are the most expensive. Rates vary, but expect to pay 1500-2000 Kč per day for a Czech-made, Škoda Felicia or similar tin can. Local rental firms are cheaper than the international chains, but their cars are decidedly worse. Try **Prague Car Rent**, Milevská 7, Praha 7 (tel. 02/6116-6511), and **Czechocar**, Palác Kultury, 5. května 65, Praha 4 (tel. 02/643-2980).

At the other end of the spectrum there's **Bohemia Travel Service**, Výstaviště, Praha 7 (tel. 2010-3625), which rents Lincoln limousines for 2400 Kč per hour (3100 Kč per hour outside of Prague).

Company	Prague	USA	UK
Avis	02/2185-1225	800/331-1212	0990/900500
Hertz	02/2223-1010	800/654-3131	0990/996699
National/Europcar	02/3536-4531	800/227-7368	0345/222525

TRAVELERS CZECH

Czech is one of the most difficult languages we have come across, just a hair milder than Mandarin Chinese. Confronted with a pair of doors marked *Vchod* and *Východ* (Entrance and Exit) you may begin to think you are in a wilderness of unpronounceable tweedledums and tweedledees. Even people who have studied the language for years still find it tough to collar the jive. But you might win some friends, or at least some smiles, by using the words and phrases below.

Here's a short lesson in the local Vulcan code.

Czech Letter	Sounds like
c	As in ca*ts*
č	As in *ch*ange
ch	As in *ch*utzpa
ď	As in *du*ty
ě	As in *ye*t
j	As in *y*et
ň	As in u*n*ion
ř	Ask a Czech!
š	As in *sh*ow
ť	As in s*tu*dent
ž	As in plea*s*ure

Numbers

English	Czech	Pronunciation
One	jeden	yeh-den
Two	dva	dvah
Three	tři	tzree
Four	čtyri	shteer-zrhe
Five	pět	pyet
Six	šest	shest
Seven	sedm	seh-dom
Eight	osm	oh-som
Nine	devět	dev-yet
Ten	deset	des-et

Days of the week

English	Czech	Pronunciation
Monday	Pondělí	pon-ďye-lee
Tuesday	Úterý	oo-te-ree
Wednesday	Středa	stzre-dah
Thursday	Čtvrtek	cht-ver-tek
Friday	Pátek	pah-tek
Saturday	Sobota	so-bo-ta
Sunday	Neděle	ned-yele

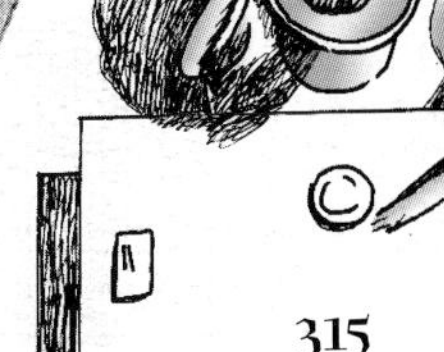

Useful Words & Phrases

English	Czech	Pronunciation
Good Day (Hello)	Dobrý den	doh-bree den
Thank You	Děkuji	d'ye-koo-yi
Yes/No	Ano/Ne	ano/neh
Please	Prosím	pro-seem
Good Bye	Na shledanou	nah-skhled-ano
Where is...?	Kde je...?	gday yeh...?
Water	Voda	voh-da
Tea	Čaj	chay
Coffee	Káva	Kah-va
How much (cost?)	Kolik to stojí?	ko-leek toh sto-yee
I can not speak Czech	Nemluvím česky	Ne-mluveem ches-ky
Where is (the metro)?	Kde je (metro)?	gday ye (metro)?
One Beer, Please	Jedno pivo, prosím	yed-no peevo, pro-seem
Another one, please	Ješte jedno, prosim	yesh-ti-ye, pro-seem
A glass of wine	Skleničku vína	skle-neetch-koo veena
Please give me the bill	Zaplatím, prosím	za-pla-teem, pro-seem
menu please	Jídelní lístek, prosím	Yidel-nee lees-tek pro-seem
Where are the toilets?	Kde jsou toalety?	gday sow to-ah-lety?
Is this (seat) free?	Je to (místo) volné?	Ye to (meestho) vol-neh?

Hello, Comrade!
Čau, kámoši!

Please treat my wife more politely
Prosím, chovejte se k mé ženě slušněji

We kicked your ass in football/ hockey/basketball
Dali jsme vám na prdel ve fotbale/ hokeji/basketu

There is an appalling stench from the adjoining table
Jde sem strašnej smrad od vedlejšího stolu

I have broken my dentures and need a dentist
Potřebuju zubaře, zlomila se mi zubní protéza

Hey! Nice goatee
Hej! Pěkná bradka

May I have your fax number?
Dáte mi vaše faxové číslo?

Do you have any scares or tattoos I should know about?
Máš nějaký jizvy nebo tetování, o kterých bych měl vědět?

Do you have anything for rectal cramps?
Máte něco na hemeroidy?

Where is the drinks trolley?
Kde je vozík s nápoji?

I'm just a stupid tourist
Jsem jenom pitomej turista

ESSENTIAL 411

CURRENCY EXCHANGE See Chapter 2/Money.

CUSTOMS REQUIREMENTS Each adult visitor may bring into the Czech Republic free of duty: one liter of alcohol over 44-proof, and two liters under 44-proof; 200 cigarettes or 50 cigars or 8.82 ounces (250 grams) of smoking tobacco.

There are no restrictions on the movement of currency and few laws restricting the importation of plants and food; you can legally show up at Prague's airport with a smoked mackerel.

US customs allows returning Americans duty-free import of $400 worth of merchandise, 200 cigarettes or 100 cigars and one liter of spirits. Above these amounts, travelers are assessed a flat 10% tax on the next $1000 worth of goods. When you shop big in Prague, keep the receipts to show customs officials.

DOCUMENT REGULATIONS Americans, British, and most Euros don't need a visa to enter the Czech Republic; only a passport with an expiration date at least six months later than the scheduled end of your visit is required. Citizens of most other countries, including Canada, Australia and South Africa, must obtain a visa from a Czech embassy or consulate. VISA RULES MAY CHANGE AT ANY TIME; Check with a Czech embassy prior to departure.

ELECTRICITY Czech runs on 220V, 50 cycles and a two-prong outlet that differs from the US and UK. American appliances must be plugged into converters; Most British appliances only need adapters, but some may also need a transformer if it's not already built into the device. We don't know where you can buy a US-Europe adapter in Prague.

INTERNET/COMPUTERS If you have trouble jacking-in, visit **Cybeteria**, Štepánská 18, Praha 1 (tel. 2423-3024; www.cybeteria.cz), an internet cafe with Web access. Other good Internet spots include **Internet Café** Prague, in Pasáž Metro, Národní 25, Praha 1; and **Bohemia Bagel**, Masná 2, Praha 1 (tel. 2481-2560).

The local Prague access number for **CompuServe** is (tel. 2210-1010). There is still no local number for **AOL** or **The Microsoft Network.**

Local firms renting computers include **Corporate Systems Consulting**, Sokolská 22, Praha 2 (tel. 2210-8109); and **Happy Comp**, Sudoměřská 25, Praha 3 (tel. 627-3740).

MEDICAL REQUIREMENTS Inoculations are not usually required to enter the Czech Republic.

MONEY See Chapter 2 for local exchange-office information. What's a Czech crown worth? For today's exchange rates, check-out *www. avantguide. com.*

PUBLIC HOLIDAYS New Years Day (January 1st); Easter Sunday and Monday (mid-April); Labor Day (May 1st); Liberation Day (May 8th); Cyril & Methodius Memorial

Day (July 5th); Jan Hus Memorial Day (July 6th); Czechoslovak Independence Day (October 28th); Christmas Eve (December 24th); Christmas (December 25th-26th).

TAX Unlike the United States where tax is tacked on at the register, in the Czech Republic Value-Added Tax (DPH) is already figured into the ticket price of most items. Restaurants always include DPH in menu prices. There is no additional airport tax upon departure, and tax is included in most hotel rates.

TELEPHONES To call Prague **from the US**, dial 011 (international code), 420 (the Czech Republic's country code), 2 (Prague's area code) and the four-to eight-digit local telephone number. To call Prague **from the UK**, dial 00 (international code), 420 (the Czech Republic's country code), 2 (Prague's area code) and the four-to eight-digit local telephone number. For information using on phones in Prague, see Chapter 2.

TIME Prague is one hour ahead of Greenwich Mean Time (GMT+1); 6 hours ahead of US Eastern Standard Time. **Daylight Savings Time** moves the clock ahead one hour, from the last Sunday in March through the last Saturday in September.

VIDEO PAL standard.

INTERNATiONAL SYSTEMS Of MEASUREMENTS

LENGTH

1 inch = 2.54 centimeters
1 foot = 12 inches = 30.48 centimeters = 0.305 meters
1 yard = 3 feet = 0.915 meters
1 mile = 5,280 feet = 1.609 kilometer

Miles To Kilometers
Multiply the number of miles by 1.61 (100 miles x 1.61 = 161 km.)

Kilometers To Miles
Multiply the number of kilometers by .62 (100km x .62 = 62 miles)

LIQUID VOLUME

1 fluid ounce = .03 liters
1 pint = 16 fluid ounces = .47 liter
1 quart = 2 pints = .94 liter
1 US gallon = 4 quarts = 3.79 liter = 83 Imperial gallons

US Gallons To Liters
Multiply the number of gallons by 3.79 (10 gals. x 3.79 = 37.9 liters)

US Gallons To Imperial Gallons
Multiply the number of US gallons by .83 (10 US gals. x .83 = 8.3 Imperial gals.)

Liters To US Gallons
Multiply the number of liters by .26 (10 liters x .26 = 2.6 US gals.)

Imperial Gallons To US Gallons
Multiply the number of Imperial gallons by 1.2
(10 Imperial gals. x 1.2 = 12 US gals.)

WEiGhT

1 ounce = 28.35 grams
1 pound = 16 ounces = 453.6 grams = .45 kg
1 ton = 2,000 pounds = 907 kilograms = .91 metric ton

Pounds To Kilograms
Multiply the number of pounds by .45 (10 lbs. x .45 = 4.5 kgs.)

Kilograms To Pounds
Multiply the number of kilograms by 2.2 (10kgs. x 2.2 = 22 lbs.)

AREA

1 acre = 0.41 hectares
1 square mile = 640 acres = 2.59 hectares = 2.6 kilometers

Acres To Hectares
Multiply the number of acres by .41 (10 acres x .41 = 4.1ha).

Square Miles To Square Kilometers
Multiply the number of square miles by 2.6 (10 sq. mi. x 2.6 = 26km2)

Hectares To Acres
Multiply the number of hectares by 2.47 (10ha x 2.47 = 24.7 acres).

Square Kilometers To Square Miles
Multiply the number of square kilometers by .39 (100km2 x .39 = 39 sq. mi.).

TEMPERATURE

Degrees Fahrenheit To Degrees Celsius
Subtract 32 from °F, multiply by 5, then divide by 9 (85°F - 32 x 5 ÷ 9 = 29.4°C).

Degrees Celsius To Degrees Fahrenheit
Multiply °C by 9, divide by 5, and add 32 (20°C x 9 ÷ 5 + 32 = 68°F).

CLOThiNG CONVERSiON ChART

Women's Clothes

UK	8	10	12	14	16
US	6	8	10	12	14
Euro	38	40	42	44	46

Women's Shoes

UK	3	4	5	6	7	8	9
US	5	6	7	8	9	10	11
Euro	36	37	38	39	40	41	42

Men's Clothes

UK	38	40	42	44	46
US	38	40	42	44	46
Euro	48	50/52	54	56	58/60

Men's Shoes

UK	8	9	10	11	12
US	9	10	11	12	13
Euro	42	43	44	45	46

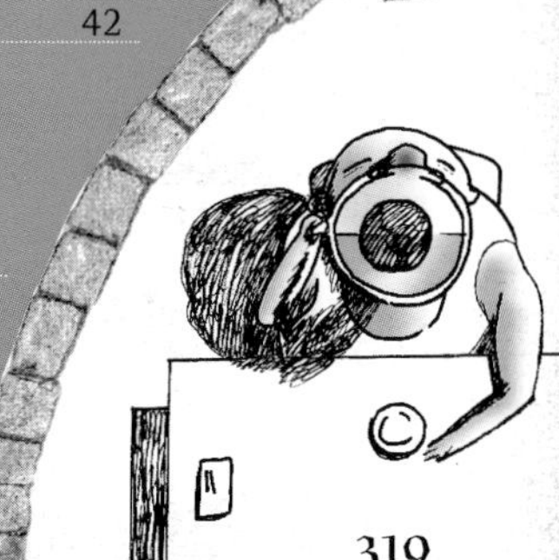

DO YOU WANT TO SPEAK CZECH?
qualified, native Czech speaker offers individual Czech lessons covering grammar, conversation, literature & colloquial expressions.
Explanation in English or Italian.
If interested, please phone tel: 67311573
6731157
Angličtina
t: (02) 717 20 885
Mobil: 0607 144 960
vistice, Laubach Certifiká
angličtiny, dva roky prax
Blahs
Where? How?
A 4-week "mini" course for
advanced English speakers
speakers and Czechs)
Starts Sun., Feb. 4, for 4 week
Offered by Charles University

×¿?× iNdEXES

Contact o

Room for Rent

in

Strossmayervo

Namesti

4.500 ck / mouth

I'm an American living in Prague one year

FLAT

0 Kcs

book iNdEX

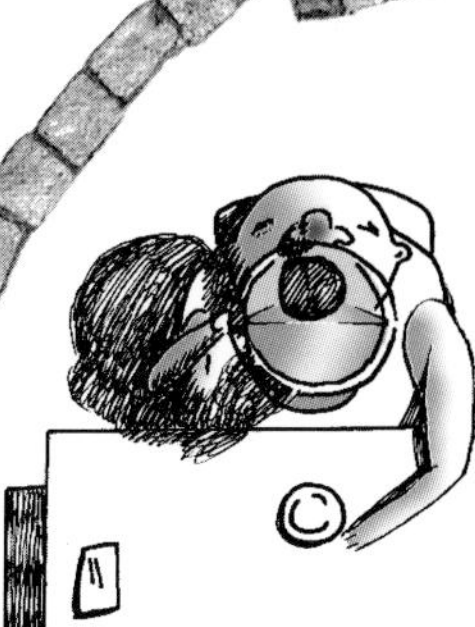

iNdEX

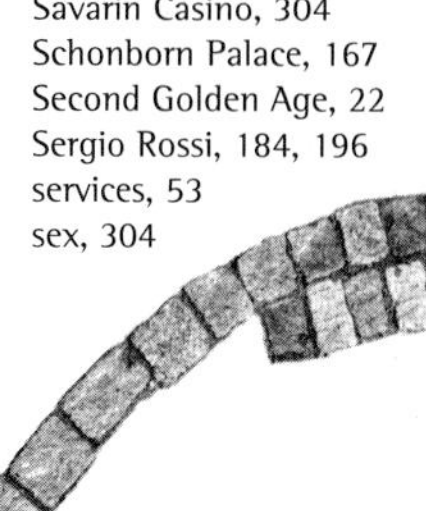
iNdEX

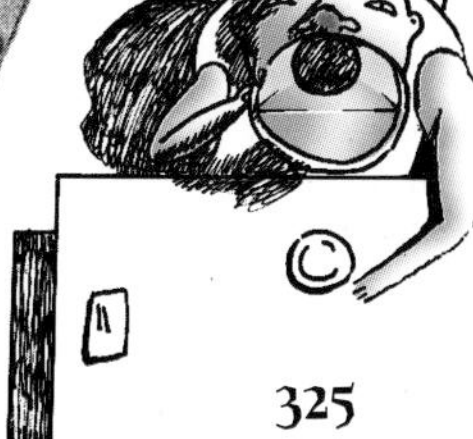

INDEX